God's Truth

Essays to commemorate the
twenty-fifth anniversary of
the publication of
Honest to God

Edited by Eric James

SCM PRESS LTD

239

British Library Cataloguing in Publication Data

God's truth: essays to commemorate the
twenty-fifth anniversary of the publication
of Honest to God.
1. Christian doctrine
I. James, Eric
230

ISBN 0–334–00585–X

First published 1988
by SCM Press Ltd,
26–30 Tottenham Road, London N1

Typeset at The Spartan Press Ltd,
Lymington, Hants
and printed in Great Britain by
Billing & Sons Ltd, Worcester

Contents

———◆———

The Contributors

Eric James is Director of Christian Action, Preacher to Gray's Inn and Honorary Canon of St Albans. In 1963 he was Vicar of St George's, Camberwell, in the Diocese of Southwark.

The Very Revd T. G. A. Baker has recently retired as Dean of Worcester. In 1963 he was Principal of Wells Theological College, Prebendary of Wells and Canon Theologian of Leicester.

Lord Beaumont of Whitley is parish priest of St Philip's, North Sheen, Surrey. In 1963 he was Secretary of the Keble Conference Group, Treasurer of the Liberal Party, Editor of *Prism* and Proprietor of *Time and Tide*.

The Very Revd Trevor Beeson is Dean of Winchester. In 1963 he was Perpetual Curate of St Chad's Conventional District, Roseworth, Stockton-on-Tees.

The Revd Dr John Bowden is Editor and Managing Director of SCM Press. In 1963 he was Assistant Curate of St Mary's, Nottingham.

The Very Revd Canon F. W. Dillistone is Fellow (Emeritus) of Oriel College, Oxford. In 1963 he was Dean of Liverpool.

The Revd Alan Ecclestone lives in retirement at Seascale, Cumbria. In 1963 he was Vicar of Holy Trinity, Darnall, Sheffield.

The Very Revd David L. Edwards is Provost of Southwark. In 1963 he was Editor of SCM Press.

The Revd Professor J. L. Houlden is Professor of Theology, King's College, London University. In 1963 he was Chaplain and Fellow of Trinity College, Oxford.

Dr Alistair Kee has recently been appointed Reader in Religious Studies at New College, Edinburgh. In 1963 he was at Union Theological Seminary, New York, working on his PhD.

Professor John Kent is Professor of Theology in the Department of Theology and Religious Studies in the University of Bristol. In 1963 he was lecturing to Methodist theological students at Hartley Victoria College, Manchester.

The Revd John Lee is Priest-in-Charge of Chiddingstone, Kent, a member of the Institute of Group Analysis and Hon. Psychotherapist in the Department of Psychological Medicine in St Bartholomew's Hospital, London. In 1963 he was a marine biologist.

The Revd Canon Dennis Nineham is living in retirement in Oxford. In 1963, he was Professor of Divinity in the University of London.

The Revd Professor J. C. O'Neill is Professor in the Department of New Testament Language, Literature and Theology in the Faculty of Divinity of the University of Edinburgh. In 1963 he was teaching New Testament at Ormond College Theological Hall, Melbourne, Australia.

The Revd Canon Ronald Preston is living in retirement in Manchester. In 1963 he was Residentiary Canon of Manchester.

The Revd Alan Race is Director of Studies, Southwark Ordination Course. In 1963 he was a pupil at Bede Hall Grammar School, Billingham-on-Tees.

Mrs Ruth Robinson is living in Arncliffe, North Yorkshire. In 1963 she was living at Blackheath.

The Rt Revd Dr P. S. M. Selby is Suffragan Bishop of Kingston. In 1963 he was an undergraduate at St John's College, Oxford.

Foreword

◆

Eric James

The publication day of *Honest to God*, 19 March 1963, was undoubtedly a watershed in the life of Bishop John Robinson. As Ruth, his wife, said: 'Life was never the same afterwards!' As a result of *Honest to God*, for instance, John received over four thousand letters. The book, with its powerful cover photograph of the German sculptor Wilhelm Lehmbruck's 'Seated Youth 1918', reminiscent of Rodin's 'Thinker', immediately became the centre of a huge controversy: television, broadcasts, cartoons, articles, letters, reviews, sermons. It sold out its first impression on the day of publication. 'No new book of serious theology has sold so quickly in the history of the world,' claimed David Edwards, then Editor and Managing Director of the publishers, SCM Press.

I have described in detail the genesis of *Honest to God*, and the story of its first weeks and months, in *A Life of Bishop John A. T. Robinson: Scholar, Pastor, Prophet. Honest to God* was followed seven months later by *The Honest to God Debate*. John was undoubtedly right to call his contribution to it 'The Debate Continues', for, as he wrote, 'The issues raised by the debate, theoretical and practical, are too big to be taken up so soon or within the scope of an essay, and the atmosphere is still too emotionally charged' (p. 232). Already it had become clear – not least to the then Archbishop of Canterbury, Michael Ramsey – that *Honest to God* was part of a larger scene. The Second Vatican Council, for instance, had opened in Rome in October 1962.

From time to time John would write articles, like his contribution to the series 'How My Mind has Changed' in the American journal *The Christian Century* of 12 November 1969 entitled 'Not Radical Enough?' (it was reprinted in *Christian Freedom in a Permissive Society*). He himself regarded his *Exploration into God* as 'my most mature book to date', and as a further contribution to 'The Debate about God'. In his Hulsean Lectures for 1969, *The Human Face of God*, John fulfilled a wish he had expressed in his contribution to *The Honest to God Debate*: 'I am deliberately not touching in this essay on questions relating to the person and work of Christ, as I should like, when time allows, to follow this up in a separate book' (p. 266).

There can be little doubt that had he lived – John being John! – he himself would have written *something* to celebrate *'Honest to God* Twenty-Five Years Later'; but, as I wrote in my biography of John, 'The saying "Man proposes but God disposes" is at least as old as Thomas à Kempis and *The Imitation of Christ*', and most of those who read this volume are unlikely to need informing that Bishop John Robinson died – after 'living with cancer' – on 5 December 1983.

Already substantial works of theology evaluating the significance of his work – including *Honest to God* – are beginning to appear. As early as 1966 there was Fr Richard McBrien's important work *The Church in the Thought of Bishop John Robinson*. For those who read Polish there is *Bog dla nas: God for us. An Ecumenical Dogmatic Study of J. A. T. Robinson's Christology* by Piotr Jackota, published by the Catholic University of Lublin in 1986. 1988 will see the publication of Alistair Kee's *The Roots of Christian Freedom: The Theology of John A. T. Robinson*. Robert Towler's analysis of the four thousand letters which John received after *Honest to God* contained in *The Need for Certainty: A Sociological Study of Conventional Religion*, published by Routledge and Kegan Paul in 1984, falls into a different category but is of considerable value. Details of John's own books and some books about him and his theology appear in the Select Bibliography and are not repeated in the notes.

A word about the aim of the book and the selection of contributors and their subjects. John Robinson asked me to be his literary executor in 1977, and I felt an obligation to initiate and edit such a volume as this: to commemorate and celebrate *Honest to God* and as an expression of gratitude for his life and work. With a few exceptions, all those invited to contribute are theologians who were much involved in the *Honest to God* debate in 1963. This alone explains the virtual absence of lay and feminine contributors. It was not least this absence – which I feel keenly – that made me press a reluctant Ruth Robinson to be a contributor (she had undoubtedly made a considerable contribution to *Honest to God*). I am grateful to all the contributors – I wish there had been space for more – but to none am I more grateful than to Ruth.

Pressure of time meant that we could not all meet together to plan the volume, or even attempt to co-ordinate our contributions by correspondence; each piece was written independently and in ignorance of the others. We did not seek to write a disciplined analysis of *Honest to God* twenty-five years later, but rather to reflect on one or other feature of it today; our concern is with the present and future rather than the past. And we have agreed that all the royalties from the book shall go to the memorial fund set up at the time of John's death which has already enabled the Cambridge Mission to Delhi (The Brotherhood of the Ascension) to build a large classroom, part of the extension to the Deenabandhu School at Shahidnagar, across the Yamuna, east of Delhi.

To the humourless, the title of our volume *God's Truth* could seem arrogant and presumptuous: it is, of course, meant to be a colloquialism to match – but not to equal – the inspired *Honest to God* (following Kipling, we might have called it, *Strewth!*). Yet it would be wrong to evacuate the title of all meaning. John Robinson was fond of quoting his Puritan namesake, pastor of the Pilgrim Fathers, who, in a memorable

sermon, said'The Lord hath more light and truth yet to break
forth out of his holy Word'. We have hope that concern for
that truth is evident in these pages.

Even for those who lived through 1963 it is not always easy
now to recapture the mood and atmosphere of twenty-five
years ago. Bernard Levin did it brilliantly in his book *The
Pendulum Years: Britain and the Sixties* (Jonathan Cape 1970) and
Philip Larkin did it in under twenty-five lines in his poem
'Annus Mirabilis' (*High Windows*, Faber and Faber 1970). Our
contributors are in the main theologians not poets; but I have
the feeling – indeed, the confident hope – that this is the kind
of creative communal celebration of *Honest to God* that would
have delighted John. In his 'Marriage of Heaven and Hell:
Proverbs of Hell', William Blake assured us that 'eternity is in
love with the productions of time'. Whatever else a commem-
oration of a twenty-fifth anniversary is, it is undeniably one
such production.

Michaelmas Day 1987

T. G. A. Baker

Is Liturgy in Good Shape?

Has liturgy come to life this century, or are we witnessing its gradual demise? The question is prompted by the title of John Robinson's little book, *Liturgy Coming to Life*, in which he describes and discusses what went on in the chapel of Clare College, Cambridge, while he was Dean. Today the ideas and phrases in this book look tired and cliché-ridden; until one realizes that the services described belong to the 1950s, and grasps the significance of the date of publication, 1960. At that time it must have come to many as a breath of very fresh air. The reader is offered the vision of the eucharist as a corporate act of worship, done rather than said, vibrantly alive at the very heart of the church's fellowship. We read of its fourfold 'shape', of the meaning of each act of the drama, of the officiant facing the people, of congregational participation, and much else that was new. The 'roots of the liturgy', a phrase which Robinson derives from an influential pamphlet of Eric James's, are in society rather than in church. It has to do with social action, the use of material things, with the common being made holy. It should be rooted in the soil of the world, and not be a 'pot-plant in the sanctuary of the church'. Robinson's enthusiasm for his theme sometimes reaches a high pitch of lyricism and, as we shall be discussing later, in all this he was ahead of his time. Nobody should be left in any doubt of the very substantial contribution which John Robinson has made to the development and enrichment of the liturgy in this country.

Yet this development is heavy with irony. *Has* it in fact fulfilled Robinson's expectations? In one respect it has, and very remarkably. Less than three decades after the liturgical experiments at Clare (which strike us now as surprisingly conservative, involving the use of the 1662 communion office, almost without revision), *everything* which Robinson has championed is not only commonplace, but is enshrined in the official service books of all the main line churches. The irony is that the hopes and expectations have been in part disappointed in the very process of fulfilment. Disenchantment has accompanied satisfaction. The sense of excitement and optimism experienced by those who, three decades ago, joined in experimental liturgies at some Anglican theological colleges, or participated at the worship of the community at Taizé, or of the seminary of the Mission de France at Pontigny, the monasteries at Bec and Maria-Laach, the parish church of S. Séverin in Paris, seems to have quite considerably evaporated. Some magic has departed. In all honesty it can hardly be said that modern worship has startlingly 'come to life', or that its roots are manifestly deep in the life of society, or of the everyday. Why? What are the unexpected and (at least in part) unforeseen developments which have taken place since the 1960s to make liturgy and worship feel so different in the 1980s? The rest of this article will be concerned with this question, and then with the prospects for the future.

The first of these imperfectly foreseen developments has been the rapidity of liturgical change, and the relatively sudden appearance of new fully authorized service books, among them the *Alternative Service Book* of the Church of England. This was seen at first as a welcome deliverance from the ever-increasing pile of disagreeable little semi-official booklets under which congregations had been suffocating for too long; deliverance also from liturgical fidgets, and an unacceptably disproportionate amount of energy spent on a task which was inevitably inward-directed and very detailed. *Not* sufficiently foreseen, either, was the considerable increase of care and sensitivity which the new books would demand from leaders of worship. Certainly there have been in some places very fruitful consultations in the introduction and presentation of these services; useful explanatory booklets have been produced in plenty. But too many congregations have too complacently settled down too soon, to a rather flat, dull and unimaginative form of worship, in which the principles underlying the new liturgies have been either uncritically accepted or inadequately assimilated. The ASB, for example, has tended to become a strait-jacket instead of a resource to be used with flexibility, and in ways suitable to each particular situation. Here is a vicar who celebrates Rite A as if it were 1662; here, an Anglo-Catholic priest who tricks it out with obsolete Roman Catholic practices to which it is antipathetic. Here, an evangelical clergyman celebrates a westward-facing rite as if he was still standing at the north end of the Table; here, a newly-ordained team-vicar, inadequately grounded in any strong tradition of liturgy or prayer, produces out of the new services a mish-mash, badly served up, indigestible, unappetizing, and lacking in nourishment – a prime example of that 'modern habit of doing ceremonial things unceremoniously' which C. S. Lewis so disliked; here, a clericalized layman during the intercessions takes the congregation on a lengthy Cook's Tour of all the world's trouble spots. But here, mercifully, an unclericalized layman or woman clothes the prayers in language which is crisp, lucid and imaginative; and here is a parish priest who, in consultation with the congregation's representatives, has worked out from all the options available a form of service suited to that congregation, carefully 'mounted', with the right combination of formality and warmth. It can be done, but alas it is too seldom done.

Another development since the 1960s has been a sense that the new services have involved a great spiritual and aesthetic impoverishment in a generation which has acquired a taste for the traditional and colourful, the grand and impressive, and sometimes the strange and exotic. The style and mood of the late 1980s, while preserving the casual elements of earlier decades, also makes room for the formal, grand, elegant and traditional. Understandably church leaders get exasperated by prejudiced and ill-informed criticisms on the part of those whose commitment is purely formal or even non-existent. It remains, however, difficult to deny that the distinguished signatories (600 of them) to the Petition presented in 1979 to the General Synod for 'the continued and loving use' of the Book of Common Prayer and the Authorized Version of the Bible scored some important points which it would be foolish for the church to ignore. John Robinson himself cared about the aesthetic element in worship, quoting with approval the Abbé Michonneau's words 'Let the liturgy be splendid', and giving a great deal of time and energy to the furnishings and redecoration of the chapels of Clare College and Trinity College at Cambridge. However, he may well have been surprised at how desolate has been the sense of loss experienced by a considerable number of sincere worshippers, not least in the realm of music, a subject on which John, being self-admittedly tone-deaf, has little to say.

A more fundamental development has been the rapidity of secularization. John Robinson wrote *Liturgy Coming to Life* during the religious 'boom' period of the 1950s, with its prevailing spirit of confidence and optimism. This confident mood may help to explain the rather aggressive dogmatism of the ASB, with its credal catalogues and bald doctrinal statements, little attempt being made to give them any contemporary resonance or relevance. But secularization has now produced a generation which has largely lost any sense of God, and for whose members (including some who still come to church) the traditional symbols of Christianity have lost the resonances and overtones they once possessed. Many a vicar might be surprised to know how many of his congregation are agnostic about some of the doctrines he expounds, and quietly do their own personal 'demythologizing' as they go along. Hence perhaps the stubborn persistence of the 'quiet eight o'clock' or 'early service', and also the growing popularity of cathedral evensong, for in these services the dogmatic element, though present, is somehow less obtrusive, and the worshipper, not being expected verbally to participate so much, is offered much greater inner space in which to enter into an experience which, while being shared, is more personal and inward. Robin Green, in his admirable book *Only Connect*, quotes Henri Nouwen: 'The mystery of love is that it protects and respects the aloneness of the other and creates the free space where he can convert his loneliness into a solitude that can be shared.'[1]

Changing attitudes to the Bible have also affected the development of liturgy. The earlier revisers of the liturgy, like John Robinson himself, were greatly influenced by the 'biblical theology' movement, based on the confidence that biblical categories of thought, and in particular the notion of 'sacred history', were fairly directly accessible to people today; and also on the confidence that there had emerged a consensus of biblical scholarship to the effect that a rigorous application of critical method to the New Testament texts now provides a solidly based foundation for a reconstruction of Christian origins sufficiently close to developed and traditional Christian doctrine to form a firm basis for the latter. But by the time the ASB was published the biblical theology movement was a spent force, and biblical study (now increasingly carried on by scholars of other faiths or none) has badly damaged a previous consensus, and is, by and large, less hospitable to orthodox Christian interpretation. That this development has been accompanied by a recrudescence of neo-fundamentalism in some quarters serves only to muddy the waters yet further. When account is taken of the fact that Bible teaching in schools has largely broken down, and that a generation has now grown up whose ignorance of the Bible is profound, then it is all the more puzzling that the church goes on using liturgy heavy with biblical quotation and allusion, as if no problem existed. It is difficult to resist the conclusion drawn by John Bowden that in worship today people have become conditioned to listening to the Bible readings as background music, rather than with close attention to the score, the only way in which the Bible can expect to have much impact in modern times. There are just too many words being thrown around. It is ironic that while John Robinson and other pioneers in liturgical revision have insisted that the eucharist is something done and not said, so many of the new eucharistic rites are as wordy as ever.

Amongst the most unexpected developments since the 1960s have been the resurgence of conservative evangelicalism, the charismatic revival, a greater polarization in 'churchmanship', and a consequent decline of the liberal elements both on the catholic and evangelical wings. At the same time the evangelicals and charismatics have aligned themselves with the catholics in adopting the eucharist, with general communion, as the central act of worship. These developments, welcome as they are in themselves, have had some less happy results; for the centrality of the eucharist, especially when combined with some extreme and unfamiliar forms of worship, has tended to be divisive, and to foster a somewhat sectarian spirit. Where the eucharist is the only service 'on offer', the increased numbers of the unconfirmed and not yet committed may feel themselves to be unchurched, so that ironically the sacrament of unity has a divisive side-effect. Add to this the relentless demand for the fullest possible congregational participation I have already spoken of, and it is easy to understand why people of an enquiring mind, reflective disposition and retiring temperament feel somewhat left out in the cold. It is a difficult time for 'dissidents' in the church today. There are quite a lot of them, and they are sometimes made to feel like traitors to the cause. This may be one reason, not the only one, why some reflective, honest and serious Christians have quietly given up church-going altogether. Equally disturbing is the tendency in much modern worship for fellowship to be transmuted into matiness, a trend exemplified by the chatter and clatter which often accompanies the 'Peace', a ceremony in former times performed in stylized or hieratic fashion. John Robinson once made a strong protest against this tendency in these words:

' . . . the great New Testament word *koinonia* . . . has as its primary reference . . . not our fellowship with each other, but our participation in God or Christ or the Spirit. The New Testament knows nothing about generating feelings of fellowship as a way to God. We are built up into the Body of Christ by feeding upon his supernatural life and in no other way. A religion of "fellowship" is as much an abomination as "solitary Christianity".'[2] Archbishop Ramsey, it will be remembered, voiced similar sentiments.

But it is in the matter of the 'house church' that recent developments have been most unexpected, and maybe most disturbing of all. In his biography, Eric James quotes from a compline address which Robinson gave at Wells Theological College back in 1949, in which he spoke strongly (perhaps too strongly) of the vital importance of the house church, i.e. the smallest possible unit of Christian existence, which he called the 'church in the basement', and of the need for theological colleges and the like to contribute to the kind of informal liturgy suitable to the 'basement' level of Christian living. Many of us may recall experiences in such small groups of a depth of relationship, an openness, a transcending of denominational barriers and doctrinal differences, all expressing itself from time to time in acts of worship (eucharistic or not) which represented the insights, hopes and difficulties of the group with an immediacy not found in formal liturgy. The liturgy of such groups was neither traditional nor revised, but creative. There was nothing in the least sectarian or schismatic about them; they were concerned more with being human than being religious; they could be light-hearted, witty; certainly ecclesiastical regulations were broken, but the members remained otherwise loyal to their own tradition. Today at the tail-end of the century things are much changed. Too often 'house churches', so far from being open and enquiring in style, are associated with attitudes which are doctrinally rigid, ethically naive or puritanical, and potentially exclusivist, sometimes to the point of schism. The house church movement today has to some extent been hijacked by those whose aims and interests are very different from those who initiated it. Happily many groups exist which are basically well-intentioned and helpful to their members, but there are some others which have been invaded by unwelcome visitors.

What of the future? Having compared the present state of affairs with those obtaining when John Robinson's ministry was in its heyday, we now enquire what things may be like in the twenty-first century. What is said now is immediately applicable to the Church of England, but much of it may be found relevant to other and much larger communions.

A modest revision of the ASB may be expected early in the new century, giving opportunity for the removal or revision of some at least of the infelicities of its original. But before going further it is only fair to emphasize that all those involved in the monumental task of producing the ASB, *given their terms of reference*, were unsparing and more than generous in the way they undertook it, with a result which was probably the best possible in the circumstances, and a great deal better than some had feared. In spite of this, or perhaps because of it, we may hope and expect that this time the prayers will be based firmly on the compositions of individuals with literary gifts and liturgical flair, rather than on committee concoctions. (What about a competition for the best *anaphora*?) Participation of the whole church in the revision, it is to be hoped, will not be judged to necessitate detailed debate in full Synod, nor the right of any or every individual to make representation direct to Synod. The result may well be services more succinct, and a prayer book significantly smaller. Even so, it will still be desirable for congregations to produce their own versions of the principal services, so as to avoid the interruption of the flow of the liturgy by the announcements of page numbers, and other stage directions, a practice so utterly devastating to the atmosphere of worship. Even a smaller edition of the ASB will be a book for the home and the vestry, but not for the pew.

The revisers may be expected to feel more keenly the need to reflect recent and continuing developments in theological understanding and enquiry. Sensitivity to increasing religious pluralism in society will cause the Christo-centrism of the ASB services to be expressed more judiciously. Changes in the social status of women in society and the church itself will result in the removal of language which is quite unnecessarily 'sexist', although any full-scale revision along these lines would be too far-reaching in its implications to be a practical proposition at the present time. The new revisers will be able to draw on the insights of various recent reports of succeeding Doctrine Commissions. Although formal association with the Board for Social Responsibility might not be productive, it may reasonably be expected that the revised services will be richer in resonances and overtones which relate to the great social, political and economic issues of our day – world poverty, gross inequalities between nations and within nations (including our own), the environment, race relations, human rights, medical ethics, the bomb.[3] They will also make more positive connections with all the various, everyday experiences of personal living, including those which are frightening, dark and destructive, and with some of the great archetypal symbols which belong to all humanity. One of the great merits of Robin Green's book, mentioned just now, is that it reminds us of the need for liturgy to reflect *all* aspects of the human condition including the dark side, and that may mean restoring some of the stark and robust realism character- istic of the Book of Common Prayer, against which the ASB prayers may appear rather too 'bright'. In the same way, public liturgies of any kind should make full allowance for the longing in the human heart for the 'numinous', the transcend- ent. There needs to be opportunity for movement, splen- dour, symbol, colour and drama. In finding new expression for the powerful and archetypal symbols and myths, liturgists need to call on the assistance of poets, musicians, sculptors, artists, choreographers. Let the services be neither highbrow nor philistine, but capable of presentation in both the simple and the grand manner. One of the secrets of good liturgy is its ability to combine the hieratic with the human, mystery with merriment, solemnity with warmth. As for music, there are at present not a few useful popular settings for the new services, but most of them, like so much else in contemporary culture, are eminently disposable. What needs also to be recognized is that modern liturgy can be combined quite happily with the kind of serious cathedral-type music this country is so good at producing. At the same time, contemporary composers should be encouraged to write settings for the new texts, some of which lend themselves quite well to musical expression and, being ecumenical, may in time develop the same kind of universality and familiarity as the traditional versions.[4]

Since secularization has resulted in a growing penumbra on the edge of the churches, whose members are not confirmed, and may not even have been baptized in infancy, we may expect that the next generation of liturgical revisers will be less preoccupied with the eucharist, and will turn their attention more to non-eucharistic worship, including the occasional offices (baptism, marriage, funerals), where the need is already being felt for forms of service which are yet more sensitive to changing patterns of religious observance, rapidly changing mores in matters of sex and marriage, and a population increasingly ignorant of the Bible and Christian faith. There will have to be greater flexibility in use. Careful attention must be paid to the increasing spread of so-called 'family services' on Sunday mornings. While it is easy to see the need for such services, and admire the way some of them are conducted, there are problems. What is the place of such services in the overall strategy of the parish? What is supposed to happen to the children when they grow up, and with the parents who bring them? If the service is the only one available, is it acceptable to deprive a whole parish of the opportunity of worshipping according to the authorized liturgy of the church? That problem is to some extent overcome if the family service is also a eucharist; but even then there are the unmarried, the unhappily married, the one-parent families, the divorced, the children of broken homes, the elderly living alone, the homosexuals. It is hardly surprising that these often feel most terribly excluded, especially when, as is too often the case, the whole tone of the 'family service' is insufferably cloying and cosy. It is salutary to bear in mind that much of the ministry of Jesus was directed at those on the margins of society, that his attitude to the family seems to have been ambivalent, and that the family unit is capable of being stifling and destructive, as well as liberating and creative. All this is not to say that 'family services' do not have their place; they evidently do, but they should be subject to a proper critique.

So there will be much work to be done in the provision of non-eucharistic services for use in parish churches. Happily a good omen for the future is the success of 'Lent, Holy Week and Easter: Services and Prayers' authorized by the bishops in 1984, and followed up by a careful education programme mounted by the Liturgical Commission. Since these services, though authorized, are optional, it has been possible to be much more adventurous in the choice of material to be included. What has been provided is in fact not so much a prayer book as a directory of worship, a manual intended to be used 'with selectivity, sensitivity and imagination', to quote its introduction, providing resources from which choices can be made. Whatever the merits or demerits of its contents, the principles and procedures it enshrines are the right ones. It opens up the possibility of services becoming a joint effort between clergy and congregation, between those who lead the worship and those who request it.

Since we are learning to welcome rather than to resist variety in liturgy, it may be that the time has come to take a fresh look at the pattern of Sunday morning worship. One possible pattern might be a 'parish eucharist' as a base, followed by a kind of *à la carte* menu from which choice could be made, consisting of such things, for example, as a children's church, a Bible study group, a prayer meeting, a discussion session, conducted meditation, Taizé type worship, youth groups, community action meetings and so on. This would involve a much greater commitment to the use of the major part of Sunday morning, as is not uncommon in the United States, but might be more difficult here because of the strong tradition of Sunday midday family dinner. Where it proved impracticable, or if, under pressure of secularization, the traditional Sunday were totally to collapse, then it might be desirable to provide on weekday evenings a variety of *worship* opportunities, instead of an exclusive diet of discussion groups, meetings and the like.

Another need likely to persist into the next century is the provision of good, imaginative para-liturgies for special occasions. Paradoxically, the demand for these seems to have increased alongside an increase in secularization. The list is a long one, and includes memorial services, forms of worship for national occasions, especially Remembrance Sunday, anniversaries of schools, colleges, and many associations both religious and secular who wish to celebrate their aims and ideals, and affirm their identities, youth 'events', pilgrimages, carol services, and so on. That the list sounds dreary is itself an indication of the lack of imagination with which these services are all too often associated. But if those responsible for devising such services are in full consultation with those who request them, if both are agreed about what is to be said to God, if the resultant service is more than a casual response to inherited expectations, more than a reverential sanctification of particular social codes and unexamined values and assumptions, if there is pattern and flow, if all available resources (of music, literature, perhaps drama or dance) are used with sensitivity, then such occasions can really come alive, powerfully expressing how the loving action of God may be detected in the particular aspect of the human condition that is being celebrated. For many of the participants these are the only occasions when they brush up against the Christian religion. Good examples of such things on the national scale have been the service in Canterbury cathedral on the occasion of the Pope's visit, and in that same Cathedral the 'Thanksgiving for the Ministries of Women in the Anglican Communion' held in April 1986, together with the service in St Paul's to mark the ending of the Falklands war. At a more popular level, some programmes in the television production 'Songs of Praise' are less of an exercise in sentimental nostalgia and more a medium for Christian proclamation. Cathedrals and large parish churches are amassing a great deal of valuable expertise in these fields. Smaller parishes likewise might be encouraged to adventure more, since their admittedly more limited resources are compensated by the greater intimacy they can offer.

An even more pressing need is the provision of much more careful training in the conduct of worship on the part of both clergy and laity. There is a notion around that, while the sermon must be prepared with much care, the liturgy can be left to look after itself. It cannot. If the liturgy is really to *connect* with where people are in their lives, and to be in integral relation to the pastoral ministry of the clergy, then it has to be imaginatively devised and conducted in a way which combines professional skill with plain commonsense. Almost a lifetime's involvement in ministerial training has convinced me that a serious imbalance exists between the time allotted to the conduct of worship and all the other many (too many?) aspects of training, even at the level of such severely practical (but not thereby unimportant) things as the choice of suitable hymns (at the right pitch and not too long:), readings that can be heard, ceremonial which is both seemly and significant, bodily postures and gestures given the attention they deserve.

The need for what Dr Alec Vidler once called the parachurch, i.e. small unstructured and unpublicized groups on the borders of the main line churches, is likely to be just as great, or greater, in the next century than it is now. John Robinson was surely right in his contention that, whatever may have been true in the past, the 'church in the basement' is necessary to the church's health, and not least in its capacity to generate the kind of creative liturgy which will help preserve public liturgy from petrification. If the house church movement is going through a rather unlovely, reactionary phase just now, that is all the more reason why it should continue to be nourished by those who may bring to it a more open and enquiring mind.

The reason why these reflections are not particularly radical is that they presuppose that the church of the twenty-first century is going to be in fairly direct continuity with the church of today, and that the worship of that church will be a recognizable development with what is here now. That cannot be taken for granted. A number of things could happen on the stage of world history seriously to rupture that continuity. So might a further increase in the speed and direction of secularization. In the 1960s the Roman Catholic theologian Charles Davis believed that quite soon the whole idea of public worship as now known would become so alien to the social habits and mental presuppositions of the population that the practice of 'going to church' would wither away except for the die-hards. That melancholy prediction has not proved correct, but there are certain signs which still point in that direction. It may be that the ever increasing pace of cultural change will produce a new culture whose interpretative 'models' of reality will be so alien to those governing the world of traditional liturgy that the latter can survive only after a development more radical than any known so far. Then there are the many signs of decadence pervading the whole of Western society. If decadence be defined as the attempt to maintain, at great expense and inconvenience, old traditions from which the meaning has departed, then traditional dogmas and liturgies begin to look problematic. Perhaps in their present form they have had their day, and must be left behind. That in itself would not spell disaster for Christianity since, under God, all institutions and customs, however hallowed by time and long usage, are ultimately provisional. We may have to reckon with a change in patterns of worship (originating perhaps in Africa, South America or China) which is so radical as to amount to a mutation. We cannot tell. But if so, it will still be true that no new development is ever valid unless it has roots in the rich soil which has nurtured what has grown there before. The liturgies which now exist in our churches are rooted deep in the rich soil of long established yet ever changing traditions, customs and practices, including the reforms and revisions of this present century. Even in the unlikely event of the worship of tomorrow's church turning out to be so radically different from our own as to be hardly recognizable, still the liturgies of today which will provide its seed-bed need to be carefully and lovingly cherished.

Tim Beaumont

John Robinson and the Radical in Politics

John Robinson had no doubts as to his general stance in the field of politics, and since, as far as I can judge, it was where I stand also, I have the less compunction in daring to write about it.

I use the word 'daring' since I am under no illusion about the difficulty of 'praying in aid' the dead. It is one thing to affirm that John thought this and that about events which occurred in his lifetime, since we have his written works as evidence one way or the other. But it is quite another thing to suggest how he would have reacted to events which occurred after his death, and it is yet another to look forward and talk about his attitudes to problems which had not yet loomed on the political horizon by the time he died.

I have three reasons for thinking that John and I thought alike on political matters. The first is that I agree almost entirely with what he says in those of his published works which deal with politics; the second is that we came from the same general background and shared the same approach to the Establishment; the third is that it explains very clearly why, without either of us making a specific effort to do so, we ran into each other at two- or three-yearly intervals and, having done so, were able to pick up our conversations where we had left them off without strain or difficulty.

Whether we were engaged in 'reforming' the structures of the Church of England as members of the 'Keble Conference Group' in the 1960s, helping the Homosexual (later 'Sexual') Law Reform Society in the 1970s or keeping a watchful eye on the conscience of the Liberal Party thereafter, we spoke one another's language. (Which is not to say that I had John's theological insights – at least not until I had lifted them from him!)

And indeed the very fact that I feel that we did agree while he was alive is a danger signal. It is quite clear to me that God and I agree on most matters of importance, so it is only too easy to assume that John concurs! I mention all this here so as to spare the reader the constant repetition of qualifications and cautions which I would otherwise have had to insert later on in the text.

I have said that we came from the same background and shared the same approach, and the truth of that may not seem immediately obvious. But John has explained (*inter alia* in *Christian Freedom in a Permissive Society*) that he was a radical, and the nature of his radicalism and what he said there applies to his attitude to both religion and politics.

First of all, he contrasts the radical with both the reformer and the revolutionary, and although his comments and conclusions involved to my mind some elusive movement between different meanings of the word 'radical', and even in differing concepts of 'roots', I find myself at home in the argument.

According to it, the reformer is someone who pastes over the cracks, an operation which he justifies because in the occasional moment when he thinks at all deeply he – particularly the Tory Reformer – sees society (and most societies, such as, say, the church) as forming a thin veneer of civilization over a bubbling inferno of anarchy and evil which is always threatening to break through (and looking at the European scene between 1918 and 1939 or the scene in South East Asia since 1947 it is difficult to fault him). So when he sees an institution in place and more or less effective, his main desire is to ensure that it goes on working. Indeed, his automatic response to almost any criticism of an extant institution (such as the House of Lords or the British electoral system) is to say: 'Well, it works, so let it alone or, at the very most, make the minimum changes needed to escape ridicule.' Any enquiry as to how well it actually works and in comparison to what is regarded as almost as irrelevant as the suggestion that the institution is logically indefensible.

The revolutionary, on the other hand, sees mainly the corruption in (almost) any institution and sees the need to dig it up and burn it lest the spores of the infection spread. He then plans to replace it with some perfect machinery (which in a fallen world proves to be impossible).

But the radical is a true gardener. He wants to see an institution grow according to its true (Platonic) nature, along the lines for which God intended it, and to that end he will go down to the roots for evidence and come up with some surprising findings.

And of course it helps if the radical himself is involved with the plant – I warned you that the metaphor might skid badly; I am much less adroit than John at hiding the skidmarks. By birth, breeding and temperament John was unmistakably a member of the Establishment of the Church of England, and was proud of the fact. I share his views on radicalism and am just as unmistakably a member of the British political establishment. (My father was a Tory MP, both my grandfathers Liberal MPs – one of them Chief Whip in the Liberal Government of 1906 – and my ancestors on the male side have sat in the Commons for six generations!)

So it was not very surprising (not that I worked this out at the time) that we should look at both national politics and the internal politics of the Church of England in much the same kind of way.

The only surprising thing was that we strayed out of our respective fields and that he became involved in secular politics and I in the politics of organized religion.

John was involved in secular politics because he saw the

gospel as primarily kingdom-orientated. Jesus preached a kingdom which was not only coming but which he had already ushered in by proclamation and signs. The early church continued to await the full coming of the kingdom, and the fact that it did not fully come within the lifetimes of Paul or John did not mean that it was not going to arrive. It was – and is – the vocation of all Christians to wait and work for the coming of that kingdom.

The kingdom would be built (humanly speaking) in two modes, both of which were essential. One mode was the spread of the gospel of love by individuals, by words and actions. The other mode was by the building up of institutions which more and more fitted into the pattern of the kingdom, and that mode demanded involvement in politics.

But although both modes were necessary, the balance between them was changing. The second mode takes on a greater and greater importance. The coming of the kingdom depends more and more on politics and less and less on preaching. The history of the church, according to John, had gone through a stage of the conversion of groups of people (households, tribes, nations), then a stage of individual conversions (during the great individualistic period in the West from the dawn of Protestantism till some time in this century), and was now culminating in a period of the conversion of institutions. Great evangelical campaigns do not seem to be on the agenda of the Holy Spirit these days; the conversion of institutions to form a network which can be used by the kingdom is.

It may be that it was a lot easier to believe this in the optimistic 1960s than it is now, towards the end of the 1980s, although John himself was always aware of 'the exceeding sinfulness of sin' and emphasized that the Christian virtue of hope was very different from optimism. As he said in his last sermon, hope comes from the enduring of suffering. 'Suffering, as Paul says, trains us to endure, and endurance brings proof that we have stood the test, and this proof is the ground of hope – in the God who can bring resurrection out and through the other side of death.'

And although the prospect of the conversion of institutions may not seem very near, nevertheless it need not be completely abandoned. God sent us Marxism (as John once remarked) as a corrective in an area where the church had conspicuously failed ('heresies are born only when some aspect of the truth is persistently being ignored or suppressed by the orthodox'). It may be that Thatcherism is part of the divine corrective treatment for some of the failures of socialism in the 1960s.

Given that we must alter our institutions, is the Christian to be involved, and if so, how? Here I must quote a passage from the *Epistle to Diognetus*, 'penned by an unknown writer probably within fifty years of the New Testament itself', which John was to include more than once in his published works:

Christians are not distinguished from the rest of mankind either in locality or in speech or in customs. For they dwell not somewhere in cities of their own, neither do they use some different language, nor practise an extraordinary kind of life. . . . But while they dwell in cities of Greeks and barbarians as the lot of each is cast, and follow the native customs in dress and food and the other arrangements of life, yet the constitution of their own citizenship, which they set forth, is marvellous, and confessedly contradicts expectation. They dwell in their own countries, but only as sojourners; they bear their share in all things as citizens, and they enjoy all hardships as strangers. Every foreign country is a fatherland to them and every fatherland is foreign. . . . They obey the established laws, and they surpass the laws in their own lives . . . in a word, what the soul is in a body, thus the Christians are in the world. . . . The world is enclosed in the body, and yet itself holds the body together; so Christians are kept in the world as in a prison house, and yet they themselves hold the world together. . . . So great is the office for which God has appointed them and which it is not lawful for them to decline.

If we are to bear our share in all things as citizens, in a democracy, this involves taking part in politics, and radicals would certainly say that it involves membership of a political party. John rejected Conservatism at an early age and joined the Labour Party. He worked and campaigned for it but became disillusioned, and finally left it over the Kenyan Asians Bill in 1967. On that occasion both major parties ganged up to dishonour a pledge of citizenship which had been given to the Asian minority in East Africa by a previous British government. John, now finding himself without a political party and believing, as I have said, that Christians should be involved, rang me up one afternoon – I remember his voice on the end of the phone – and asked me how he should join the Liberal Party. I told him, and having joined the Cambridge City Liberal Party, he remained a member – as far as I know – for the rest of his life. I used to ask them occasionally about him, and they always acknowledged his definite, if slightly quiescent, support.

The quiescence in constituency politics is not surprising. It is not in any intelligent Christian to be a 'good' Party person, although he or she may and should be a loyal one, and John's relationship with any political party was bound to be uneasy. He was persistently cynical about the ease with which a party in permanent opposition could afford to take moral stands, but there was a strain of genuine radicalism running through the Liberal Party at the time, which had nearly been eclipsed in the Labour Party, and which he found sympathetic.

If he were alive today I suspect he would have found it difficult to stomach the lurch to the right (or rather to centrism) which marked the formation of the Alliance, and he might well be attracted to the leadership which Neil Kinnock has given to the Labour Party. But if I read his philosophy correctly, it would have taken a traumatic betrayal such as that of the Kenyan Asian bills to make him change parties again. It is true that in a gloomy moment in 1976 he got as far as writing a letter to *The Guardian* announcing his resignation from the Liberal Party on the grounds that 'they seem to do nothing else but unite with the Conservatives to try and bring the

Government down and so carry Mrs Thatcher and her friends to power, than which I cannot see anything more calamitous at this moment for the health and peace of the nation'. But he never sent the letter, and it may be that the rather naive and therefore untypical understanding of the enforced role of a third Party in the British electoral system which it reveals did not endure the examination of the next morning.

But, moving from the general scene to particular issues, what did John see as the points at which God was hammering in our society in the 1960s, and what would he think were the equivalents today?

First, without doubt, came issues of injustice and inequality, particularly those which were institutionalized, because 'there is no such thing as Jew and Greek, slave and freeman, male and female, for you are all one in Jesus Christ'.

In October 1963, for instance, five months after the publication of *Honest to God*, the Rivonia trials began in South Africa of a number of anti-apartheid activists which resulted in life sentences for eight men – six Africans, one Indian and one European. Seven men remain in prison, of whom Nelson Mandela is the most celebrated. On Sunday afternoon, 14 June 1964, John was one of those who spoke in the protest meeting in Trafalgar Square – with Bertrand Russell, Elwyn Jones, Fenner Brockway, David Ennals, Angus Wilson, Andrew Faulds, Tony Benn and others.

The network of convention and law which John wanted to see society weave, which would, so to speak, by tightening its mesh sweep ever more and more fish into the kingdom of heaven, had a lot to do with human rights. The black man or woman in South Africa or Brixton or Watts, the homosexual, the poor; these were the people for whom John worked in the 1960s and these would be the people he would be working for today, although priorities might have altered.

It is, of course, one of the dangers of attempting to discern where the Holy Spirit is pushing and then placing yourself at his disposal that you often appear to be identifying merely with fashionable causes. I believe that John, although of course he attracted such accusations, can be cleared of them if we realize how often he took up the causes before they were fashionable. He had a moral sensitivity which got him there considerably before most others of his background.

If I were asked (as the Editor of this book has asked me) to hazard a guess as to what cause John might be involved in today, I would take it for granted that he would be involved in the problems of the inner cities (as indeed he was to a certain extent while he was alive) and perhaps more widely in the disadvantaged twenty-five per cent of our society, those – roughly speaking – suffering from two or more kinds of deprivation (unemployment, disability, one-parent families, sub-standard housing, etc.). Slightly less obviously, I think he might be involved with the appalling conditions in our prisons, which are a disgrace to any country even remotely claiming to be either Christian or civilized. He had already been a strong campaigner against the death penalty, and used regularly to visit a Cambridge graduate serving a life sentence in prison for murder.

He would also, I think, be involved in ecological issues, and would have been of considerable help during a recent period, now happily – I believe – over, when the church had not sufficiently authoritative biblical scholars to buttress and substantiate its instincts in this field.

And if I were to stick my neck out even further and hazard a guess as to the issues of the immediate future which those of us who increasingly see ourselves as John's disciples should be involved in, the field is, by definition, uncharted, but I think that I would look in an area which had hardly become visible in John's lifetime except to Conservatives. 'With the permissive society and the welfare state,' said Conservatives, 'is coming a breakdown of family life, and the result of that is crime, alienation and a general collapse of decent life as we know it.' Now in the 1960s it was possible to believe that education would combat these dangers. It is beyond the scope of this contribution to discuss whether such a belief was naive; suffice it to say that it was disappointed.

But we are now confronted with a growing crisis and it is not entirely clear how we are to strengthen the family and the community to deal with the problems that are arising. This is where I miss John, and I have not yet come across any more than a glimmer of insight in the murk into which the Christian Left seems to have run on this issue.

I find nothing very helpful in the conventional policies of the political parties, nor in the claims of Mrs Thatcher to be the champion of the family, justified though some of them are to a limited extent.

But the one glimmer I do find is in the recent theological and practical analysis of modern Work Practice by Christian Schumacher,[1] where he suggests that the restructuring of work patterns which have had a consistently injurious effect since the coming of the Industrial Revolution might have a revitalizing effect on the family, and he gives examples of cases where the reorganizing of factory work has given a new lease of life to workers' relationships with their families.

Christian Schumacher (Fritz's son) is a practising work engineer, and I for one can see this as the kind of issue on to which John might have latched, expounding the biblical background and linking it up with the kind of (possibly cooperative) political industrial policy which is needed and then hammering away at it.

But that, sadly, is now the work for us. What is clear is that when I first met John twenty-seven years ago it was still possible to find seemingly intelligent men and women arguing that religion and politics do not mix. Now it is not, and much of the credit belongs to him.

I remember him once volunteering to act as a kamikaze pilot in Church Assembly (as Synod was then called, when we both served in it), putting forward an extreme view of a topic compared to which the studiedly mildly-expressed views of us other radicals would look an eminently reasonable compromise which the establishment could accept. It was a tactic of which he was a master, not merely in Church Assembly, and with it he achieved a lot. Politics was not John's native country, but he 'bore his share in all things as a citizen and endured all hardships as a stranger'. And it was a pleasure to do business with him.

Trevor Beeson

◆

Reform or Renewal?

The publication of John Robinson's *Honest to God* in 1963 is now widely recognized as but one, albeit the most dramatic, manifestation of a movement of thought and demand for action which was the chief characteristic of church life in Britain throughout the 1960s. Significantly, *Honest to God* was soon followed by *The New Reformation?*, in which Robinson turned his attention to the church and discussed the various reforms that he believed to be essential if the Christian community in Britain was to be renewed and enabled to carry out its mission effectively in a society that was becoming increasingly secularized. Although *The New Reformation?* did not achieve the massive sales of its predecessor, it attracted a good deal of attention and spoke with considerable power, and encouragement, to many people, both inside and outside the churches, who hoped that ancient ecclesiastical institutions might in some way be stirred into new life and begin to express the Christian gospel in more dynamic terms. Later, the ecumenical fortnightly *New Christian* marked the 450th anniversary of the Lutheran Reformation by publishing its own '95 Theses of the New Reformation'. This was of course no more than a provocative piece of journalism, but it reflected certain hopes and aspirations at that time, and twenty years later the theses offer a fairly accurate guide to the outlook of the liberal Christian reformer.

The reasons for the turbulence in the British churches have yet to be fully analysed and explained, and the valiant but unsuccessful attempts of David Perman, in *Change and the Churches*, and Adrian Hastings, in *A History of English Christianity 1920–85*, are perhaps an indication that it is still too early to be sure what was really taking place. It is, for example, sometimes suggested that the minor religious revival of the 1950s led to the emergence of a new breed of clergy and articulate laity whose convictions and enthusiasms brought about a demand for a more lively and better organized church. Something similar was experienced after the First World War when returning army chaplains and others had campaigned, with some degree of success, for greater democracy in the Church of England. Another explanation, which goes somewhat deeper, is that the outlook and actions of the church were the religious expression of a liberal reforming spirit in British society as a whole which led to the election of the Wilson government in 1964 and which caused the decade to be described, superficially, as 'The Swinging '60s'. Here it may be noted that over the last 100 years, and possibly before that, the atmosphere within the Church of England has often been strikingly similar to that prevailing in the social and political life of the nation to which it has so many historical and cultural links.

The weakness of these explanations, however, is that they overlook the international dimension of the church's life and what was taking place outside Britain during the 1960s. In the United States, where the proportion of church attenders in the population was some four or five times greater than in Britain, the demand for church reform and for new expressions of Christian life was no less great. The Trappist monk Thomas Merton, whose writings had nurtured the spirituality of a whole generation of conservative Roman Catholics, himself moved to a quite different understanding of the Christian faith and described John Robinson's *The New*

Reformation? as far more significant than *Honest to God*. Two books by Harvey Cox, *The Secular City* and *A Feast of Fools*, crossed the Atlantic in the other direction far more success-fully than the work of most American theologians and became highly influential among British church reformers. There was common ground in spirit, if not in actual circumstances.

Much more impressive and significant than any of this was the tremendous upheaval taking place within the Roman Catholic Church and finding expression in the Second Vatican Council, which occupied the years 1962–65. If to the Anglican and Protestant observer the Council's reforms seemed an altogether too modest attempt at ecclesiastical *agg-iornamento*, the fact remained that what was proposed, and even more important the changes in theological understand-ing, amounted to something very close to a 'New Reforma-tion' in the Roman Catholic communion. Locally, in European countries such as Holland and France where the Roman Catholic Church was faced with, and indeed continues to be faced with, problems and opportunities markedly similar to those of the Church of England, reform was very much in the air and a great deal of experiment was taking place. Hopes ran high, and the visitor to one of the reforming Dutch parishes or to a group of worker-priests in France came home greatly excited; it is interesting and frustrating to speculate on how these examples of a renewed Catholicism might have de-veloped had they not fallen victim to Roman authoritarianism.

It is against this international background that church life in Britain during the 1960s needs to be examined and assessed. It simply will not do to dismiss Bishop John Robinson as a 'Media Bishop' (*Observer*, 11 October 1987) when he was seeking to interpret to English readers some of the thinking of major European and American theologians, and trying to face up to religious and philosophical questions that were ex-ercising the minds of many thoughtful people in every part of the developed world. Equally, it will not do to dismiss the reforming efforts of the 1960s, fumbling and inadequate though these may have been, as no more than the exhibition-ism of a few 'trendy' clergymen from Cambridge, when the

British churches, without fully realizing the fact, were caught up in a movement towards change that was affecting Christian communities in many parts of the world.

In Britain the first signs of desire for change appeared with the emergence in 1949 of the Parish and People movement in the Church of England. Once again it is tempting to associate this with the zeal of the liveliest among the ex-service chaplains, and some of them were certainly to be found among the pioneers of Parish and People, but this movement had deep theological roots, planted by some of the most important scholars of the inter-war years, and its twofold aim of putting the eucharist at the centre of the church's life, and of involving the laity more fully in this act of worship, had close affinities with a similar development in France, Germany and Belgium. Throughout the 1950s Parish and People grew in number and influence. The Parish Communion, with its mixture of simplicity, drama and togetherness, proved to be a popular service. In no way was it controversial: on the contrary, it seemed capable of drawing together the high, low and broad strands within the Church of England. By the end of the decade Parish and People had 1,500 subscribing members, including a large number of bishops, a magazine circulation of over 2,000, and flourishing regional groups as well as popular annual conferences.

About this time there was a division of opinion within the movement. Some of the pioneering members believed that the work of Parish and People had been accomplished and that its modest organization, managed by a country priest in the diocese of Oxford, could now be wound up. No one could doubt that the Parish Communion had largely replaced Matins and the High Mass as the main Sunday morning service, and that such a change, accomplished in a little over ten years in a notably conservative church, was indeed remarkable. But others among the leaders of Parish and People were much less happy with the situation, and felt that the movement still had a great deal to do. There was ample evidence that the Parish Communion had been adopted in many places simply because it seemed to be 'a nice service', and without much recognition of its implications for the community life and the mission of the local church. Those who saw new approaches to baptism, congregational decision-making, evangelism and social responsibility as a necessary concomitant of the Sunday eucharist were fearful that the Church of England's complacency had not really been overcome, and that nothing significant would be achieved without a long haul of education and experiment.

It was while this debate was taking place within Parish and People that the smaller but more dynamic Keble Conference Group arrived on the scene with its proposals for the reforming of the parochial system and its new ideas about the deployment and payment of the clergy. The suggestion, made in 1963, that the two organizations should merge to form one force for renewal in every part of the church's life seemed to offer a solution to two problems. It would move Parish and People away from its preoccupation with liturgical matters, and at the same time provide the Keble Conference reformers with a much more respectable platform and a much larger constituency. Thus the merger took place, engendering high hopes among its sponsors, and providing the organization, which retained the name Parish and People, that was to be the spearhead of reform in the Church of England for the next six years. Much smaller groups of a similar kind had sprung up in the Methodist, Congregational and Baptist churches, while the emergence of a flourishing, but equally ephemeral, Catholic Renewal movement awaited the end of the Vatican Council and the provocation of the encyclical *Humanae Vitae*.

Underlying the detailed programmes of the reform movements there was a threefold aim grounded in certain convictions about the nature of the Christian faith itself, and about the place of the church in the purpose of God. It may well be the case that the vision was not shared by everyone who became involved in these movements, but it certainly provided the motivation of their leaders and a high proportion of their members.

First, the church's internal life must be reformed in order that it might be better equipped for its mission in the world.

There was to be no tinkering with the machinery of church government for its own sake or to match the blueprint of an ideal Christian community. The parochial system needed to be modified and the clergy more sensibly deployed for no other reason than that of enabling the church, the Spirit-filled Body of Christ, to be a more effective instrument of God's loving purpose in the world.

Second, the movement towards Christian unity must be accelerated. The church could not be a sign and servant of the kingdom of God, and a means of reconciliation in society as a whole, while there were such sharp divisions in its own ranks. The nature of the church and the demands of mission required unity. It was also to be anticipated that the sharing of insights and traditions would lead to the great enrichment of all the uniting communities, and the sharing of buildings and other physical resources, including ministerial man and woman-power, would be more economical and efficient.

Third, the whole of the church's life must be reorientated, so that the church, at every level of its life, might engage more significantly in the affairs of the secular world and, hopefully, bring Christian insights to bear on the developing life of individuals and communities. It was emphasized that the servant church existed for the sake of the world, not the world for the sake of the church, and, in a phrase borrowed from an important study project of the World Council of Churches, it was asserted that the world must provide the church with its main agenda.

These, then, were the basic convictions of the 1960s reformers, and their belief that the church needed to be changed so that the Christian faith might be more widely and deeply propagated linked them with the 'new theologians' of that time whose objective was the same. Not every theologian was concerned with church reform, and many members of Parish and People were far more conservative in their doctrinal beliefs than John Robinson, Ronald Gregor Smith and Alistair Kee, but they occupied common ground in their acceptance of the missionary imperative and the need for renewal.

The published aims and objects of the new, or renewed, Parish and People movement were as follows:

1. A contemporary theology, spirituality and ethic in
   (a) The liturgy and its setting.
   (b) Ecumenical partnership.
   (c) Religious sociology, industrial mission and Christian social action.
2. The constitutional, administrative and financial reform of the church in
   (a) The supply and training of the ministry – ordained and lay, male and female.
   (b) Group and team ministry, and supplementary ministries.
   (c) The deployment, pay and pensions of the ministry.
   (d) Synodical government.

This was a sizeable programme and a reflection of the need to unite the diverse elements within Parish and People, rather than the result of a realistic assessment of what might be achieved by one full-time Director, an office secretary and about 1,500 members, virtually all of whom had their hands more than full with ecclesiastical or secular responsibilities.

The Revd Eric James, who resigned from his Camberwell parish in order to become Director of the movement, was undaunted by the scale of his assignment and quickly set to work, visiting all the Church of England's dioceses to take the temperature of the reforming atmosphere and, wherever possible, establish local groups to spread the message and provide support for the reformers. After the enthusiasm and excitement of central committee meetings and so forth, Eric James found the zeal for reform much less marked in the provinces. The meetings he addressed were mainly clerical in composition and it soon became evident that an alarmingly high proportion of those who had been keen on liturgical change were more than happy with the *status quo* in other areas of church life. Efforts to paint a picture of the likely consequences of failure to effect significant reform in these areas led to the defensive, and inaccurate, charge that the

Director of Parish and People was no more than a prophet of doom and gloom. It was going to be much harder work than the leaders of Parish and People had bargained for.

Nonetheless, things soon began to move. Groups were set up in every diocese, regional and national conferences were well supported, pamphlets and books were published, and *New Christian*, the unofficial journal of the movement, reached a fortnightly circulation of 11,000. On the political front, a number of able clergy and laity, including the Director himself, were elected to the Church Assembly on a reform ticket, and made such an impact on its deliberations that it soon became necessary for some of their number to be appointed to the various official commissions and committees. In one form or another the items and issues that were of special concern to Parish and People found their way on to the agenda of the Assembly, and there were many lively debates, but progress, when discernible, was always far too slow and much too limited for the serious reformer. Then came what Peter Jagger, in his valuable *History of the Parish and People Movement*, described as 'An Unexpected Death'. Eric James resigned from the Directorship soon after his appointment as a Residentiary Canon of Southwark Cathedral in September 1966, though he continued in an honorary capacity until 1969; others on the Central Committee had less time to spare; some believed that the reform of the church's institutional life was a lost cause and that it would be better to concentrate on the formation of small groups that would become parallel or even alternative churches; yet more believed that God was calling them to his service in social agencies and relief work, rather than in full-time church employment.

The crisis now being experienced in Parish and People was also being felt in the Methodist Renewal Group and a number of other ailing denominational and ecumenical reform organizations. It was therefore decided to merge all these groups and, after necessary negotiations and preparations occupying most of 1969, a new movement known as One for Christian Renewal emerged in January 1970. A rump of Parish and People continued for a time, in order to provide support for

those of its members who were still in the Church Assembly,
but this was soon re-named the Open Synod Group, and
another small organization that now uses the name of Parish
and People, and publishes pamphlets on church reform, is in
no sense a descendant of the movement of the 1950s and
1960s. One for Christian Renewal tried hard to fan the dying
embers of reform, but it was too late to make a new blaze, and
with the demise of Parish and People the Church of England
lost the one coherent group of its members that was committed to real change. Did it expire through faintness of heart or
was it effectively killed by the sheer weight and inertia of the
institution it was seeking to reform?

In fact, the movement of reform initiated or encouraged by
Parish and People continued in various ways throughout the
1970s and is not yet ended. To some assessment of what has
happened in the Church of England during these years we
now turn.

Although 'The liturgy and its setting' appeared in the
prospectus of 1963, mainly to satisfy the old hands of Parish
and People, liturgical revision did not loom large in the minds
of the movement's new leaders. For one thing, the Parish
Communion battle had already been won and the official
Liturgical Commission was now busy with the process of
revision and experiment that was to lead to the publication in
1980 of the *Alternative Service Book*. Opinion may vary about
the merits of this book (see the contribution by T. G. A. Baker
above), but by and large it represented what the liturgical
reformers of the 1950s were seeking, and in the present
situation of something approaching liturgical chaos those who
need something more radical do not appear to feel unduly
inhibited. What was not foreseen by those of us who pressed
for liturgical change was the extent to which such change
would effectively sever the connection between the Church of
England and the very large number of English people who
attend worship in their parish church only occasionally but
nonetheless regard themselves as Christians and even church
members. It was recognized that the weekly gathering of a
congregation around an altar would in due course lead to a

deeper sense of coherence and community – this was one of
the objects of the exercise – and it was expected that this would
in turn lead to a greater concern for the mission of the church
in the parish and the forging of stronger links with both the
occasional worshipper and the non-worshipper. In most
places the missionary dimension of the Parish Communion
movement has not been realized and the new services seem to
be isolating congregations even further from the communities
in which they are set. There can, of course, be no turning the
clock back to 1662 or even to 1928, and some of the most lively
and effective parishes are making good use of the *Alternative
Service Book*, but the Church of England has a serious problem
on its hands with its nominal members, and this now requires
urgent attention if England's national, or folk, church is not to
become a much smaller Anglican sect.

During the 1960s the concept of 'ecumenical partnership'
was by no means restricted to the union of major denominations through the acceptance of carefully devised
schemes. It was fully recognized that such schemes would be
useless without a readiness to work together on the part of
local congregations, and that even without official negotiations and agreements there was still the possibility of
ecumenical partnership at most levels of the church's life.
Nonetheless, the full union of the divided churches was an
important objective and here there has been deep disappointment and much frustration. The failure of the Church of
England to accept good proposals for union with the Methodist Church and later a creative covenant scheme involving
much closer links with the United Reformed Church and the
Churches of Christ, as well as the Methodists, was a most
serious set-back to the ecumenical cause. This has been
compensated for neither by the coming together of the
Congregational and Presbyterian churches in England, nor by
the considerable work of the Anglican/Roman Catholic International Theological Commission. The United Reformed
Church has in fact lost ground numerically since it came into
being in 1973 and there is, as yet, no sign that the sharing of
insights and resources has had an invigorating effect on the

former Presbyterians and Congregationalists. The mere fact of
the existence of ARCIC, let alone the degree of agreement
reached by its members, is, when viewed historically, something of a miracle. But the contents of its documents reflect a
view of the church, especially of its authority, which is a long
way removed from that which seemed to be gaining ground in
the 1960s, and even the ARCIC agreements are regarded as
revolutionary, if not heretical, by the Vatican. So several more
miracles will be needed, or failing this a new and very
different sort of Pope, before significant practical progress
becomes possible.

In this rather depressing ecumenical situation, the news
from Swanwick in September 1987 was heralded as a ray of
real hope. Church leaders, including Cardinal Basil Hume and
other members of the Roman Catholic hierarchy, entered into
a new commitment to the quest for unity and offered, or at
least recognized, the possibility of a new way forward. The
failure of the official unity schemes had not inhibited ecumenical growth in many localities and a Lent study course in 1986
entitled 'Not Strangers, but Pilgrims' attracted no fewer than
one million participants, from all the churches, meeting in
house groups. The involvement of local radio stations contributed significantly to the success of the project. The 1970s and
1980s also saw some flowering of Local Ecumenical Projects
which enable different churches to work together in ways not
normally possible elsewhere, and by mid-1987 some 540 LEPs
had come into being. Faced with the evidence of this degree of
local growth, the church leaders decided that it would be
better to foster this approach to unity, rather than promote
new official schemes, and also proposed the setting up of a
new national ecumenical body, to replace the British Council
of Churches and to which the Roman Catholic Church might
happily belong. It is hoped that the number of Local Ecumenical Projects will increase to at least 1,000 by 1990, and that new
county bodies, with a full-time officer, will be formed to co-
ordinate and stimulate ecumenical activity in their areas. The
possibility of one church acting, nationally, on behalf of all the
others on specific matters, such as education or medical

ethics, is also envisaged. The general idea seems to be to by-pass synodical procedures for a period of, say, ten years, in order to encourage practical collaboration at the local level and to create a climate of opinion in which some sort of official scheme is once again embarked upon. This approach will, of course, need more, not less, commitment to the cause of church unity, and finding the right balance between the claims of legitimate diversity and necessary union will be no easier than it has ever been.

Holy worldliness and concern for the secular was one of the chief themes of the 1960s, and among the reformers this led to interest in religious sociology, industrial mission and Christian social action. Religious sociology, in its mid-twentieth-century form, had been pioneered in France where, for example, it was shown from statistics covering more than 100 years that the level of attendance at Mass was closely related to social conditions, even to particular forms of industry. There was also the belief that the units of church life, parish boundaries and so forth ought to be adjusted to take account of the size and shape of modern communities. Research was needed to discover the true *zone humaine* before the church could plan its mission to suburbs, towns and regions. Nothing much came of this in Britain, nor for that matter in France, partly because few people believed that sociological factors of this sort were significant, and partly because it became impossible to conceive of the church making the massive adjustments to its life that the new thinking would inevitably demand.

Industrial mission certainly had much greater support, though a trauma over a change of policy in the Sheffield Industrial Mission was an alarming reminder of the degree to which even a substantial piece of new work was at the mercy of episcopal whim. The number of industrial mission teams (40) and the number of clergy involved in industrial mission (125 full-time and 113 part-time) has in fact remained about the same. The hoped-for shift of emphasis from residential ministry to mission in other key areas of human life has not, however, taken place, and is unlikely to do so now that the parochial system is under strain through shortage of money and clergy. It is also evident that the insights gained during some forty years of industrial mission work have not penetrated the missionary thinking of the church as a whole, and the industrial chaplains remain no more than a tolerated minority.

In the realm of Christian social action it is impossible to obtain facts and figures about projects, but there appears to have been a significant increase in the church's involvement in social work, especially in areas of deprivation and urgent need. The accusation, sometimes heard, that the church is now more concerned with social work than with 'preaching the Gospel' is wildly wrong, but there has been enough movement in this direction to give it some credibility among the ill-informed. Certainly pronouncements by bishops about political, economic and social matters have greatly increased in number, if not always in quality. The combination of a bench of bishops consisting of men whose ministry was at a formative stage in the 1960s and a government of the radical Right has also created the totally unexpected, and unprecedented, situation in which the church's leadership appears to be distinctly left-wing and out of sympathy with a Conservative government which has been returned with huge majorities at three successive general elections. There is nothing in this, of course, to disappoint the reformer who has always believed that the church should be concerned about every part of human life, and should not hesitate to comment on political and social developments that threaten the well-being of individuals and communities.

A difficulty has arisen, however, from the fact that the political and social comment of bishops and others does not always appear to be related to any coherent theological understanding of human nature and destiny. By the end of the 1960s it had become increasingly evident that the effort of that decade to move the church towards a much greater concern for secular issues had not been accompanied by an equally necessary effort to rediscover the biblical and theological foundations of such a concern. Indeed, the theological excavations of the time tended to shake, rather than reinforce, these foundations. In consequence, the criticism that the church's pronouncements were simply of a secular character, and had no more authority than the views expressed by the leader-writer of a liberal newspaper, was not without some validity. The continuing failure of church leaders to spell out the religious basis of their criticisms of particular government policies, allied sometimes to a failure to appreciate the complexity of certain social and economic problems, still makes them vulnerable to the rejoinder of the politician that they have strayed from their proper domain and that their comments are altogether unhelpful.

An attempt to dismiss on these grounds the report of the Archbishop of Canterbury's Commission on Urban Priority Areas *Faith in the City*, published in 1985, was, however, a spectacular failure. Once again, the theological groundwork was quite shallow, but the analysis of the deteriorating situation in Britain's inner cities indicated that the church knew, from experience and careful study, what it was talking about and had a much better understanding than most politicians of the nature of the problems and their possible solution. The authority of the report was also enhanced by the fact that a substantial part of it was addressed to the church and offered a major challenge to the church to put its own inner-city house in order. The response to the appeal for £18 million for a new Church Urban Fund, and the way in which this money is used and the church's human resources redeployed, will give a clearer indication of just how seriously the Church of England, let alone the government, is taking a report of the highest quality.

The inability of the church to make any significant impact on the great urban areas was the chief reason for the concern of the Keble Conference about the deployment and payment of the clergy, and in due course this became the major item on the church's agenda. It was evident from the Paul Report, published in 1964, that the majority of the Church of England's clergy were ministering in places where the majority of English people were not living. It also revealed that many of these country clergymen were lonely, and that those in the cities were dispirited by the insuperable problems history had bequeathed to them. The work of E. R. Wickham in Sheffield indicated the barrenness of the inner-city landscape, and the historical and social reasons for the crisis facing the church in these areas, while from across the Atlantic came warning of the temptation to the church to retreat into 'suburban captivity'. No one believed that the redeployment of the clergy would of itself solve these problems, but some freedom to move the church's full-time servants to the areas of greatest need, and to provide an organization that would enable them to work most effectively, was seen as an essential first step. The establishing of pioneer group and team ministries in both rural and urban areas suggested that this would be the way forward.

After much debate, and not a little frustration, the necessary legal and administrative changes were secured, and although the reformers did not get everything they wanted the parochial system of the Church of England was provided with a potential flexibility never previously available. That which could not be obtained willingly by theological and ecclesiastical debate in the 1960s soon became compulsory through economic necessity and a sharp decline in the number of active clergy in the 1970s. Hence the near-decimation of the country parishes in the space of a mere decade, the setting-up of group and team ministries in many areas, and the emergence of a non-stipendiary ordained ministry, prepared by local ministerial training schemes. For a church so rooted in tradition and so resistant to change, what has taken place is remarkable. The question that now has to be asked is: why are the fruits of this revolution so meagre? For it is plain for all to see that in 1988 the Church of England is no stronger than it was two decades earlier, and that in certain respects it is a good deal weaker.

As always, there is no simple answer to the question and no easy solution of the problem. It must be noted first that the numerical strength, ordained and lay, of the Church of England has continued to decline and that an organization designed for a much larger membership, active and nominal, has inevitably been under great stress. Lest anyone is tempted to believe that the decline is due to the particular follies of the Church of England, it should also be noted that during this period something similar has been taking place in other major churches throughout Western Europe, and that in some respects, especially in France, the position is more serious. In England the decline has not been uniform, and there are considerable variations between the different regions and even within regions. Some parishes remain relatively strong and vigorous. The cathedrals have never before been visited by so many people or been so well equipped to minister to them. New, creative work is going on here and there, and the Church of England still has over one million people worshipping in its parish churches every Sunday. This represents less than three per cent of the population, but it is a large number all the same. Again, it has to be recognized that the fruits of a radical change in missionary strategy are hardly likely to appear overnight. 'Take no thought of the harvest, but only of proper sowing', counsels T. S. Eliot.

What is not at all evident, however, is that the administrative changes within the Church of England have been prompted by any rethinking of missionary strategy. Rather have they been produced as desperate measures designed to ensure the survival of a church under dangerous threat – a classic example of doing the right thing for the wrong reason. This difference of approach is of the greatest significance. The enthusiastic reformers of the 1960s were motivated by missionary considerations. We believed that if the church's administration became more flexible this would set the church free to respond more vigorously to the promptings of the Holy Spirit and enable it to embark upon a new mission to the nation. In other words the motivation was dynamic rather than defensive. Defensive action has produced a church which is leaner and more tidily dressed than it was twenty years ago, yet no less uncertain as to the way in which it should be moving, and even more likely to fall flat on its face.

At no point is the danger of this greater than in its handling of the question of the place of women in the church. The number of women who occupy the pews of parish churches and undertake much of the drudgery of church maintenance continues to be very much higher than that of men. Even among young people, nearly twice as many girls as boys are confirmed every year. Yet women still have no significant place in the leadership of the Church of England and their influence on its institutional life is minimal. The admission of women to the diaconate was a step in the right direction, though many are working hard to ensure that it was a final step. That women will one day be ordained to the priesthood and eventually to the episcopate is now impossible to doubt, but it is seventeen years since Archbishop Michael Ramsey said that the theological argument against the ordination of women could no longer be sustained and that their entry into the priesthood was only a matter of time. Some matters of church reform can take their time, and normally are required to do so, but as the Church of England prepares to enter the last decade of the twentieth century it cannot delay the ordination of women much longer without destroying completely its credibility as an institution committed to the unity in Christ of the whole of the human race. Moreover, the church desperately needs feminine insights for the revival of its own corporate life.

Hardly less urgent is the need for the Church of England to reassess its place in the rural scene. The critical nature of the situation in the cities, and the need to apply greater resources to urban areas, has encouraged some overlooking of the extent to which the church has neglected, or even severed, its rural roots. In some areas the removal of the clergy, the selling of vicarages and the infrequent use of ancient churches has had a disastrous effect both on the Christian mission and on the community life of disintegrating villages. The problems here are immense but not yet beyond solution if the Church of England is prepared to move quickly and think again about the nature of Christian leadership and priesthood in small rural communities.

The prospects of moving quickly in any part of the church's

life have not been enhanced by the arrival of synodical government. The old Church Assembly was an unrepresentative body and needed to be replaced if there was to be greater involvement and more accountability in church government. Hence the interest of the 1960s reformers in proposals for national, diocesan and deanery synods. But what was not foreseen then was how cumbersome and time-consuming the whole apparatus would become and how a system of government that required something akin to a referendum of the whole church for any significant change would destroy any effective episcopal leadership. Neither was it foreseen that the domination of the Crown Appointments Commission by General Synod nominees would lead to undue influence by pressure groups on the appointment of bishops. Both the synodical procedures and the Crown Appointments Commission should be regarded as first attempts to reform the government of the late twentieth-century church, and be open to early review.

The fact that the years of liberal reform have not been accompanied by much in the way of liberal renewal must not be allowed to obscure another fact, namely that a real renewal has been taking place within the evangelical wing of the Church of England. This is to be welcomed and regarded as a sign of hope. The 'new evangelicals' are much less fundamentalist than their predecessors, have a greater understanding of sacramental worship and, in many cases, a deeper commitment to social reform. They still flourish best in comfortable, well-heeled parishes and appear to have no serious problems over right-wing governments, but they are on the move, and if their numbers continue to increase they will have much greater influence and responsibility in the Church of England than for many years past. Far from welcome is emergence of those extreme versions of evangelicalism which have found expression in the charismatic movement and the house church movement. There is sad irony in the fact that the desire of the 1960s for greater freedom for the movement of the Holy Spirit in the churches should have been replaced by something that is irrational, divisive

and largely escapist. Equally, the sectarian and often intoler-
ant character of the house church movement bears no resemblance to the search for small, authentic, local expressions of
the church led in the 1950s and 1960s by men like Ernest
Southcott.

The lesson of all this is that where a vacuum appears in the
life of the Christian community some strange and often
undesirable things often appear to fill it. It is now plain that
the reforming movement of the 1960s lacked sufficient power
of dynamic renewal to enable it to lead the church as a whole
to exploit the opportunities that reform might offer. There
were those at the time, John Robinson among them, who
insisted that mere reform was not enough and that the quest
must be for a much more radical understanding of the nature
of the Christian faith and a much more radical expression of
this faith in the life of the church. The difference between the
reformer and the revolutionary is of course well known and of
long standing, and it is never easy, at least not at the time of
action, to discern which of the two is right. What is clear,
however, from the experience of the 1960s is that the renewal
and reinvigoration of the church is not something that can be
organized and does not necessarily result from sensible, or
even inspired, reform. Such reform may be needed, but the
awakening itself requires waiting on the Spirit, rather than
waiting on the Synod, and above all a renewed commitment to
him who is the source of all life and therefore of all true
renewal.

John Bowden

Honesty is not Enough

I remember, as clearly as the death of President Kennedy, the time I first heard of *Honest to God*. I was curate of a city church in Nottingham, and was often invited up to the university when there were visitors to the theology department. That March Saturday evening, in the senior common room, David Edwards, Editor and Managing Director of SCM Press, had come up to talk. He told us of the radical new book which John Robinson, Bishop of Woolwich, had written, and of the furore that it was likely to cause: 'He may well lose his job.'

There next morning at Sunday breakfast was *The Observer*, with its banner headline 'Our Image of God must Go', and on the Monday I was at our local bookshop the moment it opened, persuading the friendly assistant to let me buy on the day before publication one of the select 6,000 copies which formed the first impression of *Honest to God*.

I took it home and read it and – to be as honest as its author tried to be – I was not bowled over. To those who had been at certain Anglican theological colleges at the end of the 1950s, the ideas expressed in *Honest to God* were not new; having left behind us university courses which all too often did not acknowledge that anything important in theology had happened after the Council of Chalcedon in AD 451, we revelled in the thought of Bonhoeffer, Bultmann and Tillich, who by then were after all established modern classics: Tillich's *The Shaking of the Foundations* had appeared in 1949; Bonhoeffer's *Letters and Papers from Prison* and Bultmann's *Kerygma and Myth* in 1953. Most of what was said in *Honest to God* was familiar stuff. What made it different was first – and this was no mean feat – that John Robinson had got everyone talking about God: on radio and television, in the national newspapers, and indeed in the pubs; secondly, that he had put these disparate theologians, and much else, together in one small paperback; and thirdly, that he was a bishop. All this suggested that something new and revolutionary might actually be about to happen.

Two things became clear to me after talking with other people who had bought *Honest to God*. Of those I talked with, the majority of non-theologians who bought it found it very hard going indeed, and many of them never got to the end. To judge from much of the published lay comment, including the many letters to the author, those who did read it and commented were often projecting their own hopes and thoughts on to the book rather than reading what it actually said: the reaction was emotional rather than rational. The majority of theologians who read it seemed to find its combination of such different theologians strange and, when it emerged that this mixture was to be combined with a very conservative and by then somewhat dated biblical theology (James Barr's death sentence on that movement, *The Semantics of Biblical Language*, had appeared in 1961), felt that John Robinson's position just would not do.

Nowhere was this twofold reaction clearer than at a conference on 'The New Theology' held at St Anne's College, Oxford, I think, in 1964. There were gathered those hopefuls who felt that they might be at the dawn of a new beginning in Christian thought and practice, and there too were the professionals, keen to press the author of *Honest to God* on those points where they felt he was evasive, inconsistent or even self-contradictory. The disappointment of the lay radicals was manifest when they discovered, meeting John Robinson face to face, that in temperament he really was an Anglican bishop and was in no way prepared to abandon his biblical theology, for all the radical questions he was asking in other directions. And the frustration of the professionals was manifest when towards the end of a question-and-answer session aimed at clarifying John Robinson's position, at which he had parried just about every question they had put to him with 'I think that we must remain open on that point', the philosopher J. L. Lucas stood up and remarked, 'I would like to remind the Bishop that a vessel which is open on all sides is incapable of containing anything.'

The initial diffuseness, the lack of rigour, in the *Honest to God* debate was not helped by the fact that in his next book, *The New Reformation?*, John Robinson moved on to rather different ground. That was not surprising, since he did not have, and indeed did not claim to have, the philosophical and theological training to enable him to take further the questions he had raised. That bomb had gone off, and pieces seemed to be flying everywhere, but there was no obvious programme for further development, not least because what had happened with the publication of *Honest to God* had had such a high degree of emotional and personal content. The topic of the new book was important enough: the church and above all 'the stripping of the structures' which, it was argued, needed to be done if the church was to bring new life to a new age. But since much of the *Honest to God* public consisted of those who had already lost patience with the church or were in some way alienated from it, this topic proved less interesting than that of God, and so began a gradual decline in interest which reduced John Robinson's readership to more conventional dimensions, where it subsequently remained. More seriously, the new book signally lacked what would have made it really valuable: any specific programme for the way in which the structures should be stripped and what should take their place. And what can be expected if you put everything into a melting pot which is open on all sides took place: it ran away into the sand.

And so it was that only two or three years later, well before the 'sixties' revolution had reached its climax in 1968, that church and theology were already returning, passion apparently spent, to more deeply embedded habits and patterns, marking a relapse to a conservatism which has deepened steadily until at the end of the 1980s the churches are inherently far more conservative than they were in the 1950s, and a situation where theological understanding and competence has decreased appallingly – as witness the pathetic level of recent public debate centred on the Bishop of Durham. I personally have to live with the fact that the result of my more than twenty years of involvement in publishing – at a financial profit – theology in the tradition of *Honest to God* is a church which seems to get more reactionary every day.

Our present situation is not without its oddities and paradoxes. The curate who was forewarned about *Honest to God* that night in 1963 (and who at the time was a regular, anonymous, reviewer for the *Church Times*) is now in charge of SCM Press; the then apparently radical editor of SCM Press is a pillar of orthodoxy, and no issue of the *Church Times* is complete without an article or review by him. No one lost their job. One of the most conservative figures of the 1960s, David Jenkins, whose *Guide to the Debate about God* and 1966 Bampton Lectures *The Glory of Man* are classic statements of orthodoxy, has now become the *bête noir* of a church which has completely forgotten Bultmann and Tillich, and for whom Bonhoeffer is primarily a devotional writer. And to all outward apearances a whole generation of 1960s radicals has just disappeared, giving place within the Church of England, at any rate, to an atmosphere dominated by constant infighting between party groups redolent more of the nineteenth century than the twentieth.

Yet at the same time it has sometimes come to feel more dangerous, at least to some of the sensitive, to be a Christian. Nowhere is speech quite as free as it used to be, and it seems inconceivable that the sort of debate which took off after *Honest to God* could be carried on nowadays in the same sort of atmosphere. With religion a factor in so many situations of war or racial tension, from Latin America to the Middle East, with the influence of fundamentalist Christians in the United States leading in some areas to a *de facto* censorship of thought, and with churches often finding their political position to the left of a government (the Church of England is always necessarily political, but that fact only emerges when its stated views are critical of the government), religion has taken on a new profile in national and world affairs, very different from that which it had in the days of so-called 'secular man'. And it is becoming evident that any substantial degree of questioning in certain areas is going to be costly in all kinds of ways, not least for clergy with a lifetime to spend in the paid employment of the church. For we are in the era not only of cuts in churches and universities but also of the 'safe' appointment – and not just (the odd mishap apart) to the bench of bishops.

This may explain to some degree why although many of those involved in the *Honest to God* debate are still comparatively young and active, that debate now seems to be generally regarded as a temporary aberration, just one feature of the 'swinging sixties'. There is a good case for keeping your head down and your views to yourself if you want to stay in the church's ministry; and if you are a lay person who joins the major exodus of thinking professional people (teachers, doctors, social workers and so on) from the churches which has been such a disturbing feature of the last twenty years, you will find no forum within which you can communicate your views anyway.

But that does not really explain the present theological climate. It would certainly be unfair to see the Church of England as being made up of so many Vicars of Bray. (Though there is no mistaking the pull of the traditional Anglican way of life which cast a spell not least on John Robinson himself in his last years. Those who have never felt it and have many still unanswered questions about it have some justification for feeling betrayed.) Nor is it the case that since *Honest to God* theology itself has substantially changed direction and is now pointing the church back to more conservative ways. The old questions still remain basically unanswered, and in many areas of belief problems still continue to mount unheeded. For all the claims that the tide has now turned, in a church whose practice and attitudes have become more conservative over twenty years, there are remarkably few substantial and intellectually attractive restatements of Christian belief which counter successfully the now well-established criticisms of it. What we have seems rather to amount to either apathy or deliberate disregard of these questions, with little attempt to push through them and face the consequences. Perhaps that is why theological writing, in Britain, at any rate, is at such a low ebb.

For the position is that despite attempts to revive it, biblical theology has remained dead: increasing study of the Old Testament and archaeological discoveries in the Near East have led many Old Testament specialists to feel that they know less, rather than more, about their subject; New Testament scholarship is in a state of stagnation, not really knowing what to do with a canonical book to which more lip-service than real attention is paid. No viable answer has really been produced to the challenge of Christian doctrine posed by the sort of doctrinal criticism represented by *The Myth of God Incarnate*, published in 1977, and the approach inspired by historical relativism which underlies it. New disciplines like narrative theology, canonical criticism, structuralism and post-structuralism are essentially élitist, and their significance still remains nebulous except to their most devoted followers. The unexploded bomb of the inter-relationship of world religions (does or does not Christianity claim to be superior to all other religions by virtue of the 'revelation' in Jesus: if not, does its theology not need to be revised drastically?) is still ticking away insistently, but no one seems keen to attempt to defuse it.

One thing is abundantly clear: there is no way of putting the pieces in which theology now is together again in such a way that they add up to the old answers in some miraculously new form and can give justification to present structures. Yet if there is anything other than a mere concern to survive at all costs behind their current official attitudes, precisely that seems to be the presupposition of the institutional churches. And so we have the situation that the institutions are looking to theologians for the kind of statements that in all honesty just cannot be made, and the conclusions of those who think most deeply about the nature of Christianity and other religions and believe in God diverge so widely from what the institutional churches are looking for that no place can be found for them in those churches. In other words, structures and theological exploration have fallen apart to such a degree that the former are now supported by little more than an ideology (in the worst sense of the term) and the latter has no structures to which to relate. And that is putting it mildly. If you cannot feel at home in the church there is only one place to go – into the wilderness. There is no alternative. This tension is avoided in a way which recent events show not to have changed since the time of *Honest to God*. These things may be admitted, but in hardback rather than paperback, by a professor but not by a bishop, in private but not in public. And that means that this intolerable situation just continues and, simply by continuing, gets worse. The much-vaunted Anglican tolerance had its black underside: by refusing to recognize more openly the very real conflict that has now existed for more than a century, the Church of England is remaining in existence (a steadily declining existence) in a state of apathy and anti-intellectualism. At times the conflicts within the Roman Catholic church look preferable, because they are indications that at least someone is thinking hard.

What it means really to face the tensions produced by modern theological and critical research has been shown by a long line of figures who have paid a greater or lesser price for their thinking: one might mention, as examples, David Friedrich Strauss, W. Robertson Smith, George Tyrrell, Leonardo Boff and John Hick, all of whom suffered some form of disciplining from their church which brought them pain. And perhaps most significant of all, in the last century there was the famous Old Testament scholar Julius Wellhausen, who when surrendering his chair in Old Testament to take up a junior post as lecturer in Semitic studies, wrote to the Prussian Minister of Education:

> Your Excellency will perhaps remember that in Easter 1880 I requested, if it were at all possible, to be transferred into the Faculty of Philosophy. At the same time I tried to set out the reasons for my request. I became a theologian because I was interested in the academic study of the Bible. It then gradually dawned on me that a professor of theology also has the practical task of preparing students in the Protestant Church, and I was not up to this practical task. Despite every restraint on my part, I was making my pupils more unsuitable for it. Since then, my theological professorship has been a heavy burden on my conscience.

For a great many theologians, that situation has not essentially changed. But now it needs to be put in a different way. Certainly the churches have in many areas drifted too far away from the truth. But in that situation honesty is not enough: considering one's personal position and going where one's conscience leads, or living an unhappy compromise within the existing structures. If there is to be any hope for the Christian churches the structures have to be changed. Honesty is not enough, and thinking and writing is not enough. Part of any theological exploration must be to be involved in some action: for those still within the structures, to see how they can be changed in the light of the truth; for those outside them to come together and attempt to create new alternative structures. And one of the weaknesses of critical theology has been to ignore this problem.

There are, of course, areas of theology of which that comment is not true, notably liberation theology and those areas in European and American theology where theological concern focuses on a particular issue, like the ordination of women or the celibacy of the priesthood in the Roman Catholic Church. Here the aim is quite specific, and in liberation theology the normal approach of theologians is in fact turned upside down: liberation theology is a new way of doing theology – it is always described as a 'second act'; the *praxis*, which includes issues of structure, comes first and the theology is reflection on it. So it cannot avoid taking structures into account, otherwise it would not be a theology of liberation. But areas of tension are not the best foundations on which to build theology, and liberation theology still has to face many of the issues that were on the agenda of *Honest to God*: liberation theology, for example, must one day come to grips with the problems of biblical criticism and the nature of Christian life after 'liberation'; those concerned for the ordination of women or a married priesthood in the Roman Catholic Church need to tackle more deeply the question 'What is a priest?'

So one characteristic of the position among those critical of Christianity today and concerned to bring about change is the existence of two very different approaches, neither of which by itself is enough, and both of which, left to themselves, will either get nowhere or produce just a different ideology. On the one hand the question 'what does it mean?' or the answer 'it depends what you mean' are not very useful for achieving revolutions, yet on the other the aims and slogans of liberation theology, while containing a good deal of truth, are dangerous over-simplifications that are themselves in need of criticism.

One of David Jenkins' classic sayings, which I think dates back to the 1960s, was: 'The Church of England is all in favour of change as long as it doesn't make any difference.' For all his radical statements, in this connection as in much else John Robinson was more than a little a true son of the Church of England, and although *Honest to God* begins and ends with his favourite image of letting everything go into the melting, I at any rate have the sneaking feeling that the temperature of the furnace is not quite high enough for the process to work properly.

Or perhaps it is that the metaphor in the end proved too seductive and distracted attention from the quite specific questions which needed to be asked about where the 'new Reformation' was to lead and what it was to require.

I can write as I have done only because by virtue of having spent most of my working life as a theological publisher, I largely stand outside the structures of which I have been writing rather than within them. If I were more involved my perspective would doubtless be different. But one has to write of what one sees, even if being to some extent an outsider on the one hand brings freedom from many of the tensions faced by those within the structures of the church and makes it difficult to take part in any more active programme for change there.

But there are other structures, which the churches all too often forget, and which have to be struggled with just as vigorously. For example, it is a commonplace that we live in a secular, media-dominated age. Against that background what will be the form of the future communication of Christianity?

A wealth of possibilities for communication is available – but they are predominantly under the control of others. Only in a country like the United States can the churches secure a strong foothold in media like television, and then they do so at a high price. In England, since *Honest to God* the possibilities of communicating Christianity in all its aspects through the media have been much reduced; particularly in the areas of publishing and bookselling and religious journals and news-papers the situation has deteriorated very seriously indeed, and with cuts in university theology and religious education the situation will in due course get very much worse. How will theological ideas be communicated? What can be done? Unless that kind of question can be answered, practically, we will certainly soon be entering a theological dark age.

There is need for vision not only inside the churches but outside them. Vision and a concern actually to make some differences where there is a crying need for change. Honesty is quite manifestly not enough; more people are going to have to do some fighting.

F. W. Dillistone

Recasting the Mould

Honest to God introduced countless readers to the works of three German theologians whose names were probably quite unfamiliar to them: Paul Tillich, Rudolf Bultmann and Dietrich Bonhoeffer. John Robinson had already distinguished himself as a New Testament scholar and in that field Bultmann had become famous. His attempts to separate the gospel from the mythological framework of the ancient world and to express it in the language of the modern world seemed a legitimate procedure if it could be effected. Further, the career of Bonhoeffer had been such as to challenge many of the assumptions about Christianity which had hitherto been taken for granted. Particularly in the areas of worship and ethical practice there were accepted traditions which were now seriously called into question by his letters from prison. John wrote with passionate sympathy about these two men. The terms 'myth' and 'religion' needed an altogether fresh examination. Thus a considerable part of his book was directed towards the framing of a new liturgy and a new morality.

But it is with his treatment of the philosophy and theology of Paul Tillich that I am chiefly concerned, especially as the place of *symbolism* in human forms of expression was at the very heart of Tillich's system. By 1963 Tillich had gained a large audience in Germany and America, but only in fairly restricted theological circles had his writings become known in England. It was John who by appealing to Tillich's printed sermons first brought his language and imagery about God into the ambit of more popular comprehension.

I shall begin by noticing a rather remarkable parallel between the early upbringing of the two men. Tillich was born and brought up within the context of what could be called traditional Lutheran orthodoxy and orthopraxis. His father was a distinguished Superintendent (having semi-episcopal authority), in a mediaeval walled town of Eastern Germany where the fine Gothic church and its adjoining school stood at the centre of its social life. The boy grew up in a kind of sanctified enclosure and at first had little contact with the modern world. The classical and mediaeval worlds, with their religious associations, were very real to him, and this treasured context was breached only by two minor external influences.

The first, strangely powerful to the growing boy, came through the family's annual holiday excursion to the Baltic sea shore. There, it has been recorded, young Paul would build a great sandcastle, climb to the top of it, and sit for a while in rapt contemplation of the unbroken vista ahead of him: the water, the deep, the far horizon, the ultimate boundary. Already he was fascinated by an experience which, though not put into words, would continue with him until, years later, he established a holiday home at the tip of Long Island and again gazed out to sea. There was also the dark forest near his home which was pervaded by an air of mystery. Such were the indelible impressions due to find expression imaginatively in his theology.

The second memorable experience was provided by occasional visits with his father to the great city of Berlin, now one of the most famous centres of nineteenth-century artistic culture. Here he began to be aware of human activities different from those of the limited religious circle to which he belonged. Could theology and culture be somehow related or combined?

What has all this to do with John Robinson? I think of John growing up in the mediaeval surroundings of Canterbury, educated in the attractive rural setting of Marlborough, with its classical tradition and ethos characteristic of the nineteenth-century public school: then Cambridge and Wells with all their religious buildings and traditions. The context was not the same as that of late nineteenth-century eastern Germany, but there were strong parallels. What John's feeling for nature was in his early years I do not know, but it was probably not without a touch of romance. Certainly in the years at Cambridge he could hardly have failed to feel the tension between his religious background and the changing cultural scene.

Between 1914 and 1934 Tillich passed through a succession of almost shattering experiences. His service as chaplain in the German trenches, his discovery of the solace of contemplating examples of great art, his political involvements, first with Religious Socialism then in opposition to National Socialism, his movement towards a more existentialist philosophy – all these affected his outlook and gained expression in his developing systematic theology. Through all this development, however, one concept was central and determinative. It was the concept of the *symbol* and the way in which *symbolism* belongs to the very essence of a truly human life. An animal can respond to stimuli of the senses, even to signals such as a threat or a command from a human source; a machine can perform a round of motions automatically, responding to a switch or a given programme; a human being can behave often like an animal or a machine: only, however, while truly human can an individual form *symbols* to express his or her world, a world made up of relations to nature, to other humans and finally to the transcendent, the ultimate whom we call *God*.

The symbol does not act as a *direct* representation of what is perceived in nature, humanity and God, though there is always a tendency in human speech and gesture to give a literal rendering or an exact reproduction. In a measure such a tendency is natural, for the ordering of communal life demands a framework of laws appropriate to a particular time and to particular circumstances. The danger is that these laws come then to be regarded as *absolute*. No place is then left for symbols pointing towards the transcendent and the ultimate, the infinite and the eternal; nor is there place for the imagination to go beyond immediate sense-perceptions or direct stimulations. The human becomes increasingly content to live within an enclosure which seems to be sanctified by earlier achievements (a great building, a noble painting, a collection of writings, a method of manipulating nature) or by communal law (of a group or of a union or of a nation or of a league of nations). The symbol pointing towards new imagined possibilities has a hard time. The old is better. Familiar language and imagery are safer. The world can operate, it seems, only with the help of logical sequences and mechanical laws.

For Tillich, crisis came in the trenches during the First World War. He had lived within the security of the religious, social and intellectual context of the Germany of his student days. He was grounded in the works of the great philosophers, with Schelling exercising a special appeal (and this Tillich claims, meant a break with the dominant nineteenth-century German philosophical systems). Also, like Robinson later, he discovered Kierkegaard, whose writings up to that time had been largely unknown. Thus there were urgent questionings in his mind which were to receive critical reinforcement by his experiences at the front, in the art galleries of Italy, and in the political turmoil of a defeated Germany. His imagination was stirred, even fired, by the possibilities of expressing the Christian message in terms of the symbolism of a new era. Not that the former tradition and training were to be jettisoned. But the challenge of the *kairos* (a critical juncture in human affairs) was such that only a theology expressed in its relation to twentieth-century culture could any longer suffice.

This, however, would not be easy. He began to lecture and
write with an urgent reference to the German situation. Then
came his dismissal and emigration to the United States, to a
new language and a new culture. How could his theology be
expressed in this new environment? The Second World War
came and his voice had scarcely been heard in England. Not
until the series of sermons, with the striking title *The Shaking of
the Foundations* (published by SCM Press in 1949), came to be
mediated to a wide audience through the pen of John
Robinson did Tillich's emphasis on the symbol and the
imagination and the Protestant principle and the notions of
depth and ultimate concern become more generally known.
And I suppose that of them all, the one which made the
greatest appeal was that of *depth*. Not height but depth. The
gazing out to sea, the imagining of unlimited depth, the depth
of the unconscious, the ground, the foundation, the hidden
mystery – could this prove to be the new symbolic expression
of our turning towards God? Was the divine grasp of us to be
mediated through experiences of depth rather than of transcendent height?

The move from Cambridge to the South Bank may not have
been as dramatic as that of Tillich in moving from the heights
of pre-war Berlin culture to the near despair of post-war
Germany. But certainly there came a critical change for John.
Not that he had been unprepared in some of his reading and
thinking. Though surrounded, as I have suggested, by
traditional Anglican buildings, though familiar with the
traditional Anglican liturgy and trained in the classical disciplines, he had also, from the time of his graduate study in
Cambridge, become well acquainted with Kant and Buber and
Kierkegaard, none of whom fitted into the Platonic scheme of
things. It is true that in pursuit of his New Testament studies
he had written a major monograph on *The Body* and its
symbolism, while in Clare he was experimenting in revision of
eucharistic practices. But there was nothing so far that could
be called radical (a favourite word with John, which suggested
a concern about roots or foundation).

Becoming a bishop in South London immersed him in an

almost entirely different culture, politically and economically
and in many respects religiously. Were the foundations being
shaken? Was he being challenged to discover new symbols to
express his new experiences?

Interestingly the most prominent symbol to appear in
Honest to God is to be found in the title of the final chapter:
'Recasting the Mould'. This is a symbol which has been
frequently used in political circles. A new party, we have been
told, will break the accepted traditional mould of the English
political system. Yet John had no desire to found a new party
within the church. Rather, he wanted to break the mould of a
past age in which he believed Christianity had been encased.

'It will doubtless seem to some,' he writes, 'that I have by
implication abandoned the Christian faith and practice
altogether. On the contrary, I believe that *unless* we are
prepared for the kind of revolution of which I have spoken it
will come to be abandoned. And that will be because it is
moulded, in the form we know it, by a cast of thought that
belongs to a past age – the cast of thought which, with their
different emphases, Bultmann describes as "mythological",
Tillich as "supranaturalist", and Bonhoeffer as "religious"' (p.
123).

Mould, form, cast of thought. With these terms John
associated first the rigorous dependence of orthodox Jews on
Law as an encasing mould, then the devotion of pagan Greeks
on *images* and particularly mental images. In each case a vivid
example was provided of the human struggles to speak of
God, to picture God, by enclosing him within a formula or a
visible structure. Such a struggle is not to be lightly condemned. It can serve tentatively, experimentally, even temporally.
But once the mould becomes cast, fixed, indispensable, the
form becomes a sign belonging to a past age and an earlier
culture instead of a symbol pointing towards the uncondi-
tional and the ultimate.

The symbol-system represented by breaking the mould,
perhaps by recasting or transforming it, is fairly familiar. It is
linked with the old problem of form and content: can the
precise content in a jar or vessel be preserved when the form,

the casing, is radically changed? John deals with the problem in a less familiar way in *The Honest to God Debate* by asking what happens when a country decides to revalue its currency (pp. 243ff.). There is a crisis of some kind. (We have been aware of them ever since the Armistice in 1918: amongst the most dramatic have been the currency crisis in Germany in the 1920s and the great depression in America, affecting the Western world, in 1929.) The traditionally accepted means of exchange are threatened. Paper money is issued but becomes of less and less value. Where is the exchange rate, the gold standard, the support of the central bank, and so on?

John employs this situation symbolically to point towards what can happen or is actually happening in the history of Christianity. 'Doctrinal formulations, moral codes, liturgical forms . . . are, as it were, the paper money with which the business of communication is regularly conducted. They are backed in the last resort by certain commitments, certain "promises to pay" of which they are the token and expression.' These symbols represent 'not truths in themselves out of the context of any personal response, but a relationship-in-trust to the various aspects of the truth as it is in Jesus'. Thus a symbol can well be defined as a relationship-in-trust. It does not aspire to stand for some isolated objective reality. Nor does it do service for an isolated subjective inner state. A symbol is always a two-way affair, the expression of a *relation*. In economics it is the relation between the standard of exchange and the paper money. In theology it is the relation between formal doctrines and liturgies on the one side and the reality of God in Christ on the other. John's concern was that the living symbols of the Christian faith are in constant danger of becoming mere signs of orthodoxy, mere labels of belonging to 'the circle of a religious in-group'. It cannot, I think, be sufficiently stressed that in the view of a philosopher such as Susanne Langer, the symbol is the medium of *relation*. 'Relations are known to us primarily through words, our most ready and powerful symbols.'[1]

If this is true of words, images are not far behind in second place. Indeed the proliferation of images through modern techniques may make them the more powerful symbols of our time. Be that as it may, her linkage between symbols and relations is entirely in line with Tillich's and John's formulation. Content and form cannot be set up in separate compartments. It is the office and function of the symbol to *relate* content to form, message to medium, depth to existential expression, again and again and again. There is no final solution in this world. John's achievement was to open the way for a too rigid mould to be broken and for fresh symbols to express the relation of the traditional to the world of contemporary culture.

Honest to God was a very impressive book when it appeared. It did much to introduce readers to a different culture and to countries which had been devastated by war. It raised questions about popular images of God and helped to break through the insularity which had long been the danger of traditional Anglicanism. The question arises, however, whether at that stage John was aware of the full implications of the symbolic character which he was advocating for the doctrines and ethical standards subscribed to within his own church. In a revealing passage in *Honest to God* John exclaims: 'What looks like being required of us, reluctant as we may be for the effort involved, is a radically new mould or *meta-morphosis*, of Christian belief and practice. Such a recasting will, I am convinced, leave the fundamental truth of the Gospel unaffected. But it means that we have to be prepared for *everything* to go into the melting – even our most cherished religious categories and moral absolutes. And the first thing we must be ready to let go is our image of God himself' (p. 124).

Such a statement, though impressively honest, leaves me asking questions. Radical (uprooting and transplanting)? Recasting mould (breaking and re-making)? A new meta-morphosis (who will do the re-shaping?)? Melting (*everything* into the melting-pot? What will emerge?)? Letting go an image (does a clearly-shaped corporately-held image exist?)? All these questions are far from easy to answer. But the most difficult question of all concerns 'the fundamental truth of the Gospel'. How was this constituted? How expressed? How transmitted? How can any such 'fundamental truth' be unaffected by changes of place and time? The most urgent question of all: how can we today, who speak a particular language and are members of a particular culture, speak about or portray visually the 'truth of the gospel' except in *symbolic* (not final or absolute or literal or static) ways? The 'fundamental truth' cannot be enshrined or objectified in iconic form. It can only be symbolized and re-symbolized by being *related*: the past to the present, the Palestinian to the Indian (or some other location), the Greek language to the English, Roman culture to that of modern science. This I believe to have been John's central concern, but his use of the terms 'fundamental' and 'unaffected' seems to me to be seriously open to question. They can so easily be expanded into inerrancy and fundamentalism, whereas John's whole concern was to move towards openness and freedom, dynamic qualities which can only live within the context of symbolism and relationship.

One further submission I wish to make about symbols. Commonly *two* expressions have been used to indicate the relation of a symbol to ultimate or transcendent reality. One is to 'participate in'; the other is to 'point to'. Both of these occur in Tillich's doctrine of the symbol. But there is, I think, a subtle difference. The first emphasizes the *continuity* between the symbol and that to which it is related, and I think this was the more prominent aspect within John's own background of thought and experience. In his 'exploration into God' he regarded *panentheism* as the best term to describe his own theological position. The symbolic system within which he had been reared, and to which his primary allegiance still belonged, entailed no obvious break with the world of theism. So much within his Anglican inheritance *participated* in the divine, possessed *analogies* with divine realities, was capable of being employed to inspire others to share in the immanent life of the Spirit. This method of analogy (and an analogy is one form of symbol) can be valuable and powerful in enabling the human imagination to transcend the immediate and be related to the infinite.

Yet there is also the language-form which speaks of a symbol *pointing to* some transcendent or ultimate reality. The emphasis here is on *discontinuity*. There is a flash of likeness, though the dominant feature is that of distance, distinctiveness, even unlikeness. Often surprisingly, often unexpectedly, especially in periods of crisis and disorder, there comes a flash of connection, of relation between the bondage of earth and the vision of heaven.

> O world invisible, we view thee,
> O world intangible, we touch thee,
> O world unknowable, we know thee,
> Inapprehensible, we clutch thee!

Did John, when confined to his bed, catch a glimpse of the traffic between Heaven and Charing Cross?

> Yea, in the night, my Soul, my daughter,
> Cry – clinging Heaven by the hems;
> And lo, Christ walking on the water
> Not of Genesareth, but Thames![2]

The flash, the disclosure, the sudden apprehension, suggests another kind of symbol – the metaphor – in which the relationship is that of pointing towards, though not participating in. To be sure, pointing towards may be almost entirely reflexive: the seeing of red or green on a traffic light, with appropriate action immediately. But metaphor is concerned with a decisive response, not to an automatic signal but rather to a new possibility, an unexpectedly gracious action, a sudden spanning of what appeared to be an unbridgeable gulf. It is this aspect of experience which has captured the attention of many Christian scholars since *Honest to God* was published. The wonder of Jesus' parables pointing to God's surprising activity, the metaphorical disclosures of the workings of divine grace, the acceptance by God of the wretchedly unacceptable – all these are examples of the way in which symbols can express the relation of *pointing to* though not of identifying with. Humans can be justified by faith as they hear the good news of salvation through a cross, as they view the man whose touch could bring healing even to the leper, the apparently hopeless case.

John attained world-wide publicity as the publishers rolled off copies of *Honest to God*. He never ceased to carry on his work of relating himself to new situations or rather to the One who is active in every *new* situation. Of his subsequent writings I found none more surprising than his Teape lectures, given in India and published under the title *Truth is Two-Eyed*. I say surprising, because John had a conservative streak in him, shown specially in his examination of the New Testament writings. He was not averse to raising questions with his revered teacher C. H. Dodd on certain aspects of the historical tradition in the Fourth Gospel.

But India, with its long established and still continuing lack of interest in so-called 'facts' of history; India, with its religious literature and worship-practices rich in philosophical, mystical and mythical associations: could 'the fundamental truth of the Gospel' be related to what seemed to be a totally alien theological and philosophical background?

Astonishingly John took up the challenge, not lightly or half-heartedly, but with a determination to engage in a careful study of Hinduism and its treasured scriptures, together with an open-ended dialogue with those who had first-hand experience of Hinduism and its contacts with Christianity. The invitation to give the lectures was received in 1976: the book containing their substance was published in 1979, some forty years after John began to study theology seriously.

The title is honest and arresting. Truth cannot be expressed in univocal, single-eyed terms. Just as the scientific quest has led to the doctrine of *complementarity* (light e.g. being regarded sometimes as waves, sometimes as particles), so the theological quest should cease to be a struggle for some unified, orthodox, single vision of reality, but rather it should be prepared to confess that no one-eyed expression can ever be sufficient: only a double symbolism, sometimes participating in the transcendent, sometimes pointing to the ultimate, can make theological authenticity or advance possible. Myth and history, mysticism and prophetism, analogy and metaphor, essentialism and existentialism, such are some of the expressions of the two-eyed approach advocated in John's book.

His final lecture closed with this kind of appeal. By exposure to India and the East, he urged, we in the West will have a better chance of gaining that 'two-eyed' vision of truth and praxis which combines the mystical and the prophetic, the 'unitive' and the 'communitive': or in the terms which I have suggested, the 'participating in' and the 'pointing to'. The quotation with which he ends his book is taken from the writings of the Indian theologian P. Chenchiah. It uses a common experience in the art of the photographer to symbolize what may happen to us as we seek today to apprehend more fully the connection between the Jesus of history and the Christ of faith: 'The negative plate of Jesus, developed in a solution of Hinduism, brings out hitherto unknown features of the portrait and this may prove exactly the "Gospel" for our time.'[3]

It is a striking suggestion. What, however, constitutes this 'negative plate of Jesus'? No such plate exists. What we do have is a series of gospel testimonies which do indeed bear a certain resemblance to photographs taken by different people in different situations. These can certainly be examined and compared and a dominant form of testimony to Jesus of Nazareth may then be constructed.

But can this then be 'developed' within a solution of Hinduism or for that matter of Hellenism or scholasticism or of any other cultural-linguistic complex? Such a possible procedure raises serious doubts. There can surely be no 'development' of a quasi-mechanical kind (from negative plate to positive reproduction); rather there must be a continuous, never-ending process of *relationship* between the testimonies, pointing towards the words and deeds of Jesus of Nazareth and the cultural-artistic experiences manifested within a particular system at a particular time.

Much of John's work was devoted to determining the authenticity of the testimonies to the 'things concerning Jesus'. He did this within the context of a rich acquaintance with the culture of the ancient world, the dramatic changes within British and German culture and, at the end of his career, remarkably within the Indian cultural tradition. The demanding process of *relating*, of creating revived or new symbolic forms, must go on indefinitely. John, more than most of his contemporaries, made an outstanding contribution to this quest.

Summing up, I return to John's early claim in *Honest to God*: 'I have never really doubted the fundamental truth of the Christian faith – though I have constantly found myself questioning its expression' (p. 27). Fundamental truth. Fundamental-foundation – hidden depth: truth – *veritas* – correspondence to reality. This is the abiding factor for John. The reality of the gospel or of the Christian faith which is hidden, rooted, deeply founded. How can it be *expressed* or *communicated*? Never, it would appear, directly, exactly, photographically, univocally, for it lies hidden. Yet something emerges visibly, outwardly above the foundation. It can be a superstructure built of wood, hay, straw or even of gold, silver and fine stone and therefore ready in time to perish. What then is the *expression* which will endure? This was John's problem as it was that of Tillich, Bultmann and Bonhoeffer. Bultmann was prepared for a stripping away of all mythological elements leaving only the death-resurrection *kerygma*; Bonhoeffer for the removal of all 'religious' or pseudo-religious elements, leaving only the *man for others*, the earthly representative of the crucified God; Tillich for the abandonment of traditional, supernaturalistic language, verbal or visual, with the clear recognition that the outward *expression* must always be symbolic, whether the key-terms be 'new being' or 'spiritual presence'. Thus in each case we find witnesses to the *foundation* struggling for forms of *expression* to represent more adequately and vividly the gospel or the faith to which by faith they had given their full allegiance.

The significance of John's part in this struggle is surely that he could not and did not attempt to achieve it finally or once for all. In *Honest to God* he used numerous modern symbols, always emphasizing his own eagerness to keep *personal* relationships in the forefront. He could use terms like long-stop, stopgap, wavelength, melting-pot, clue, map, projection in a religious context, but these were, I think, subsidiary to his chief concern. His central aims were expressed through the titles of two later books: *Exploration into God* and *Truth is Two-Eyed*. He never ceased from being an explorer: his exploration had to take account of two kinds of vision, that which tried to express reality in terms of intimate, inner relationship and that which complementarily sought to speak of God in terms of disclosure or encounter. A word which has been used to encompass the former is co-inherence; to denote the latter has been reciprocity or interaction. The perilous swamps on either side of the journey are absorption, and isolation. The first, surrendering to the culture surrounding it; the second, establishing its own independent structure. Symbols represent freedom to interrelate and to intercommunicate. In both of these undertakings John showed himself to be a courageous explorer and a creative interpreter of the Christian faith.

Alan Ecclestone

Religious Truth Must be Lived

Half a century ago, in a book entitled *The Modern Mind*, Michael Roberts wrote: 'It is the fact of prayer which makes the language of religion necessary, and it is prayer that distinguishes religion from moral, philosophical and aesthetic sentiment. It is the daily counterpart of conversion: we may say it is an act of supreme mental honesty, reaching beyond the conscious mind to the world of hidden motives, that it allows us to realize our deepest and most lasting desires and to set in order the contradictions and confusions within ourselves; that it involves at the one moment the most strenuous effort of honesty and the most complete relaxation.'[1]

With that in mind I felt that I understood better why Shakespeare had Hamlet saying, 'Look you, I'll go pray'; but it was the repetition of the word honesty that gave me a starting point from which to ask some questions about *Honest to God* and what it said about worship and prayer. Clearly, what the praying Robinson was writing about was not a patchwork of prayers religiously sewn together but something that brought into action the whole soul of a man or woman, something that had to be lived in every particle of his or her being, whether in terror or grief, delight or joy. Liturgical prayer would be that living experience shared in by a number of people. For the one and the many the matter of honesty was all-important. I was faced by the question: how honest was *Honest to God*?

Reading the chapter entitled 'Worldly Holiness' and also the book *Liturgy Coming to Life* referred to in that chapter, I was struck by two remarkably honest confessions. As regards liturgy, John Robinson began by saying that it was not 'my line', and that at 'my theological college there was no subject that seemed to me so remote from any living concern for the Gospel and its relevance to the modern world than what was taught and examined as "liturgiology"'. And so, 'I left my theological college liturgically clueless . . . since I had never attended a single lecture in the subject, and contrived to get excused it, with a good deal else, from my ordination examination' (pp. 1f.).

That was honestly said, but it left me wondering whether that was all that needed to be said. Living in a theological college involves a man in a good deal of liturgical prayer along with all other members of the college. That is probably much more testing than, though not as easily examinable as, the things which appear in the Worship paper. Did that participation daily in the liturgical action of that body of men raise no questions or provoke no sense of unease?

On the matter of personal prayer the confession in *Honest to God* was equally candid. 'Here [in the college] were all the conditions laid on – time, space, quiet. And here were the teachers, the classics of the spiritual life, and all the aids and manuals . . . but I discovered there what I can only describe as a freemasonry of silent, profoundly discouraged, underground opposition, which felt that all that was said and written about prayer was doubtless unexceptionable, but simply did not speak to "our" condition . . . nothing else was offered in its place, and to this day we have an inferiority complex', taken along with a further comment that 'we clergy cover up the uncomfortable knowledge that they [the traditional types of spirituality] have long been failing us, and that we have failed to communicate a relevant spirituality to our people' (pp. 93f.). That, too, seemed to be bravely and

honestly said and offer good grounds for suggesting amend-
ment of life.

It was this impression that no doubt won for the book a
sympathetic response. It was a 'cri de coeur'. It reflected
pastoral concern and missionary purpose. It accorded with
the desire for liturgical reform, theological realism and the
widening of religious perspectives current in English life at the
time. Certain phrases such as 'a Copernican revolution', 'a
keeping open to the world the frontiers of the Church', 'a
radically new mould or metamorphosis of Christian belief and
practice' secured expectant if sometimes startled attention.
Metamorphosis had an encouraging sound. It suggested, not
the transformation of man into vermin as in Kafka's terrible
story or as in the Nazi 'Final Solution', but release of a
worthier, more beautiful creature from the chrysalis conditions in which it had for too long been confined. Readers could
identify with this even if they had very tenuous relations with
Christian faith or the church.

Coming from a bishop it also startled. Not since *Robert
Elsmere* caught the attention of mid-Victorian readers of novels
and moved even Mr Gladstone to review it, had such interest
in theological matters been kindled in Britain. It did not excite
the fury that gave Froude's *The Nemesis of Faith* in 1849 the
distinction of being the only book piously burned in Oxford in
the nineteenth century, but the letters, articles and debates to
which it gave rise suggested that it was timely and raised
certain hopes as well as touching some raw nerves.

On the other hand it is difficult to say what exactly it did.
Like so many religious appeals addressed to British people
since the time of the National Mission of Repentance and
Hope in 1917, through the post-war campaigns of the Industrial Christian Fellowship, the meetings of COPEC, the Ways
of Renewal, the Malvern Conference, the Report *Towards the
Conversion of England* and the various Lambeth Conferences,
its career was that of 'a bright exhalation' that drew great
attention and then faded out. One is bound to ask: Why?
Could it be, its honesty notwithstanding, that it was misconceived and misdirected in the way it tackled its problems? Did

it offer too few footholds to enable many readers to make much way forward in that difficult terrain? One remembers that Froude put his case in a passionate, even melodramatic novel which was still being reprinted in the opening years of the twentieth century. 'Foothold' reminds me of *East Coker* and the fact that Eliot's poems made a much more lasting impression upon men and women concerned about spirituality. Was John Robinson's exposition of the thinking of Tillich, Bultmann and Bonhoeffer too austerely metaphysical to provide a foundation for a response that would move from questions to commitment? Could it really help people to reach 'beyond the conscious mind to the world of hidden motives'?

I recall some words of Wallace Stevens about the poet's function as regards his readers: 'to make his imagination theirs', so that it becomes a light in their minds that helps them to live their lives. It was in that way that Jesus of Nazareth, the teller of stories, became the light to lighten nations. Outside theological circles his words reached men and women the world over and in turn moved painters, musicians, dramatists, novelists and poets to plant and reap ever newer harvests of the words once sown. Nor should the architect be forgotten. His building is no less revelation of Christ's searching glance at the world's cities today than it was when he looked at Jerusalem and wept. He is no less prophetic than Isaiah. In his book *Architecture and You* (1958) Siegfried Giedion asked, 'Why is our age so sick?'. He pointed by way of answering it to the widespread failure to conceive and create adequate symbols to convey to men moving recklessly into the world being brought into being by unparalleled technological advances a true sense of their spiritual condition. To live with failed or false symbols was to live deprived of the means to an honest self-understanding in a situation where the Faustian possession of power could not but threaten self-destruction.

John Robinson was far from being insensitive to those witnesses to the truth that must be lived. Elsewhere in his writing he made fruitful use of their work, but in *Honest to God* he was sadly neglectful of them. There is but one woman mentioned in it. It gives no sense that women have a distinctive contribution to make or that the imagery used to speak about God hitherto had been pitifully impoverished by lacking it. Had he turned to George Eliot, for example, he would have found far more rich and reliable testimony to the spiritual condition of England than in many shelves of theological treatises. Had he observed how feminine consciousness of this very thing had been quietly expressed by Dorothy Richardson, Rebecca West, Virginia Woolf, Rosamund Lehmann, Doris Lessing, to mention only a few, the kind of plea that he was making for honesty before God would have been vastly different. 'We see truth through fictions, our own and other peoples', writes Antonia Byatt in her novel *The Game* (1967). *Honest to God* is far from being unaware of this, as its attention to Tillich and Bultmann makes clear, but it gives very little strenuous effort to an examination of the fictions actually being employed not by theologians but by the rank and file members of Christian congregations and embodied in the language of liturgy.

As a consequence of this, though it makes a plea for the 'earthing' of its theology, *Honest to God* gives remarkably little by way of examples as to how this was to be done. It quotes with approval John Wren-Lewis saying that 'perhaps the ideal would be to try to revolutionize the church in question, by bringing its members to see the plain meaning of their own Gospel, but some kinds of church tradition are heavily protected against this and one must have a realistic assessment of one's revolutionary capacities'.[2] I find that 'perhaps' very difficult to take and I wish that *Honest to God* had challenged it, and insisted, as John MacMurray always did, that idealism is the great enemy of true religion. Of course no one should deceive himself by over-estimating his revolutionary capacities, but the question to be faced is whether the effort to revolutionize the church should be made as the only commitment that is honest to God. No one doubts that a great many church traditions are embattled to resist any such thing. They bestow, in the words of J. B. Metz, 'a political innocence on the status quo', and in so doing reject messianic religion out of hand and 'rob Hope of genuine expectation'. I go back

in my mind to Antonia Byatt saying firmly, 'there is no
innocent vision', and recognize that that part of the liturgy
that is penitential must bring all of us to face that fact and what
we are doing about it.

I know that John Robinson was convinced that the
'Copernican revolution' he had in mind called for a profound
shift of attention from the God 'out there' and the God in any
way separated from the context of politics, work, commerce,
warfare, leisure, health, education, sexual and ethnic relations and ecology and technological change, but there is little
weight of attention given to these things in *Honest to God*.
Bonhoeffer is quoted at length, but nothing is said of the
circumstances that brought him to imprisonment and death or
why Tillich should have been in exile. One would not guess
from its theological reflections that they were made in
twentieth-century Europe which had witnessed the starvation
and massacre of many millions of people. It must surely
prompt questions like: What sort of a world do theologians
live in? What sort of a world do they imagine that God's
people live in?

These questions must be considered in greater depth later.
Here I would recall that there were many efforts being made in
the light of the catastrophes that had overtaken Europe to
account for what had happened. Some of them were no doubt
premature and in their judgments superficial. Nevertheless,
such books as Erich Fromm's *Fear of Freedom* (1942), Karl
Mannheim's *Diagnosis of our Time* (1943), Lancelot Whyte's
Next Development in Man (1944) and Alfred Weber's *Farewell to
European History* (1947), to mention but a few, did direct
attention to the grim significance of the events of the last
twenty-five years. To ignore these things was to push
theology into a bell jar, as Sylvia Plath's novel could have
warned us. The temptation to deal with abstractions rather
than the experiences of men and women must be among the
most serious of snares besetting those who work in that field.
The warning uttered by Dom Sebastian Moore must be faced.
He asked, 'What is it that all the scholars lack?' and answered,
'It is the unremitting pressure of the human situation on Jesus.

The reason why they find many possible interpretations of his intention is that they conceive of this in a void.' A hard judgment, but cutting very near to the truth. He went on to say: 'Religion, for most of the religious, has little to do with the God who places us between the poles of sex and death and calls us there into the fire and light of His presence.'[3] Now there is much in John Robinson's work – *The Human Face of God* is a good example – which bravely answered that call, but I don't find awareness of it in *Honest to God* as something compelling. The importance of liturgical prayer could not have been more boldly stated, however, and the brief references to what John Robinson set out to do in Clare College Chapel give some indication of how he sought to help others to approach the holy meal. The true picture of it would best be found in seeing both liturgical and personal prayer as the acts of a Resistance movement as deliberate and costly as those that worked in wartime in occupied countries. Its purpose was to use things common to daily life like bread and wine in such a way that those partaking of it were drawn into quite other relations with God, with his earth, with his people and with themselves, than those which obtained elsewhere. It was to 'focus, sharpen and deepen our response to the world and to other people beyond the point of proximate concern (of liking, self-interest, limited commitment), to that of ultimate concern'. It must infuse a life-style that would be both earnest and foretaste of the life of the Kingdom of God. Of this he wrote: 'Anything that achieves this or assists towards it is Christian worship; anything that fails to do this is not Christian worship, be it ever so religious' (*Honest to God*, pp 87f.). All this was well said and honestly intended.

I am nevertheless perplexed to notice that along with these tremendous statements there was so little attention paid to what had actually been happening in a great many parish churches for upwards of forty years or more. As he readily admitted, John Robinson owed much to his introduction as a curate to a lively parish communion, but in *Honest to God* there is no reference whatever to the movement that fostered it and the experience that had been gained from it which was reviewed in the *Parish and People* Conference in 1962. There, to an extent that no college chapel experiment could compare with, something had been coming up from below, rather than received from above, for a very long time. What was important in this was the experience gained, described recently in Donald Gray's book *Earth and Altar* (1986), in the work of the League of the Kingdom of God and the Catholic Crusade, in innumerable parishes where priests and people co-operated in re-shaping liturgical practice, and quite notably from the teaching of Gabriel Hebert SSM.

There was an even more striking omission. The notes accompanying the communion service for use in Clare College Chapel were sensitively done and helpfully designed to add depth to the prayers. One sentence at the end said: 'The sharing of the bread, concluded now sacramentally, must be continued socially – and thence economically and politically.'[4] One is tempted to exclaim with either Shylock or Falstaff about that 'must' and to inquire what precisely was meant by the further statement in *Honest to God*: 'There must be what Jacques Ellul has called a distinctively Christian "style of life", and if this is not nourished all is lost' (p. 136). Some suggestions as to what this might mean and the cost of it would have been valuable.

An older generation would have thought of it in terms of the work of the Christian Social Union, launched in 1889; of the lead given by Westcott, Gore, Scott Holland, Figgis and others in their attempt to translate into social, economic and political terms the implications of Christian faith. But *Honest to God* is strangely 'unhistorically' perceptive and unenquiring about what happened to those movements. It does not examine the possibility that the consequences of a contradiction at parish levels of the sharing that was called for and the way of the competitive world would be an increasing alienation – the word that F. J. A. Hort and Karl Marx used of it – of human beings from each other, from Nature, from themselves and from God.

With Bonhoeffer so much in mind it is hard to account for this failure to look at what actually happened and the warning it might be presumed to give. I recall a German Confessional pastor, a friend of mine and as an exile ordained as an Anglican priest, telling me what it felt like for himself and his people to hold their communion services week by week for some months with a couple of Gestapo men sitting there, noting all that was said and done and by whom. It made church-goers themselves note carefully what they were doing and saying in the name of Jesus Christ when next week the church might be closed and they find themselves in Dachau.

With this in mind I want to turn now to the matter of personal prayer, already mentioned, sadly but honestly, in connection with theological college life. Perhaps the most revealing sentence is that which confessed, 'We dare not admit to others or to ourselves what non-starters we are' (p. 94). Nevertheless, John Robinson persisted in trying, and went on to say: 'I wonder whether Christian prayer is not to be *defined* in terms of penetration through the world to God rather than of withdrawal from the world to God' (p. 97). He recognized that weighty and long-standing tradition had laid great emphasis upon the going apart into silence and solitude, upon being alone with God, upon the cultivation of an interior life, but he questioned its overall validity. He saw in the great biblical tradition an affirmation of total relationship of human beings to God, of the whole man and woman in every function and activity of human life, as being the essence of true religion. Withdrawal, whether to the inner room or the wilderness, had its place in order that the true bearings of both personal and corporate life might be recovered. The exodus journey was not out of this world but towards 'a land that I will show thee where they shall build houses and inhabit them, and plant vineyards and eat of the fruit of them'. It was to recover a full sense of the beauty, goodness and truth of the creation of life on this planet that one turned to pray.

Equally strongly he contended that in his own experience he had most commonly found enlightenment when he had faced matters and wrestled his way through them in company with others. He called it a 'non-religious understanding of prayer' but, in truth, it is the most truly religious perception of prayer. I am tempted to say that he gets to this most worthwhile passage when he forgets his encounters with great theologians, valuable and important as these will have been to him, and thinks very simply about meeting people, listening to them, opening oneself to them unconditionally in love to them, taking their otherness as seriously and sensitively as possible. Perhaps it is because of being freed from any particular image of God and indeed forgetting that it is prayer that authentic praying takes over. The great theologians had done their work to the extent that they taught John Robinson to be honest with himself and to look with like honesty at the symbolic acts of prayer performed by communities in college chapels or churches.

The price of it is nothing less than all that a man has.

Hamlet: Then I would you were so honest a man.
Polonius: Honest, my Lord!
Hamlet: Ay, sir; to be honest, as this world goes, is to be
                 one man picked out of ten thousand.

And it would be truer to say, as Hamlet would no doubt very readily have agreed, that we are all 'indifferent honest' and at best apprentices to its practice, which begins, as John Robinson points out, not when men 'turn to prayer' in the conventional sense, but when they address themselves to their immediate relations with other people, to the jobs to be done, to the world in which they live and its history, to make yet further attempts to be wholly attentive to them.

What is lacking, I think, from this most valuable part of his treatment of prayer so understood is an enquiry as to why this is so difficult to do. What is it that hinders us from praying? How does it come about that deceit finds lodging in the human heart? What are we to say to those who ask us why it is hard to pray? That he was well aware of these questions is evident enough when he comments upon the 'countless people who give up praying' because they find the spaces they have allotted to prayer become emptier and emptier. He did not reject the 'rules of prayer' approach but he did suggest that it might be better for some to be guided by Kairos rather than Chronos, from the moments of truth, the crises or opportunities offered, rather than from set times.

I would turn, rather, to the treatment of these things in Iris Murdoch's lecture, *The Sovereignty of Good*, and to many passages in her novels, as notably in *Henry and Cato*, where she speaks of prayer. This connects with what we have just noted of John Robinson's meeting with people. 'Prayer,' she says, 'is properly not petition, but simply an attention to God which is a form of love.' The ability to attend properly to any feature of life is something not easily attained. It has to be acquired and learned. It must be able to overcome the fears, the obsessions and the selfishness that otherwise block the channels of perception. It is one of the functions of good art to help us to do this. 'Art transcends selfish and obsessive limitations of personality and can enlarge the sensibility of its consumer.' To meet others with an attentiveness that is not warped by fantasy, by distrust, by a sense of injury, by pride, whether as a person or as a member of a tribe, a church or a nation, is therefore the thing that prayer is endeavouring to lay hold of.

Clearly the preparation to pray becomes, as the ancient Hasidic teachers of prayer insisted, a matter of supreme importance. If we are to help one another to pray it must be by way of opening their eyes, overcoming their fears, dropping our own barriers, approaching them as persons. As such, prayer is our attempt to come somewhat nearer to the relationship which we find characterized in the relations between Jesus of Nazareth and his friends. As Fr Coventry said: 'We cannot tackle the problem of how to pray without first facing the problem of our bad or poor relationships with other people.' That applies to the theological college, the parish church, inter-faith relations, as much as it does to the inner city or international spheres.

As I look at *Honest to God* from this angle there are very obvious gaps, and it is only by recognizing these that we make any progress in learning to pray. I cite some of them now. The preface is dated November 1962, and the book appeared in the following March. Perhaps we should ask what features of that time might with some justification have been regarded as Kairos matters.

On 11 October 1962, Pope John XXIII addressed the opening session of the Second Vatican Council. Jubilant hopefulness on the part of some, consternation among others, suggested that this event might well have something of profound significance to give to the church and the world. It was not simply that no such thing had happened for almost a century, but that the kind of direction given to it from the outset was markedly different. The Pope called for 'dedication to the work which our age demands of us' and proceeded to spell out the signs of the times as coded signals of Holy Spirit. As the Council got down to business the encyclical *Pacem in Terris* (April 1963) provided a more detailed survey of the things which called for attention and the kind of attentiveness that they merited. Very soon a number of encyclicals appeared to particularize these matters. Nearly twenty-five years later it has become a debatable matter to inquire 'Whatever happened to Vatican II?' I find the absence of any reference to the calling of the Council in *Honest to God* an unfortunate thing, an opportunity missed.

Much more important, however, in view of the insistence in *Honest to God* of getting beyond 'churchiness', in being truly attentive to moments of truth in the world, were: Hiroshima and the manufacture and stockpiling of nuclear weapons; the Holocaust and an assessment of its cultural significance; the Cold War together with the wars in Korea, Viet Nam, Algeria, Suez and Latin America; apartheid in the Union of South Africa and the struggles for independence among African peoples; the movements for the emancipation of women and the revolution in sexual relations; inter-faith dialogue involving new relationships with Islam, Hinduism and Buddhism; ethnic problems arising from large-scale emigration of low-paid workers, together with those consequent upon micro-chip technology, genetic engineering and the international traffic in drugs. Any one of these constituted a formidable problem for Christian spirituality to engage with. None of them could be ignored by those who hailed Christ as the Lord of all life. Not all of these had revealed their full significance at the time of the gestation of *Honest to God*, but the major issues represented in them had been disclosed. It is the absence of questions relating to them which must constitute a problem for us today. No reader of the Gospels can be unaware of the warnings ascribed to Jesus which referred to the imminence of disaster for those who knew not the day of visitation. How then was it possible for a book which sought to subject the church to the claims of God in the world and to direct Christian spirituality to those crises which in all honesty had to be faced to be silent about these things?

The reproach falls on us all. It is now more than forty years since many of the things listed above became known to us and required of us in the matter of praying an effort more strenuous and more fundamental than any which had faced humankind before. Christian worship and prayer must now take place in a world where the threat of nuclear annihilation is a constant one and where the implications of Auschwitz for mankind as a whole have yet to be faced. None of us can hope to do more than pray about them, and the dread list I have mentioned cannot but overwhelm us. To hear Elie Wiesel's words, 'at Auschwitz, not only man died, but also the idea of man', if rightly understood, takes from us not only the 'last stay of bread and the whole stay of water' but the strength to cry. For these things press upon all of us who have our own personal tensions and sins to contend with, our own weaknesses and humiliations that drain from us what little spiritual strength we might have hoped to summon up. I could have wished that *Honest to God* had directed us much more towards honest avowal of our sick society and the extent in which we all breathe in its tainted air and drink from its polluted wells, and less towards theological and ecclesiastical matters. I wish it had spelled out in detail what things our praying had to grapple with to give meaning to our tiny parts in the tragic circumstances of our time.

Because it was by choice a theological and ecclesial book I wish it had shown more plainly how God comes into these conditions today. I do not agree with Ulrich Simon's description of it as 'a mean little book', but I think I know what he meant and why he said it. Compared with a novel like *La Peste* of Camus or narratives of the survivors of the camps, it feels all too often precious or beside the point.

On the other hand I am grateful for *Honest to God* most chiefly because it reveals the great poverty of my own prayers and because it moves me to try to be more honest about them. Even more important, and this as a very personal quirk, it set me thinking all over again why the word honesty runs through the play *Hamlet* as if it were the Divine Word itself. Could one say more to the point about God than borrow Hamlet's phrase, 'It is an honest Ghost', and remember that what spiritual strength we have comes from that source?

David L. Edwards

———————————◆———————————

Why the Conservative Backlash?

Twenty-five years from now I shall, I believe, know much more, for I shall be dead. Even when I look back to 1963 I want to claim that I have already learned quite a bit. In a life of strangely varying scenes since I published *Honest to God* as Editor of SCM Press – trying to halt the decline of the Student Christian Movement as its General Secretary 1965–66; in Cambridge, as Dean of King's College, where I tried to relate the country's most beautiful church and choir to the runaway world whose slogan was 'make love not war'; in Westminster Abbey, where I saw something of England's remaining folk religion; as Dean of Norwich, where I continued to enjoy the tradition, but in a rural setting; more recently, although still in a cathedral, surrounded by London's bitter social problems; in travel through time and space, in order to write books; in a private life, sadder and happier than I expected in 1963; in spiritual wrestlings and eye-openings – I have reflected, again and again, on the questions which *Honest to God* did so much to make public. When I read the typescript, adding the little headlines which divide the chapters, I thought it would sell like the books by Bonhoeffer, Bultmann, Tillich and Vidler which SCM Press had already published. But I have lived to learn that it was a turning point.

It has not had so much influence because it is an authoritative masterpiece of wisdom. In 1963 John Robinson knew
more than I did. Ten years older, he was an incomparably
better theologian and pastor. But his many critics said that he
was confused in his theology and muddled in his feelings and
he himself confessed that some of the tensions or contradictions ran deeply through his own personality. And that
was why *Honest to God* had such an appeal, once the non-
theological public came to hear of it. In words from a daily
newspaper which I put at the front of *The Honest to God Debate*,
'it is an agonizing and unusual spectacle – a bishop groping for
truth, admitting that he does not know all the answers'. The
fearless honesty of the man beneath the mitre, the open
puzzlement in the eyes which looked at you when they might
have been lowered safely into a theologian's technical studies,
arrested the attention of a public which had grown weary of
bland platitudes from the church's spokesmen. And the
interest was sustained, because – as I learned afresh when I
read most of the letters which flooded into the author and
when I collected the printed reviews – *Honest to God* is
thoroughly ambiguous. What its author was 'really saying'
could be debated endlessly. What its reader really felt after
reading it depended on the reader: there could be anger,
contempt, bewilderment, disappointment, relief, conversion,
the loss of faith, hungry excitement. The most perceptive way
of looking at it may be to regard it as two books: not as two
volumes which display a clear evolution of convinced
thought, or as two layers of writing where one strand of
thought is always on top, but as a single book within which
may be found an atheist's book and an evangelist's, an
iconoclast's book and a traditionalist's, the book of a rebel who
is convinced that the whole of Christianity needs to be
restated and restructured, without theism, without supernaturalism, without religion, without moral rules, and the
book of a bishop who summons his fellow-Christians to return
to their roots in the New Testament. It is, he wrote in *Honest to
God*, 'the God of our own upbringing and conversation, the
God of our fathers and our religion who is under attack' – and

he left it to his readers to decide who (or which) was the God he wished to defend. In at least one respect that little paperback is like the Bible. Almost anything can be proved by quoting from it selectively.

As I attempt an assessment as final as anything can be after a mere twenty-five years, I see that the disturbance which then troubled not only John Robinson's acute sensitivity but also a substantial part of the religious or semi-religious world was completely necessary. It would never have spread had there not already existed a very widespread unease with the conventions being questioned. The lack of smoothness in *Honest to God* was the bubbling which shows that the whole pot is on the boil.

I need not try to tell again the story of secularization in order to make the point that orthodox Christian doctrine had been thought by very many to be untrue, and traditional Christian morality had been thought by very many to be unrealistic and therefore unhealthy, long before 1963. But during and after World War II there was in many parts of Europe and North America a definite, although limited, return to a more or less traditional form of religion. Against Hitler, the idea of a Christian society had to be asserted. It also had to be asserted against Stalin during the post-war reconstruction. As is now documented in the excellent biography of John Robinson by Eric James, 'the author of *Honest to God*' was almost unrecognizable in the 1940s and 1950s.

Although he was an *enfant terrible* as a young tutor in the theological college overshadowed by Wells Cathedral, it is interesting that he accepted such an appointment. Although he was unusually determined to draw broad conclusions of contemporary and contentious relevance from his New Testament studies, it is also interesting that he was prepared to base his theology on a close examination of the Greek text, his professional concern when he became a Cambridge don. The inspiration of his doctoral thesis was a Christian philosophy of personalism, stressing the mysterious dignity of each individual 'thou' (which was to become the favourite theme of John Paul II). Influenced by the SCM and by his curacy under

Mervyn Stockwood, he also expounded a corporate, liturgical and political theology, which stressed the church as a model to society (and which was closer to the ideology of the Liturgical Movement and Catholic Action than to the revolutionary liberation theology of the Latin Americans). Thus the relevance of the New Testament for an understanding of the person and of society was what absorbed his intellectual excitement. He was never a mere conformist: when made a suffragan bishop through Stockwood's insistence, he was expected to pioneer non-residential training for priests and the advocacy of church reform. But in that Christian world where the giants were Pius XII and Karl Barth, it was tempting for many clergymen to sweep awkward questions about Christianity's truth under the carpet. In particular it was tempting in the Church of England, which in many parts of the country still operated as the Establishment. It had magnificent buildings (being rebuilt or repaired where necessary), large endowments (being supplemented by new lay giving to cure the poverty of many of the inferior clergy), ready access to the politicians (who were developing a consensus partly inspired by Archbishop William Temple), and at the helm Archbishop Geoffrey Fisher (who was concentrating on the revision of canon law). Fisher crowned Elizabeth II amid an historic pageant and left the church, he claimed, 'in good heart'. 'As a bishop,' John Robinson himself wrote in *Honest to God*, 'I could happily get on with most of my work without ever being forced to discuss such questions.'

By 1963 the climate was becoming somewhat different. The monthly *Prism* became a focus for young Anglicans angry at complacency. Older Cambridge theologians aroused much sympathy as they called for the facing of hard questions in *Soundings* and *Objections to Christian Belief*. John Robinson was not asked to contribute to these books; he was thought to be too conventional a churchman. But in fact his audience was assembling. Soon after the publication of *Honest to God* Archbishop Michael Ramsey repented of his initial aloofness or anger and reflected: 'As a Church we need to be grappling with the questions and trials of belief in the modern world.

Since the war our Church has been too inclined to be concerned with the organizing of its own life, perhaps assuming too easily that the faith may be taken for granted and needs only to be stated and commended. But we state and commend the faith only in so far as we go out and put ourselves with loving sympathy inside the doubts of the doubters, the questions of the questioners, and the loneliness of those who have lost their way.'

I have often been told that the statistical decline of the Church of England in the decade 1965–75 was due to its leadership's 'failure of nerve' epitomized by *Honest to God.* And no doubt some who gave up going to church, or thoughts of ordination, did so because they were dismayed by the doctrinal and moral chaos. An institution does look more impressive when it has a clear sense of direction – provided that enough people think the direction sensible. But some conservatives' claims that the Church of England was doing very nicely until its radical theologians spoiled everything should not be accepted as accurate. Many of the laity and quite a few of the clergy were dissatisfied with a religious situation where God was often felt to be 'out there', whether or not he was pictured as a grandfather in the sky. They would have agreed with the feelings expressed by Lord Home in an address to the General Assembly of the Church of Scotland: 'Too often the simple, basic teachings are overlaid by doctrine and dogma against which the intelligence revolts. Books like *Honest to God* show that there is a passionate desire that religion should appeal to the mind. Do not let us fear this search for the truth.' *Honest to God* often helped such people to stay in touch with the church or to return to it. But the church with which they had to come to terms certainly did not treat *Honest to God* as the fifth gospel, thus alienating all conservatives. On the contrary, the proceedings of the General Synod which was inaugurated in 1970 and the contents of the *Alternative Service Book* which was authorized in 1980 showed very little trace of the influence of 'radical' ideas in theology. It is also fair to note that churches where John Robinson was little known went through a similar time of troubles and experiments, loss and growth. In the world-wide Roman Catholic Church, for example, a dramatic decline in the numbers and confidence of the clergy, and often also in lay attendance at Mass, was often blamed on the unsettlement caused by the Second Vatican Council, although it seems more significant to ask whether the church would not have found itself in a far worse situation had the council not been unexpectedly summoned by John XXIII.

The essential truth seems to be that the Christian church changed in the 1960s for reasons which went far beyond the influence of one book or many, a group of theologians or a council of bishops – and the most important of these reasons is that Hitlerism and Stalinism had become sufficiently remote for the felt need of the myths and rituals of conservative Christianity as a shelter from the storm to be reduced. Before oil prices escalated a new optimism, even a Utopianism, was in the air. Many people felt secure enough, and had enough confident energy, to talk honestly about religious and moral truth as contrasted with religious and moral tradition. If man could reach the moon, could not the idea of God be brought down to earth? To some such people, the high promise of *Honest to God* was that it showed that some of the ablest theologians of the time were aware of the problems and had already offered a few tentative solutions.

Since 1963, the diversification of global Christianity has been its most conspicuous characteristic and I have no wish to oversimplify the picture which I tried to paint in my books *Religion and Change* and *The Futures of Christianity*. But if I confine myself to Britain, I observe that the main feature of this quarter-century has been deepening secularization. Although many good religious programmes are still included in the output of the BBC and the TV companies (maintaining a standard matched nowhere else in the world), the compulsion to devote the early part of Sunday evening on TV to religion has gone, and it is probably true that for the majority of viewers and listeners broadcast religion now means hymns heard in the background to life. Although religious education and assemblies for worship are still officially compulsory in

Britain's schools (which astonishes Americans, for example), a thorough grounding in the Bible and the doctrines of the main churches has become rare, and it is probably true that, for the majority of children, school religion now means the praise of kindness. Various statistics of religious allegiance and church-going could be cited, but it is probably true that those actively identified with the churches are now little more than a tenth of the population – and in some sections of society much less. The coverage of religion in the national news-papers is maintained by a few distinguished journalists, but Sunday in particular brings home the editorial belief that the public does not wish to read about theology or the churches. Some of the political comments of church leaders and assem-blies, and some summaries of the expert reports which prepare for such utterances, can be reported as being con-troversial, but a comparison with history soon shows how marked is the decline of explicitly religious influence on the political parties. And one result of this deepening seculariza-tion has been a decrease in the number of people in every class educated in living contact with one or other of the churches and in emotional touch with the world of the Bible. For such a population, Christmas has become a spending and eating spree celebrating family life and adorned by tales and songs from fairyland; and at Good Friday, Easter and Pentecost (for Christians, more significant festivals), it is thought eccentric to go to church.

John Robinson's biography makes clear how very eccles-iastical, and indeed clerical, his own background was, right from his birth in the precincts of Canterbury cathedral. The suggestion that he was one of the last of the heart-searching Victorian clergymen seems to me valid. Michael Ramsey's reflection in 1963, which I quoted, was surely correct in implying that a large part of the *Honest to God* public consisted of people who actively doubted and questioned the Christian tradition which they knew, or who felt lonely because they no longer walked in its way. The Student Christian Movement which influenced the young John Robinson and which I knew in the 1950s and 1960s consisted largely of young people who were interested chiefly in exploring the relevance of a faith which they held (or which still held them, despite doubts or heresies) to the intellectual movements and the political and moral questions of the day. But the development of secularization in Britain has meant that most people have been born and brought up in a world very far distant from Canterbury Cathedral, largely ignorant of the Bible and the Christian tradition, and mostly uninterested in the proposition that this tradition may be a heritage which is decisively relevant. Towards the end of the twentieth century, people have ceased to be moved existentially by the withdrawing roar of the sea of faith because they have gone back to have drinks in the plastic hotel.

As John Robinson did when he was Bishop of Woolwich, I find, now that I am Provost of Southwark cathedral, that I am surrounded by indifference to the churches, partial exceptions being the Roman Catholic Church, with its Irish base, and the black-led Pentecostal congregations. Although in this traditionally working-class area of London there has been interest in the clergy when they seem able to bring practical benefits to the people, or when their influence in national politics may work to the people's advantage (as in the report *Faith in the City*), the church's concern for an 'urban priority area' is handicapped by its own numerical weakness. But the alienation of the British from their churches is not only a factor of proletarian culture. As John Robinson did when he returned to Cambridge as Dean of Chapel in Trinity College, when I was a Cambridge don, I experienced the indifference to theology which has become characteristic of British intellectuals and which can be voiced in contempt for livings earned out of religion. The easiest field for ecclesiastical sowers to cultivate is the domestically affluent, or upwardly mobile, middle-class world – but there, what is taken with life-determining seriousness (Tillich's 'ultimate concern') tends to be money and what money can buy, with worry (Tillich's 'anxiety') concentrated on the mortgage. It is often thought that if religion is taken too seriously it leads to the kind of fanaticism seen in door-knocking Jehovah's Witnesses or more bloodily in the news from Northern Ireland and the Middle East. This was one of the considerations that led a number of theologians in the 1960s to welcome secularization. Whatever we may think of such an enthusiasm (which soon faded), we can see why the advance of secularization helps to explain how the 'New Stirring in English Christianity' which I announced in the first chapter of *The Honest to God Debate* did not for long enjoy much public interest.

Of course it is dangerous to oversimplify the concept of 'secularization'. We have been taught that by sociologists such as David Martin if we have not learned it from our own experience. Although the articulate and passionate questioning of the relevance of traditional Christianity to be found in *Honest to God* has become rare, in many ways the kind of irreligious religion contemplated in that book is often the philosophy of the British public, if not usually expressed with any great sophistication or interest. Appearances in churches for weddings and christenings, or at festivals, are fewer, but there are enough of them to show that much of the public wishes to be related to a church to some extent. There seems to be no great hostility to the religion that remains in broadcasting and the schools: rather, there is an uncommitted liking for its usually undemanding hopefulness. I must not generalize from my experience of anticlericalism, for in the course of my ministry I have met much evidence of goodwill in a 'post-Christian' situation which is certainly different from the climate of opinion in any traditionally non-Christian country. Such an attitude could not be maintained unless there were in many hearts thoughts, however vague and brief, about questions raised in *Honest to God*. What do the old, half-heard, words of religion actually mean? Is life itself ultimately meaningless? If love wins in the end, how does it do so? Is it upheld by 'God'? Is my real self the selfish self of my appetites, or is it somehow part of something better – perhaps 'God'? Why does Jesus attract by his love? Do I take enough time to think about life and love? Are my actions guided by love?

Such questions sometimes bubble up to the surface of public opinion. However, the conservative backlash in the churches and in Christian movements has created a stir much larger than any of us expected in 1963. In the Roman Catholic Church – whose regularly worshipping adherents in England may now outnumber the Church of England's – the laity have not been given power in church affairs and, in theory, have been denied the use of contraceptives. The clergy have been denied marriage and have been firmly discouraged from theological adventures. The most widely travelled Pope in history is a populist conservative in doctrine and ethics, although also faithful to the Second Vatican Council as he interprets its often ambiguous pronouncements. In the Orthodox churches the whole emphasis is on maintaining traditions. In the Protestant world the largest growth, both within the denominations and in para-church movements, has been secured by doctrinally and ethically conservative Evangelicals to whom the Bible remains 'inerrant'. In the Church of England such 'Evangelicals' are the most effective force in the colleges and the parishes (the species of 'liberal Evangelicals' having apparently diminished). 'Renewal' is no longer identified with the ecumenical movement, where the dream that the denominations would be willing to die for the sake of a radically new resurrection has been largely forgotten; the term is associated with the charismatic movement, which is new in the sense that it advocates informality, warmth, joy and love but which is not new in theology, ethics or ideas about church organization. In many quarters there is found resistance to updating proposals such as the reunion of the denominations, the recognition of some divorces or the ordination of women to the priesthood – and this resistance is not confined to the older generation. The conservative back-lash includes considerable parts of the student world and has led to talk about 'young fogeys'.

How does one account for this phenomenon? Sociologically and psychologically conservatism in religion is, of course, a reaction to some aspect of modernization which is perceived as hostile. This is obviously true of Islamic fundamentalism in reaction against Western colonialism and the clumsy pro-gramme of Westernization associated with the Shah. It is also true of Buddhist conservatism in Burma and of the orthodoxy of Israelis. Plainly this analysis also applies to the homeland of John Paul II, where the Polish national tradition is subjected to Soviet imperialism; or to the heartlands of Protestant fundamentalism in the USA, where the old simplicities are under daily attack. But I suggest that essentially this analysis is the truth about conservative religion in Britain, where sincere and strenuous efforts have been made to dissociate Christian thinking, praying and living from the crudities and barbarities of fundamentalism elsewhere. For this analysis remains true, even if one grants (as I certainly do) that a purified kind of conservative religion deserves honour among all Christians. Indeed, it is true even if one argues (as I do) that the conservative streak in a radical such as John Robinson prevailed in the end.

In Britain the conservative religious reaction has been directed against aspects of secularization which are (I agree) repulsive and dismaying. Since 1963 quite a few of us have learned anew that religion, for all its snags, may be better than the seven devils which can invade the empty heart. In philosophy, for example, religion has been sternly criticized for its tendency to be over-literal about mythology, or to be over-confident about the intelligible content of metaphysics; but there came a moment when many philosophers realized that if they pursued their debunking of religion to its logical-positivist conclusion, and confined their attention to the discussion of everyday problems in ordinary language, there would be a shortage of problems really worth discussing. In politics, religion has been criticized for its tendency to identify the kingdom of God with some ambition of a class, a nation or a race, and projects which cannot be safely financed; but there came a moment when many politicians realized that in a democracy they must be seen to care about people who are pushed to rot on the margins if left to the cruel play of market forces. In ethics, religion has been criticized for its tendency to suppress natural instincts, particularly in sex, enthroning law above love; but there came a moment when many saw that the truly moral action is often one which does not immediately gratify selfish appetites. In the 1960s this was always advocated in talk about the morals of politics; nuclear war, the industrial rape of the environment, apartheid and the exploitation of the Third World were known to be absolutely wrong whatever defences might be offered for them by practical considerations about 'the situation'. And now voices are heard taking the same strong line about morality in personal relations. The most accessible platform for such voices has been provided by the old religious tradition: 'thou shalt not . . .' An absolutist principle has been applied even to sexual relations – even before the AIDS epidemic destroyed the glamour of gay liberation and reinserted fear into heterosexual promiscuity. Chastity is now almost fashionable. Above all, some social statistics have aroused fear and can be connected with the figures showing the decline in religious belief and observance, suggesting that 'post-Christian' morality is wearing thinner and thinner. I refer, of course, to the well known statistics about crime, particularly about crimes of violence against the person; about abortions and illegitimate births; about divorces; about dependence on drugs, including alcohol and tobacco as well as chemical drugs; about compulsive gambling. Such statistics have not remained in an official publication or in the newspaper. They have devastated as they have touched almost every family in the land and they have not been a good advertisement for secularization. Often man 'come of age' seems to have become demonic and 'the Ground of our being' seems to be a selfishness far from divine, since

Humanity must perforce prey on itself
Like monsters of the deep.

Disgusted by this age, many of those who have remained deeply religious have turned to a religion which deliberately transcends and defies its environment – to a Christianity with a holy God who is to be adored and obeyed, with a definite, biblical gospel revealing salvation, with a community which by regular worship, close fellowship and strict moral standards affirms its difference from a largely secular society. There

has been a hunger for simple, positive teaching; for commitment and assurance responding to authority; for continuity
with the past. Much as in the 1940s or 1950s, many have felt a
need to believe and belong in that tradition – accentuating a
permanent characteristic of religion, which is that even people
who want to make up their own minds and shoulder their
own responsibilities in many fields also want, when at prayer,
to depend on the God who is pictured as being like a powerful
and demanding but loving parent. Specially has this been true
about many of those who have felt the need of God's grace
when personal tragedy has hit them. The funerals which still
constitute the almost universal survival of the 'folk religion' of
the British are the most dramatic illustration of a return to God
which is to be observed amid many distresses other than
bereavement. It is surely a revelation of human suffering, and
of the conservative religious answer to it, that Evangelical
bookshops are so full of stories of the quiet triumphs of
converted Christians, lay men and women, over personal
disasters. Such literature, more than anything else, explains
the power of the Evangelical message in our time of many
troubles. In the Catholic tradition the sacraments have been
loved because of their conveyance of divine power to sustain,
and it is no accident that participation in the eucharist has
become more and more popular among committed Christians. But in a book honouring John Robinson it is supremely
right to point to his own courageous response to cancer. He
had always found a place for 'disengagement' and now he was
to be disengaged from life itself. His response was fed by more
intense prayer, by a renewed love of silence, poetry and the
Psalms, by a deepened communion with the Creator through
nature and art, and by a spirituality which (like the impris-
oned Bonhoeffer's) profoundly impressed many as a trans-
figured walking with Christ along the way of the cross. When I
preached at the last Sunday Evensong over which he presided
in Cambridge, I thought it right to speak very simply about
discipleship. What I could not bring myself to say was that it
can take a death to show that God is not dead. And I believe
that John Robinson's later literary work was of one piece with

his style of dying. He loved the New Testament so much that
he wanted to argue that it was all written before AD 70 and
that the Gospels (including the Fourth) were much more
trustworthy historically than most of his fellow-scholars were
(or are) prepared to grant. He loved Jesus so much that he
took seriously the claim that the Lord's shroud, left behind in
his empty tomb, is preserved in Turin. Of course he argued
for these propositions by discussing the evidence for them:
he was always an intellectual. But what was his motivation?
It was partly a love of being in a minority; he was always an
enfant terrible. But I believe that there was an emotional factor
in his desire to defend the New Testament against sceptical
critics.

It may be pointed out that neither this dying nor this
writing was a typical activity within the church of the 1980s –
which is undeniable. But John Robinson's whole life can be
used to illustrate the importance of themes central in the
conservative Christian backlash although obscured by other
themes in *Honest to God*. In the final analysis he believed in
God, the Father and Creator (to use two partially satisfactory
images). He did not believe that 'God' is a nice word to
describe what is best in us – as he repeatedly showed in
dialogue with Don Cupitt when back in Cambridge. He
believed in Jesus, the human face of God, the window into
God, God's initiative in our salvation. He did not believe that
Jesus was only 'the Man for Others' or merely a prophet
inspired by God – as he showed in his criticisms of *The Myth
of God Incarnate* or his own book on Indian thought. He
believed in the Spirit filling the church – as he demonstrated
by his eager delight in serving clergy and congregations in
South London, Cambridge and Yorkshire. All this disappointed many who had hoped that *Honest to God* heralded
the birth of a Christianity without God, without a Revealer
and Saviour and without any structured church; a Christianity where, as the Beatles sang, 'all you need is love', where
love is god. But in addition to his growing conservatism in
biblical scholarship all this lined him up with simpler souls in
the more conservative Christian community.

I hope I have outlined the most important developments since I edited *The Honest to God Debate*. But I do not want to leave the impression that I believe that 'the questions have been answered' by conservatives. I am an impenitent radical or liberal who believes that many of the questions demand answers which are not easy for conservatives – and not easy for the conservative side of John Robinson. I have attempted to argue this point in *Essentials: A Liberal-Evangelical Dialogue*, a book of 1988 where John Stott replies to my critique of his teaching. I believe that, unless total disaster overwhelms our civilization, there will come a day when the climate will be more favourable than it is now to the exploration of these questions in dialogue between innovators and traditionalists. I am encouraged in this hope by, for example, the 1987 report of the Church of England's Doctrine Commission, *We Believe in God*. 'The one thing of which I am fairly sure,' wrote John Robinson in the Preface to *Honest to God*, 'is that, in retrospect, it will be seen to have erred in not being nearly radical enough.' He was right. Specially in comparison with the 1987 report, that short book of 1963 did not deal adequately with the roots of religious devotion and discipleship. And it did no more than state some of the agenda of the discussion about liberation, salvation, doctrine, ethics, prayer and the church – a discussion which in the centuries to come must include, in all the continents, hundreds of millions of honest Christians.

J. L. Houlden

Frontiers of Honesty

In his Sarum Lectures for 1968–69, published as *A Variety of Catholic Modernists*,[1] Alec Vidler recounted the sad story of the Abbé Turmel who, for many years after losing faith in the doctrines of Christianity, continued to carry out the public duties of a priest, and even after his excommunication in 1930 continued to wear the soutane and to say mass on Sundays for his housekeeper 'who would otherwise become crazed'. Vidler is inclined to see here a case not so much of intellectual conflict as of pathological bifurcation of personality. Be that as it may, in the light of the total intellectual, psychological and social context of French Catholicism at the beginning of the present century, it is plainly hard to draw an assured line between the two diagnoses, and Turmel may not unfairly stand as a symbol of a certain kind of tragic predicament.

He was the bright son of illiterate Brittany peasants, who owed his entire culture and education to the church. The discovery, then, that (as it seemed to him) the church taught falsehood, about the Bible in particular, placed him in the acutest of dilemmas. Simply to give up his profession as a priest and his post as a seminary professor was scarcely possible, for, in his context and at that period, this would be to forfeit his very identity; yet no recovery of faith could take place, for the arguments to effect it were unavailable. Nor could the ecclesiastical system bend to give comfort in one way or another; Turmel had indeed gone beyond any reasonable bounds of church membership, certainly as then conceived. If only an escape route had not been so difficult to find!

It was an extreme case. Here was a man without alternative resources. He sprang from no solid church dynasty and could fall back on no well-placed or liberal-minded contacts in the church establishment – as William Temple and Hensley Henson could when in comparable (though less severe) difficulties at much the same time.[2] He had no liberal university to cushion his fall or allow him to hold his new views with dignity – as many more recent English and German 'rebels' have had.[3] Honesty would have been a suicidal luxury for him. So he adopted a policy of dishonesty and rationalized it: the church had deceived him for many years by its teaching – why should he not now deceive the church?

It was then also a peculiar case. Turmel was not saying, as the leading Catholic Modernists of his day were saying: 'The traditional formulations of Christian faith and the traditional understanding of the Bible are outmoded and misleading; here is the way to formulate and understand now.' He was saying: 'I have been deceived and I am no longer a believer.' If remaining a believer is the great object, he was no longer trying to attain it. Yet who is to say whether such a one might not retain faith if new ways of perceiving and stating Christian belief were to be freely available or if authority were more patient and pliable? In more latitudinarian circumstances he might have been the kind of dissident who forsakes what those who remain believers scarcely recognize as their faith at all or abandons faith for reasons which many believers also see as difficulties but as peripheral in their bearing on 'real faith'. Some recent defections have evoked these responses:[4] may honesty not be too demanding, too conscientious?

But to return: how far Turmel's behaviour was a matter of his own personality and how far the effect of his circumstances may now be of purely historical interest. Bizarre as his case is, it

throws into relief many features of a persistent issue in the
practice of theology in relation to the church, in a way
sufficiently close to, yet sufficiently far from, present-day
Western circumstances to be both instructive and stimulating.
At its simplest, the issue is: how important is honesty in the
Christian theologian's work? What are its terms and what is its
character?

For many, both insiders and outsiders as far as faith is
concerned, the thing is clear-cut. Particularly in a pluralist
society with commonly recognized (if only vaguely defined)
criteria of evidence and truthfulness, the church is perceived
as now a voluntary society competent to make its rules and
define its membership (sometimes, as in England, with some
blurred areas derived from the past). It may once have been
different, but now no one compels people to join or to remain.
So it seems clear: if they cannot conform, they must be
outside. No one now need face the agonies of Turmel.

There is of course an immediate qualification, even when
the situation is judged at the secular level of 'the church as
voluntary society': members of such bodies may properly
attempt to change the rules and re-define the conditions of
membership, even by means of lengthy campaigns of education and persuasion. No one, however strongly he perceives
Christianity as an unchanging faith, can reasonably maintain
that in all matters such adjustment is ruled out. Plainly, as a
result of initiatives from all levels of the church, top, middle
and bottom, it has occurred constantly in the past. Plainly too,
there is an uncertain dividing line between permissible
adjustment and impermissible change which does violence to
the heartland of faith or (more prosily) commonsense Christian identifiability. The line may be felt to be discernible only
with hindsight, and the cynical observer will say that the chief
determinant of its positioning depends on whether the
aspiring reformer succeeds or fails.

Such considerations affect all kinds of bodies – political
parties and charitable societies as well as churches. They affect
bodies possessing all kinds of ethos (open or authoritarian)
and structures (democratic or hierarchical). But in the case of

the church, other factors reinforce the position of the would-be reformer who has no wish to leave the fold, notably the provisional character of all speech and formulation about God.

Religious bodies are in a strange position in this respect: the more central to faith the matter in question, the more susceptible it is to the operation of provisionality of formulation and (if the point can only be accepted) the weaker the position of the traditionalist; yet such subjects, being central, are precisely those on which, in religious bodies, the question of exclusion from membership most appropriately arises, and in relation to which awareness of the inadequacy of human talk about God is least likely to be admitted – for the very identity of the body concerned seems to be at stake.[5] That a reformer holds and seeks to commend new views on, for example, funeral procedures or the ethics of gambling, and even persists in being out of line on these matters, may seem poor grounds for raising the question of his or her integrity in relation to membership. Yet when it comes to matters which manifestly and understandably do raise that question (belief in God, understanding of the Incarnation), the issue of provisionality comes firmly into view and baffles action. Experienced and 'history-wise' authorities may be reluctant to exclude the dissident who is acting with integrity – whatever the clamour from those not given to subtlety of perception or moderation of tongue.

It is of course possible (and has in the past been usual) for church authorities to deny provisionality in the statement of belief and to insist (whether out of concern for orthodoxy or for civil order) on particular formulations as if possessing 'final' validity, but authorities thereby run serious risks: at the least, the future charge, probable on the basis of many past examples, of short-sightedness and foolishness; and more, the general depressing of credibility and the trivializing of religion that comes from enforcing belief about the transcendent encapsulated in ephemeral terms.

The matter is made worse when one knows (and these days everyone may know) the mechanisms by which churches arrive at their statements: the bureaucratic and political, rather than intellectual pressures which commonly predominate; the

calibre and type of those primarily involved, often simply
those willing to devote energy and able to devote time to the
elaborate machinations required. It takes a lofty and
penetrating conviction of the divine guidance operative in
these procedures, and of its overriding authority, to compen-
sate for this acquaintance with the earthly details – and of
course this highly theological conviction is itself subject
(please God) to the criterion of provisionality which is in
question.

For some, nevertheless, this conviction has been the determining factor: in the 1920s Abbot Cuthbert Butler of Downside
deliberately turned aside from research into Christian origins
and the New Testament because of the risk of collision with
ecclesiastical authority,[6] presumably not because of sheer
pusillanimity and cynical evasion but because of an underlying belief that 'the Church', however improbably and unim-
pressively embodied for a particular purpose, had *ultimate*
competence as the organ of Christian truth, even where there
were matters susceptible of historical investigation and
vulnerable to its uncertainties, as had now become painfully
plain.

In more modern form, some such complex of attitudes
seems to underlie certain areas of the work of a scholar like
Raymond Brown, the American Roman Catholic writer on the
New Testament whose books are so widely and deservedly
appreciated. In his study of Matthew 1–2 and Luke 1–2,[7] he
confronts, as he must, the implications of his historical
exegetical work for the doctrine of Jesus' virginal conception.
He devotes an appendix to the question and concludes that
'the *scientifically controllable* biblical evidence leaves the question of the historicity of the virginal conception unresolved'
(p. 527). The italics hint that other kinds of 'evidence' must be
available which are relevant to the matter, presumably
(though it is not clearly said) some form of magisterial church
teaching. Yet of course the setting and emergence of that
teaching in what he shows to be its many and varied forms are
themselves equally open to scientific control, and one is left
wondering how exactly it can carry force when one recognizes

that its proponents took a wholly optimistic view of historicity. Brown is left with (*a*) an *opinion* that 'it is easier to explain the New Testament evidence by positing historical basis than by positing pure theological creation' (pp. 527f.), and (*b*) a belief in the virginal conception as an 'action of God's creative power' (nevertheless 'not a phenomenon of nature' (p. 531)!) whose precise purpose seems to be elusive. Such an exercise may strike some as a determination to stay sitting on the branch while cheerfully sawing it through to breaking-point. And the purpose, or perhaps the trusted way of safety? Surely it is the conviction that in the end the magisterium *knows* in the long term if not in the short, and is anyway the sphere whereby God's purposes are spearheaded in the world.

Those who, placed outside this particular framework of theology and so this particular posture in which to discern what honesty requires, gasp at such a manner of proceeding, should reflect that some form of it may stare them in the face at any moment. Whenever, confronting the apparent need as a result of theological investigation to modify the traditional patterns of faith and so to place themselves at variance with the main stream, they nevertheless try to insist on their integrity in remaining within the fold, they may well be positing a location where their view is legitimized, even if that location is no earthly organ of the church but the very mind of God himself.

So far this discussion has concerned largely the interaction between the nonconforming or reformist theologian and the church; it has commented on some aspects of the issue of integrity that may arise. Where the dissident is employed by a modern Western secular academic institution, or (to raise the tone) feels the moral claim of the ethos such institutions represent, the issue may seem in effect non-existent: surely it settles itself. The difficulties arise purely when one is involved with the church: its rules, its heritage, its inability to move in the light of translucent evidence but only by the kind of slow, mysterious adaptability, almost invisible to the naked eye, found in the evolutionary processes of nature itself.[8] It is not surprising that the examples that have sprung most readily to mind have come from Roman Catholicism, where these factors appear most sharply in the modern world. But lay all that aside, and integrity is easy; and its claims are among the most elementary moral requirements that we know. In this sense, there are situations where a church may represent a standing temptation to immorality, if only by placing institutional survival or cohesion in one form or another above ordinary truthfulness, or fostering a style of loyalty or fellowship in which the moral priority of truthfulness is blurred or underplayed (no doubt in the interests of other 'truth' whose defensibility is precisely what is in question).

All the same, the overriding character of the high-minded academic's integrity may be challenged for better cause than that given by the aspects of ecclesiastical culture just listed (in effect, the inherited tradition). Despite all discouragement, the belief that the nature and content of theological wisdom are better understood and described by committed insiders than detached outsiders has force. It is a belief which profits, be it noted, from a shift in terminology and accent: from theological *truth* to theological *wisdom*; from something which is likely to be conceptual and to lend itself to dogmatic formulation and authoritative pronouncement to something which will extend to more elusive and even tentative expression but suggests greater depth of reflection and strength for all that. While it may be more subjective, it will also be wider in scope, embracing moral and spiritual as well as intellectual dimensions and seeking to unify them within a *mode of existence*. Such wisdom is of course far from immune to self-deception and failure to face reality – indeed it is the favourite refuge of the woolly – but at its best it presents strong credentials to opposing viewpoints and is capable of making them shrivel into superficiality, a fate to which the detached outsider is peculiarly vulnerable at its hand. Such is the wisdom that can be a quality of the insider. It is of its essence to share the experience of religion, not simply to describe it. In modern circumstances, it will at its best (and with regard to this wisdom, only the best is tolerable) be able to combine commitment with detachment from all particular forms of theological formulation and religious life, seeing them as but transient approximations to the true and the good. It is then as far as possible removed from the absolute attachment to particular forms of ministry or liturgy or architecture to which religious people are prone, while at the same time it generates intense love of whatever forms seem best for the moment. It will of course face chronically the charges of instability and weakness. Precisely this sort of wisdom, with its fusion of the intellectual, the moral and the spiritual, calls into question the claims of certain styles of integrity in theology which at first sight seem beyond challenge, for example that of the independent scholar who feels responsibilities to standards and styles of truthfulness which churches, with their multifarious membership and innate caution, sense less keenly.

We may illustrate the matter by examining it in the setting of early Christianity witnessed in the New Testament. In those documents, it is doubtful whether the question of theological honesty is ever raised in the senses most recognizable to us. They are too much a product of the intellectual developments of the past two centuries and of secularization for that to be possible. There is no sign in the New Testament of people suffering a sense of conflict between a high service of truth and evidence on the one hand and authoritative teaching on the other.

But there are instances, of which Paul, at the very fount of the tradition, is much the most striking, where questions of integrity are to be found such as are not beyond our capacity to understand with sympathy bred of experience.

The most far-reaching example concerns Paul's attempt to reconcile the universal role of Jesus with his inherited conviction concerning Jewish particularism.[9] It involved the question of the Law's validity (in part or as a whole? for some, for all, or for none? in past or in present?); it involved a mental picture of Israel's history and its role in history as a whole (top dog or under dog? privileged or discarded? with a future or only a past?); and it involved a framework for understanding God's providential ordering of things (unwavering consistency or discontinuities? discernible plans or inscrutable

counsels?). Here was a collection of issues which were far
from being theoretical puzzles one could ponder at leisure,
but were rather matters on which one's very self-understanding, the intelligibility of one's 'world' depended. For
Paul, the irruption of Jesus as God's chosen envoy and his
own belief in Jesus' consequentially urgent significance for
everybody, rendered highly problematic all conventional and
traditional assessments of that 'world'.

There have been many efforts to weld Paul's statements on
these questions into a consistent whole. To succeed in the
endeavour would be to vindicate the integrity of both Paul
and scripture, a prospect lending zeal to the task. A more
candid and realistic examination convinces many students of
Paul that the quest is misconceived. While Paul's words
make an identifiable set of points, those points are evidence
of a variety of tendencies, a number of different 'probes' into
the thought-situation which he faced. In that sense, Paul is a
man seeking integrity rather than expressing it. It is as if,
seized by the single clear conviction of Jesus' unique and
crucial significance, he was, in the letters before us, *in process*
of reorganizing other elements of his mind's truth, his
'world', around that central belief. (Whether, in the terms
available to him and as the problems then presented themselves, *any* satisfactory reorganization was possible is
another matter.)

It is of course debatable where this places Paul in relation to
theological honesty. Putting it crudely: does he win points for
accepting new truth brilliantly clear to him, even if its
implications were obscure and even confused? Or lose points
for accepting new data which did not clearly cohere with truth
already revealed and established? Was he admirably adventurous in letting his 'world' go, or a raiser of dust (still not
settled!) which can only blind the faithful pilgrim? Then: is
honesty to God a matter of acceptance of authority and
authenticated tradition in belief, or is it acceptance of 'call',
yielding a wisdom which may have its own kind of fused
integrity at a level where belief, behaviour and prayer are one?
'Against such there is no law' (Gal. 5.23).

Another example relates to Paul's moral and pastoral counselling. It is the familiar case of idol meat,[10] whether Christians should eat meat which had, en route to the butcher and the table, been the object of pagan ritual 'treatment'. We now have a very full understanding of the circumstances surrounding this matter in the life of a Greek city and we can enter into the social realities involved for a Christian group which contained members from various levels of society. Nevertheless, the question of moral strategy on which Paul rules in I Cor. 8 is plain enough: shall theological truth be acted upon regardless of the irrational susceptibilities of some members of the group? An added element in this case is that in all probability it was the richer ones who discerned the key theological truth that 'idols are nothing' and the poor who had scruples, taboo feelings, about association with pagan cults. Paul firmly subordinates the claim of theological truth to that of love for the 'weaker' members. Has he not then failed in intellectual integrity, forsaken a fundamental piece of honesty, for the sake of ignoramuses? Will not such a policy, consistently pursued, result in a religion where truth counts not at all and all manner of superstition happily gets away with it? So the honest outsider may easily think. But there is an insider's wisdom ready to speak on Paul's side (though whether it should be determinative is still up for discussion). It derives from the perceiving of realities deeper still than honesty about the truth concerning God. God has called into being a community of persons in allegiance to him in the way of Jesus. It is together that they must learn to live in relation to him, and that 'living' is not chiefly a matter of articulated truths about God's nature, but of conviction *experienced* in life together. There is more than one route by which truth may emerge and finally enter into understanding, more than one order in which wisdom may be acquired. If this is a way of now assessing Paul's judgment in this case, then it is hard to deny it the tribute of a valid kind of honesty. The modern Christian who wonders whether to abandon (as it seems) valued 'truth' in the interests of relations with those of other Christian traditions or of other faiths may find himself facing a not dissimilar set of considerations.

The challenges facing the Christian of the present day who wishes to combine commitment with integrity in the face of discouragement or conflict are in many ways not much like those discernible in the career of Paul. There are, however, as I have hinted, sufficient similarities to give pause to those who are apt to go for simple resolutions in one direction or another. Religious honesty is a complex quality: not synonymous with speaking one's mind in all circumstances, or with uttering every new thought in a field where criteria of excellence are not wholly clear or easy to come by, still less with enjoying intellectual excitement; more a matter of weighing all relevant considerations, then combining firmness with tentativeness, strength with provisionality, clarity with scepticism, because of the character of our knowledge of God and our pilgrim-like relationship with him.

Alistair Kee

Mystery and Politics. The Explorations Continue

During 1987 I re-read all of John Robinson's major works, as preparation for the book I was writing on his thought. Although I had read many of them as they came out over the years, examining them together within a relatively short period produced a very different perception of his work. My original impression was that he treated many subjects but did not have one coherent position. This seemed particularly true in the contrast between the conservatism of his biblical studies and the more radical stance of his theological works. However, reading them together convinced me that his position overall was fundamentally consistent. They exhibit a distinctive dialectic through which he was both loyal to the past and free to explore the reinterpretation of the Bible, doctrine, liturgy, organization and structures, as well as moral and social issues. 'Exploration' is indeed the best way to describe his work. In each aspect it was provisional, not in the sense of uncertain or incomplete, but in being responsive to the situation of rapid social, cultural, intellectual, and economic change. In such times it is necessary to have roots in the tradition, but to be so confident of these as not to be rooted to the spot, to be liberated to encounter God already ahead of us, not left somewhere behind.

When I mentioned to various people that I had been writing a book about the work of John Robinson, there were two types of reaction. The first was from those who were appalled that it was twenty-five years since the publication of *Honest to God*. Never! It can't be! The second was from people under thirty who were completely unmoved by the announcement, as if I had reported that my research subject was the history of weeding the garden, 1758–1875. My interest was not in getting the past right, or writing some definitive account of the works of a churchman and scholar of the recent past. It was rather to open up in a timely way some of the paths of exploration first mapped out by John Robinson; to invite those who remember *Honest to God* to continue with these fundamental questions, and for a new generation, to invite them to take up matters which have become not less but more urgent in the intervening time. I wish to illustrate this by taking up four issues which are prominent in John Robinson's work, and which have become even more important today.

1. *Naming the mystery*

We live in a time of constant change. Things are not going to settle down; indeed, if anything, even the speed of change is going to increase. We can see this decade by decade, and it affects religion and the way of being religious, as everything else. The 1950s, the post-war decade, was one in which there was optimism in the churches about the impact they were about to make on society. In 1959, John Robinson addressed a confirmation class with these challenging words: 'You are coming into active membership of the church at a time when great things are afoot. I believe that in England we may be at a turning of the tide.' But a decade later, at the end of the 1960s, he was able to look back ironically on this reading of the situation. 'The tide was indeed imperceptibly on the turn. But 1960 was to represent the high-water mark, not the low-water mark!'[1] And this at the end of the decade of *Honest to God*. Why, after all the thought, energy and effort which characterized that frenetic period, was the decline in church membership not reversed or at least halted? And the question is even more urgent today, when by the statistics provided by the churches themselves this crisis is deepening year by year.

The answer to such a fundamental question must lie, appropriately, at the most fundamental level of the Christian religion, the doctrine of God. It has been amply demonstrated that secondary matters, such as reorganization of ecclesiastical structures, or rewording of liturgy, make no significant impact on the problem. So many things were changed, often radically, in the life and practice of the churches in the 1960s and 1970s, and yet the doctrine of God did not change in any way. In consequence, while there has been renewal within the churches, Christian faith has not been made credible to those outside. This was the impasse of the period: only a radical revision of the doctrine of God would solve the problem, yet this was the one element of Christian faith which apparently could not be reinterpreted. It is difficult to find an appropriate illustration, but it is as if a body called UK Mystery Tours plc decided it had to make a more effective presentation to the public. Its organization was streamlined, with the help of a firm of consultants; its staff got a new uniform; a more informal style of language was adopted ('Hi, I'm Jeni, thank you for calling UKMT'); and, of course, a main frame computer was installed. The employees loved it, though one or two of the traditionalists took early retirement. How frustrating: even fewer people showed any interest in the product. Tragic really, since most people are fascinated by mystery and ready for it. But at this stage in the twentieth century going to Barnsley was not their idea of a mystery and that was all UKMT would offer. Take it or leave it.

The tragedy is that people today intuitively know that there is more to life than colour-supplement consumerism or tabloid voyeurism. In the film *Educating Rita* the main character is trying to break out of the constrictions of the traditional life on offer to her. Afraid that she is becoming alienated from her family, she returns one evening to the warmth of the pub and sits beside her mother during the ritual sing-along. Why can't she be like that, at peace with her life? But she is even more disturbed when she sees her mother's tears, and hears her despairing words: 'There must be better songs to sing than this.' The tragedy is that many people know there must be more to life, but 'God' does not represent more. The religion on offer does not hold out for them the promise of a new life: they see it as but an aspect of the old.

It is one of John Robinson's contributions to tackling this issue that he begins where people are, and what is most real to them. If people do not believe there is anything more to life than this, that there are no better songs, then that is an end of religion. But much more important, there is an end to anything that deserves to be called human. Wherever people are conscious that there is more to life than this, there is a question, a sense of mystery. That is the reality, and few people would question it. They do not ask whether this reality exists or not, but how it is to be understood, and how it can be brought about in their lives.

But this is not new. In every society which deserves to be called human the same question is pursued, in widely different terms, depending on the level of culture and consciousness of the period. Within the Christian tradition the matter has been explored as the doctrine of God, but the doctrine has been very much a function of the culture and consciousness of the times. In the Bible, the doctrine is expressed in mythological terms, as if the mystery were a supernatural being dwelling in a realm above the earth, reaching down to it from time to time. People were not wrong to think of the mystery in this way, but it would be quite wrong for us to do so, since we do not share this mythological way of thinking in the rest of our lives. The history of Christian doctrine has been dominated not by mythological thinking, but by the thought-forms of Greek metaphysics. For people who share this way of thinking, the mystery is timeless and immutable, standing in complete contrast to all that we know to be characteristic of the human world. Nor were people wrong to speak in this way if they shared that metaphysical world-view, but it would be quite wrong for us to continue to describe the mystery in this way, for we do not inhabit their world.

It is from this sense of mystery that religion arises. Each generation must describe the mystery as experienced under new circumstances. We rightly regard our understanding of the world as more accurate than previous world-views. We should have a more accurate and appropriate account of the mystery which lies at the heart of reality. It is therefore entirely misleading to pose the question in the form: Does God exist? In *Honest to God* John Robinson insisted that we should start the other way around. 'God is, by definition, ultimate reality. And one cannot argue whether ultimate reality *exists*. One can only ask what ultimate reality is like – whether, for instance, in the last analysis what lies at the heart of things and governs their working is to be described in personal or impersonal categories' (p. 29).

A mythical being in another realm might or might not exist, and the world would continue unchanged, as would our lives. An immutable being incapable of being affected by our lives might or might not exist, and the history of the world would continue to evolve and to change, as would our lives. The fact that people can argue about the existence of such a being, either mythological or metaphysical – or not even feel moved to discuss the possibility – only indicates that these ways of thinking are quite foreign to us today. The question is not whether such a being exists, but how we today experience the mystery and how we should best describe it in the thought forms of our time. It is this latter form of the question which has proved impossible to answer. The explorations of the previous decades have come to an end indecisively because theologians have not been able to break away from the combination of the biblical, mythological or the classical metaphysical models. Or rather such attempts as there have been, notably process theology based on neo-classical metaphysics, have not been generally accepted as adequately describing the mystery. This is the most excruciatingly difficult task which lies before theology, and relatively little thought is now being given to it. Yet if religion is still an important factor in society a century from now it will be because this problem has been solved and a new way of describing the mystery formulated which incorporates the experience of previous eras, but takes account of the new experiences of the modern world.

2. *The inclusive Christ*

The speed of change distinguishes this time from all others. Previously things moved relatively slowly and individuals and societies had time to absorb changes and come to terms with them. It is one of the assumptions of classical ontology that change is unreal or unimportant, and that the things of religion are unchanging. Change has therefore been seen as a distraction from or a threat to religion. Nothing could be further from a biblical understanding. The God of history causes change and makes himself known through it. He is the creator of the new and is not to be defended against it. He is to be sought coming from the future, not in limbo outside the flow of events. He is the God of hope not nostalgia. And this is a good example of why the mystery can no longer be described in the categories of a world view which was suspicious of change. Otherwise religion will be synonymous with reaction. Rudolf Otto describes a not dissimilar situation which illustrates the danger. The example concerns the position of religion with respect to the German Romantic movement of the late eighteenth century. 'A mighty torrent of the powers, talents, and strivings of the human spirit surged forward. Only one human interest seemed to be laggard amid this universal stir and excitement and it was precisely the interest which for so long had been the first, indeed almost the only one: religion.'[2] Religion, which had previously been the primary way of exploring reality, penetrating the mystery, was now regarded as an obstacle to the quest. Otto, in suitably Romantic categories, describes the characteristics of the explorer. 'One was cultured and full of ideals; one was aesthetic, and one was moral. But one was no longer religious' (p. ix).

These words were written in Otto's Introduction to Schleiermacher's work *On Religion: Speeches to its Cultured Despisers*, itself a contribution to the Romantic movement, and published in 1799. Although John Robinson does not discuss Schleiermacher, there are close parallels in their objectives. Schleiermacher was concerned that the most creative and sensitive people of his day regarded themselves as having gone beyond religion, as if it were a feature of more primitive times. He wished to do two things at once. First, he sought to present religion as something which still lay ahead of them if they thought to explore what is real and worthwhile. They have mistaken religion itself for the trappings of religion. These trappings correspond to the culture and consciousness of previous times. But religion itself they have yet to explore. They must not be put off by the externals. Secondly, the roots of religion are to be found in human experience. They are not being asked to believe things which are foreign to the modern world. Rather they have to consider their deepest understanding of how things are, the mystery of reality. That is the core of religion, and religious beliefs, doctrines, codes and rituals are all attempts to express this core, the deep things of experience.

There is a parallel here with John Robinson's attempt to direct people to those things they can affirm, their deepest experiences of how things are. There is no reason why in the modern world we should be tied to describing the mystery in the thought-forms of a world-view which in every other respect we have come to reject.

A second parallel is that both Schleiermacher and John Robinson were committed Christians, and therefore found the most comprehensive way to explore the mystery to be in terms of Jesus Christ. But in both cases they proceeded from the general to the particular. If Christ is the Word made flesh, that means that it is in his life that the mystery is most clearly revealed. 'He who has seen me, has seen the Father' (John 14.9). This is the mythological, biblical manner of expressing the faith, and we today must find its equivalent, which will allow our contemporaries to affirm the same faith. (I illustrate

this with a quotation from the Fourth Gospel, since John
Robinson considered that his Bampton Lectures, *The Priority of
John*, was the first critical work since Schleiermacher to
advocate the priority of the Johannine tradition.)

I have mentioned the work of Schleiermacher, since he can
be regarded as one of the main contributors to the rise of the
phenomenology of religion. He makes the important distinction between the core of religion, religion in itself, and the
manifestations of religion, the various ways in which this core
is expressed in any age or culture. This opens up the
possibility of being true to religion while declining to hold to it
in the terms of previous generations. It is the characteristic of
John Robinson's position that he is absolutely rooted in
Christian faith, and because of this is free to explore the
appropriate forms in which it is to be confessed today. This is
in no sense disloyalty to the past. It depends on the past. In
several places he makes the point that to discard the tradition,
to cut one's roots, is literally to be *déraciné*, which is the
opposite of radical. It is the freedom of the Christian to sit
loose to the law of tradition – as a law. The tradition was made
for man, not man for the tradition.

In this respect there is a further parallel between Schleiermacher and John Robinson, for although he never consciously
attempted to formulate a phenomenology of religion, there
are two aspects of his thought which point in this direction.
The first has already been indicated, namely focussing on the
mystery of reality as the core of religion, rather than on a
timeless definition – whether mythological or ontological –
which must be confessed today. The second concerns the
relationship between Christianity and other world religions.
As we should expect, he concentrates on the modern experience of the mystery. This was a subject which John Robinson
took up in the Teape Lectures, delivered in various centres in
India, on the broad field of Christianity and Hinduism, and
published as *Truth is Two-eyed*. All religions have to be judged
by their capacity to express and explore this mystery, on how
they deal with such matters as suffering, evil, the contemporary understanding – sociologically and psychologically – of

what it means to be a human being. But there is another aspect, which derives from his affirmation of Christ as the unique and final expression of the mystery. Whereas in the days of missionary triumphalism this would mean that all other religions are either wrong, or are to be fulfilled in Christianity, John Robinson makes a very different point, namely that Christ does not belong to Christianity. He quotes V. Chakkarai with approval: 'To believe that God is best defined by Christ is not to believe that God is confined to Christ' (p. 129). Christ is greater than Christianity, and he can wear the clothes of other religions. Just as it was not necessary to become a Jew in order to become a Christian, it may no longer be necessary to become a Christian in order to affirm the mystery in his terms.

In these days of inter-religious ecumenism, when it is quite clear that no one religion is going to conquer the hearts of the world, Christians must find a very different way of confessing the uniqueness of Christ. John Robinson returned to the issue in a lecture delivered in Hamilton, Ontario, in 1982, published in *Where Three Ways Meet*: 'No other task, I believe, is more urgent for the church today, than to learn how to restate its conviction of the centrality of Christ both in relation to other faiths and in relation to insights of modern psychology without on the one hand being imperialistic and triumphalist . . . or lapsing into a helpless syncretism, in which all religions and all insights are as good as each other or can be regarded ultimately as saying the same thing (which they are not)' (p. 12). Exploration of the inclusive Christ is even more urgent today.

3. Political theology

How can something so vague as 'the mystery of reality' be seen to be in continuity with the mythological or metaphysical ways of speaking about God? John Robinson's answer at first seems incredible: the mystery is personal. But what he means can be exemplified in the field of morality. We know what it is to do what is right, even when it is uncomfortable or costly. It

could mean destroying something dear to us, risking a
friendship. On occasion it could mean putting a career in
jeopardy. In its most extreme form, to do what we know to be
right might mean risking death itself. If we have not faced all
of these situations personally, we can understand accounts
given by other people who have. Now why does this kind of
action make sense? Or rather, why does its making sense
overrule every other criterion by which it makes no sense at
all? Why do we know that to avoid this demand would be
somehow to diminish ourselves as human beings or de-
humanize others?

We call it a demand, but that is a word associated with what
is required by another human being. Although we can speak
of the moral law within, to use Kant's phrase, if truth be told it
is not a law at all, in two respects. It is not a law in the sense
that we are not here dealing with a series of actions which are
always right or always wrong. Rather we are dealing with
situations in which we are to do the right thing by ourselves or
with respect to other people. It is only called a law in the
loosest sense. But more importantly, if it could be established
that there was such a law in the universe, why on earth,
literally, should we bother to obey it? Even Kant could give no
reason, and had to postulate a God who would provide a
reason, in terms of a life hereafter, of rewards and punishments. But we acknowledge the demands – if we do – without
regard to rewards or punishments. We admire those who
choose death rather than a dehumanized life. In all this we are
in the realms of personal relations. If there is such a demand
on each of us, which is inadequately described as a law, then
the best and most apt way we have of describing it is to say it is
the demand of a person, to be a person and to enable others to
be persons. Hence when John Robinson says that reality, the
mystery, is personal, he is seeking to describe one of the most
fundamental experiences of our lives.

But reality is personal in a more immediate sense. The
demand to do the right is not with respect to some Thou
standing outside the world, over against the world, in a
mythological or metaphysical mode. Rather the demand is

always in respect of another person, a thou. It is John Robinson's contention that we meet the Thou in the thou. In traditional language, we meet God in our neighbour. It is in our social lives that we encounter God – or not at all. Now there is something profoundly biblical about this, although it is not expressed in mythological language. If true, it means that religion is an inherently social form of life. It is not a private mode. It means that all theology is social theology, even political theology. There is no neutral gap between the world and God, in which we can seek him, by turning away from our social responsibilities.

Even worship is to be understood in this manner. *Leitourgia* was originally a secular word for public works which a citizen undertook. It was social action. Nothing could describe the eucharist better: social action. 'Do this, in remembrance of me.' The verb is active and plural.

But already in the 1960s theology was becoming political theology for quite different reasons. It was not, as in Europe, a conclusion arrived at by discussion. In the third world, but especially in Latin America, theology was discovered to be political theology. In societies much more deeply and visibly divided than in Europe, wealth and power, law and order, served the interests of a small minority at the expense of the suffering of the majority. The situation was not new, and for the most part the Catholic Church was identified with the institutions of wealth and power. Indeed it was one of them. The situation was not new, but there was a new consciousness, in part created by recent influence of Marxist critical theory. As Sartre points out, the intolerable is only experienced as intolerable when we are made aware that an alternative is possible. The Church was not in charge of the situation, but it was challenged about where it stood. Three options lay before it. Would it continue to associate itself with the structures and institutions which legalized injustice and perpetuated the suffering of the poor? Put this way the answer must be, No. Would it change sides and take the part of the poor, to defend them against their oppressors? Although individual bishops might adopt this position, the church as an institution could not. A third possibility was that it could be even-handed, blessing and judging both sides as appropriate. In practice, to be even-handed in an unequal situation is to favour the *status quo* and therefore to be a party to injustice. (A fourth possibility was later to be to defined by writers such as Jon Sobrino and Leonardo Boff, that the church should not remain as one of the powerful institutions of society even to use its power on behalf of the poor. 'A church *for* the poor, is not yet necessarily a church *of* or *from* the poor.'[3])

These were the choices forced on the Catholic Church, and finally on all the churches in Latin America, in the 1960s and 1970s. It was not a matter of theory. The theology which justified the *status quo* was just as much a political theology as the theology which justified revolution. And perhaps the most political theology of all was that which declared that the church must keep out of politics. Eventually the new thinking was identified by the title 'liberation theology', and for those who had eyes to see the initiative in theology had passed to the Third World, first to Latin America but then to Asia and to Africa. It was not just an extension of the old agenda. It was a new perspective from which the old agenda was judged. It was a new method by which the old procedures were condemned. It may have begun with economic and political issues, but it came to deal systematically with doctrine, with ethics, spirituality and with the basic organization of Christian communities.

Reactions to liberation theology divide broadly into two groups. First there are those who know little of it and assume it is not for them. It is thought to be all about revolution and joining guerilla bands in the mountains. But even those who know better often assume that it is only a special kind of ethics or spirituality. They do not understand that it is a new way of doing theology, and a critique of what in Europe is assumed to be the only way. In some respects John Robinson anticipated these criticisms, especially of European theology's dependence on Greek metaphysical assumptions about God and the world. There is, however, another, smaller group, which is so impressed by liberation theology that they wish to introduce it into this country, largely in its original form and without criticism. Although there have been many criticisms of liberation theology from the traditional side, there have been few radical criticisms. One such is the 'fraternal criticism' offered by the Spanish theologian Alfredo Fierro, and it concerns the relationship between political theology and the issues of belief discussed here at the outset.

In many fields there is a somewhat patronizing attitude towards the Third World. They are on the same road that we in the West have pioneered, except that they are well behind and struggling to catch up. While in some respects this is true, many liberation theologians take a critical view of Western life, especially its lack of spirituality, and are working to make sure that their own societies progress by a rather different route. It is therefore not certain that these societies will pass through stages which we have already reached, or that theologians will have to address themselves to our questions. However that may be, one of the most obvious differences between Latin American and European theologies is their attitude towards secularization. Liberation theologians, so original and incisive on many issues, are unable to understand the high priority given in Europe to such matters as belief in God. It is simply not a problem for them or for their Christian communities. They become irritated by such discussions and see in them further evidence that European theology is inherently incapable of becoming truly social or political. Consequently, although liberation theologians are radical on a whole series of matters, on this one they are curiously quiescent. Fierro criticizes Latin American theologians for failing to pay attention to critical theology, and specifically refers to the work of Rudolf Bultmann and John Robinson. 'Gutíerrez's theology of liberation is a leftist orthodoxy. It makes a subversive application of a dogmatics that remains at bottom little altered and quite traditional.'[4] On the fundamental issues it is 'a theology of subversive orthodoxy'.

Fierro also raises the question of what will happen to liberation theology when (if) Latin American societies become secular? Then there will be an increasing number of people whose secular consciousness will mean that they cannot understand talk about the God of history, the God of the poor. Even if this theology can be largely purified of Greek metaphysical assumptions, such assertions are highly mythological, and will not be appropriate in societies which are increasingly secular, scientific and industrial. Liberation theology has a great deal to contribute to European theology, to make it more truly biblical, even if there are fundamental issues, already raised in Europe, which it has yet to face. It cannot solve the crisis in European religion, but it can contribute to a better understanding of the fact that all theology is fundamentally political theology.

4. *Privatized religion*

If the 1960s and 1970s were characterized by liberation, by progressive and broadly left-thinking initiatives, the 1980s have been characterized by a strong reaction against such trends. The reaction has affected the same spectrum of religion, morality, social and economic life, and the organization of institutions and communities. It is to be observed in Christianity, throughout the north Atlantic countries, but it is not essentially Christian. It is found also in other world religions. Nor is it an essentially religious movement. It is an ethos which now permeates political life. If the previous decades were deeply influenced by socialist thinking, this is predominantly capitalist. It is not a revival of old conservatism, but a neo-conservatism which is often dismissive of and abusive towards an older more humane conservatism. In *Christian Freedom in a Permissive Society* John Robinson says that he 'was brought up an unthinking Tory' (p. 89). But soon he began to move to the Labour Party and then the Social Democratic Party. No party was ideal, but he felt an obligation to be involved actively in political life, rather than to enjoy the luxury of a pure life above all that kind of thing. He was able to identify the new ethos very early. As he commented in *The Roots of a Radical*: 'Symbolic of the Seventies are what I call my "three M's", Malcolm Muggeridge, Mary Whitehouse and Margaret Thatcher. Though I have nothing against any of them personally and indeed admire them for the courage of their convictions, I can never make up my mind which most represents all that my soul abhors' (p. 4).

The neo-conservative ethos undermines the social understanding of religion at both superficial and profound levels. Sociologists used to speak of modern life as being characterized by privatization. Religion, for example, became an element in the private life of the individual, not affecting social or political values. Johannes Metz, one of the founders of political theology in Europe, declared that political theology should aim to bring privatized religion to an end.[5] Since then the word 'privatize' has become identified with neo-conservative economic policies. Industry, which was within social control, to ensure that it contributed to the formation of a certain type of society, is now increasingly sold off into private (in practice corporate) hands, to assist in the creation of a very different kind of society. It is therefore fitting that in this neo-conservative culture, the privatization of religion is regarded as a good thing. It has implications for all aspects of religion.

Although neo-conservatism is not Luddite, indeed it is frequently associated with adventure capital and the promotion of sunrise industries, paradoxically it is often found to co-exist with the ancient world-view. Many of those who in their jobs are on the frontiers of technology seem quite happy to continue with highly mythological doctrines which are entirely incompatible with a modern scientific understanding of the world. Whatever psychological needs such a reassertion of the tradition serves, it goes back on everything that has been said about finding God in the new, and seeking new ways of speaking about the mystery. But it also breaks the link between the Thou and the thous, and reintroduces that characteristic gap between God and the world in which a specifically religious sphere can be established. Eric James has summed it up well. 'The great danger is that liturgy creates a world of things over against the secular, instead of a vision of the sacredness of the secular.'[6] But if true of worship, it also has wider ramifications.

Privatized religion can display an entrepreneurial attitude. Increasingly in this country we hear the echoes of that form of American evangelism in which it is asserted that if you are right with God, your career will take off. The association of material well-being with God's blessing, and misfortune and suffering with God's punishment, was rejected in the Book of Job, and again by Jesus (e.g. John 9.3), but it is too strong a part of the neo-conservative world view to be rejected simply on these grounds.

Religion on this view should not be involved in politics: it is about the individual soul and God. This has immediate relevance in the social sphere. In American neo-conservatism, repeated increasingly in this country, there is a preference for charity as opposed to welfare. It is argued, or perhaps just asserted, that there is a welfare mentality that is deeply degrading and debilitating for the recipients. But those in need should not be forgotten, and Christians should attend to charity. This argument would be stronger if sin were also privatized, that is, if evil were only expressed in deliberate and overt actions committed by individuals. But we know that evil is also institutionalized, so that individuals can with integrity and clear conscience operate impersonal policies which advance the interests of the rich and powerful against the interests of the poor and weak. It is not only the institutions of state centralism which have to be criticized. But privatized religion, in adopting the thoroughly unbiblical position of declaring that religion must be kept out of politics, stills the voice of prophetic criticism against capitalist institutions.

Finally, privatized religion also represents the return to the competitive triumphalism of a previous age, very often with a rejection of other religions in terms which have racist overtones. Who could seriously take courage from such a religious revival? It represents a further postponement of the day when the serious issues raised in the 1960s can be taken up once again and explored with courage, with creativity and above all with faith in the mystery revealed in Jesus Christ.

John Kent

The Shadow of a Grove of
Chestnut Trees

At the time when *Honest to God* was published 'radical theology' seemed likely to dominate the English Protestant theological landscape indefinitely: by the late 1980s, however, it had clearly been marginalized by a weak form of what asserted itself to be 'orthodoxy'. This was the case, not only in the Protestant churches but also in the Church of Rome, where the more 'liberal' theological shift which some thought would follow the Vatican Council did not take place, but where theologians like Hans Küng, Edward Schillebeeckx, Charles Curran and Archbishop Hunthausen were severely disciplined by the Vatican. What had happened? Contemporary history is not easy to write, not least because evidence is not always available with which to test the assumptions of the narrative line which is bound to have set itself up under the pressure of events. Some explanations may be suggested, however. These all lead to the same, encouraging conclusion, that the eclipse of 'radical theology' will be temporary, because the intellectual problems which were raised or revived by the theological radicals of the post-war period have not been solved, either by the disciplinary offensive of the papal curia (reminiscent of the methods used at the beginning of the century to silence the Catholic Modernists), or by the weak academic counter-attack which has developed in Protestant circles during the Thatcher years. I say *intellectual* problems deliberately, because in the days of the *Honest to God* debate there were other kinds of ecclesiastical and politico-religious 'radicalism' which asked for liturgical and institutional changes in the mainstream on pragmatic rather than dogmatic grounds. *Honest to God* itself had much to say about the unsatisfactory nature of the individual's religious life in the post-war churches of England; and a non-church movement briefly expressed the gut feeling, never far from the surface of Western Christianity after the middle of the eighteenth century, that membership of 'the church' was not necessary in order to be a Christian. Politically and ecclesiastically, however, very few radical changes resulted from these activities. The churches avoided direct political intervention, and their place was taken by conservative religious pressure-groups which concentrated on single-issue politics, like opposition to contraception and abortion, or support for television censorship, badly disguised as a concern for public morality – it is easy to forget that Mrs Whitehouse was already well-known in 1965. Liturgical reformers seemed to concentrate on removing Latin from the Roman Mass and English from the standard translation of the Bible as well as from the Prayer Books of the Protestant churches. Radical theology, with its basic rejection of 'orthodox' certainty, a certainty which expressed through hierarchical, masculine church orders a Barthian belief in the absoluteness of the Christian revelation, in a God who condescends to us through a revelation which cannot be translated into terms other than its own, which we can either accept or reject but certainly not qualify – radical theology was out on its own, and was unlikely to appeal to more than a minority in the churches. For a brief period, however, that minority flourished centre-stage.

If one seeks to explain why radical theology withdrew to the wings during the 1980s, one has to begin by asking what was the deeper reason for the success of the radicals in the *Honest to God* years. Fundamental for the Christian intellectuals most concerned was the tendency of the modern Western consciousness to find the religious and especially Christian uses of language less and less convincing. Such language, talk about the Trinity, sin, the divinity of Jesus as the Christ, atonement, salvation, human depravity and so forth, remained everywhere in use in the churches of the 1960s. But, as J. S. Bezzant wrote for example, in *Objections to Christian Belief*, in 1963, the year of *Honest to God*'s publication, 'the root of the doctrine of human depravity is not in direct experience but in the much more dubious statements of the Bible, reinforced by Augustine, regarded as revelation of propositional truth'.[1] Orthodox theologians, relying on a doctrine of unique divine revelation, and on a second, highly disputable doctrine that 'authority' had been divinely given to 'the Church' to rule on the meaning of disputed theological statements, were not accustomed to press the question of truth against such propositions. To quote Bezzant again from the 1960s: 'There is an essential but easily concealed and overlooked implication in claiming that anything is true: it is that there are sufficient grounds for knowing or for reasonable belief that it is true. This is at once evident if we envisage the opposite statement, "This is true, but I have no grounds for knowing or believing that it is true", which is absurd. . . . Unintelligible or humanly unassimilable alleged revelation, whatever else it may be, is not revelation' (pp. 101–9).

Paul van Buren took the argument a stage further, also in 1963: 'The empiricist in us finds the heart of the difficulty not in what is said about God, but in the very talking about God at all. We do not know what "God" is, and we cannot understand how the word "God" is being used. It seems to function as a name, yet theologians tell us that we cannot use it as we do other names, to refer to something quite specific. If it is meant to refer to an existential encounter, a point of view, or the speaker's self-understanding, surely a more appropriate expression could be found. The problem is not solved by substituting other words for the word "God". . . . The problem of the Gospel in a secular age is a problem of the logic of its apparently meaningless language . . .'[2]

Radical theologians like John Robinson, Paul van Buren and John Bezzant were acutely conscious of the habit of mind which Nietzsche had detected years before in both religious and philosophical teachers: 'Such assertions and promises as those of the antique philosophers concerning the unity of virtue and happiness, or the Christian, "But seek ye first the Kingdom of Heaven and its righteousness and all these things shall be added unto you", have never been made with total honesty and yet always without a bad conscience: one has advanced such propositions, which one very much desires to be true, boldly in the face of all appearance and has felt no religious or moral pang of conscience – for one had transcended reality *in honorem majorem* of virtue or of God and without any selfish motive. Many worthy people still stand at this level of truthfulness: when they *feel* themselves selfless they think that they are permitted to trouble themselves less about truth.'[3]

Nietzsche meant that Christianity had not kept its promises, that the history of the churches offered no evidence that Christianity was a liberating force in human life, but he also meant that the religious use of language had become parasitic on its own modern claim to 'metaphorical' status, as though the statement that 'my love is like a red, red rose' *must* be both intelligible and true because one was willing to use the words, and as though metaphor, in this like the allegedly inspired biblical text which had preceded it as the basis of theological statements, carried its own mysterious guarantee of truth. Radical theology appealed as an attitude and as a method to a comparatively small group of people who found the use of religious language in the 'orthodox' manner unbearably authoritarian, a demand that the reader-hearer-believer subordinate the actual experience of religion, and of the Christian religion in particular, to a specified vocabulary, whether the words employed appeared to fit what was the case or not. The practice of a critical theology was much older than the twentieth century (this was part of the point of introducing the quotation from Nietzsche); in more recent terms, the radical theologians were exercising their own version of a 'hermeneutic of suspicion' before feminist theology gave a new sharpness to the method.

This intense if specialized interest in the sources and legitimization of religious statements prospered in the British religious sub-culture between 1945 and about 1970 because the immediate effect of the loss of empire, imperial wealth and the great-power status was more than just a 'sensation of having lost an empire and having failed to find a role'. That comment may well have been true in some administrative circles, but elsewhere there emerged and lingered for a few years, during which the apparatus of the British welfare state was set up, a vision of a changed, milder society which would turn its back on the authoritarianism, inequality, snobbery and politico-military incompetence which the ruling élites had displayed so thoroughly in the first half of the century. Symbolically, that tradition had culminated in the fall of Singapore. Indeed, a temporary though far from total freedom from the dead hand of traditional authority was a phenomenon to be found in most Western democratic countries in the aftermath of World War Two, and a similar atmosphere of cultural experiment developed in the United States as the Vietnam War revealed the limitations of American imperial power and of the American governing classes. It is a commonplace of New Right thinking in the 1980s that the British welfare state was a disastrous political error of direction forced by the Labour Party on an unsuspecting society exhausted by a long war; what exhaustion really produced, however, when combined with the natural scepticism of the governed classes, was a brief openness to change – and this was a climate in which critical theology was able to grow. The 'liberal Protestant' and 'Catholic Modernist' questions which both the Barthian and the ecumenical theologians supposed that they had more or less permanently removed from the agenda surfaced once more and became widely discussed, partly through the impact of *Honest to God*. At that stage religious radicalism divided: some radical theologians paid more attention to abstract questions such as christology and ecclesiology; others were more enamoured of the chance to apply their anti-dogmatism to the field of Christian ethics in general and of sexual behaviour in particular. Part of the animus which 'orthodoxy' has shown towards critical theology in recent years probably stemmed from a realization that radical theology helped to make the misnamed 'permissive society' intellectually respectable.

To the extent that radical theology implied a critical attitude towards 'authority', certainty and hierarchy, one would not have expected it to have remained popular in the Britain of the 1980s. The political shift to the Right, whatever its deeper causes, involved the formation of a society in which theologians were supposed to bear the double duty of not criticizing either the church or the state, though the state might properly comment on the activities of the church because, whereas the state had been purged of every kind of left-wing thinking and theological radicalism, ecclesiastical bodies, and not least those in cities like Durham and Liverpool, advocated an alternative public morality. Mrs Thatcher's state represented the triumph of a counter-revolution which had rejected the civilizing values of toleration and discussion in favour of a centralized dogmatism which was highly *secular* in its practical application. The old conservative order, much beloved of television, the conservationists and the owners of large 'historical' country houses, but which nevertheless had collapsed in the 1940s when the British effectively *lost* World War Two, had failed to protect its client sub-culture – that is, everyone who did not *feel* themselves to belong either to the 'working-classes' or to a dissenting sub-culture of intellectuals – against a sudden post-war inrush of 'socialist' legislation, and that old, incompetent conservatism had therefore to be replaced with a new and more powerful form of the state which would rank 'order' above law, the 'family' above the individual, censorship above tolerance, wealth above virtue, privilege above compassion, 'white' above 'non-white' and propaganda above education (because education, properly organized, may encourage the undesirable critical faculties). There was nothing novel about such a society; it was probably the standard form of human association throughout modern history, nor was there anything new in the experience of rejection which critical theologians had to accept. What we need to look at now is which forces within the ecclesiastical sub-culture worked against the survival of the radicals and which worked in their favour. There was never any question, however, of 'orthodoxy' completely silencing radicalism: the success of 'orthodoxy' at the institutional level is always the best guarantee of radicalism's re-emergence.

What has worked against radical theology in the churches has been the recognition of the unpredictable consequences of any apparently irreversible acceptance of critical-theological attitudes. The life of the institutions themselves, and therefore the identity and importance of those who control them, has been at stake throughout, but even apart from this there was always a sense that the survival of Christianity itself (not of religion) as a coherent, significant force in modern society was also at stake. The advance of radical theology does not mean, as many Protestant theologians seem to have believed, simply re-establishing 'orthodoxy' on surer if radical foundations, the base altered but the superstructure miraculously unchanged. There is no convenient 'essence of Christianity', however exiguous, which can be used to prop up the existing order, to save the appearances. Radical theology implies, for example, ethical uncertainty, the use, however inadequately, of a sensitive educated judgment in particular situations, and not the legal application of allegedly revealed norms – and also the inevitable scandals of particularity when strict adherence to the rule clashes with the social obligations of the church. That element of uncertainty has always lain at the heart of the conflict: true critical theology deserves John Henry Newman's label of 'undogmatic'. That is why the idea of papal infallibility, for instance, or its popular Protestant substitute, the 'infallibility of the church', belongs, as far as radicalism is concerned, to a world of dead ideas which cannot be taken seriously, either in itself or in terms of the ecumenical *ecclesia* which so many ecclesiastics of all denominations have been working so hard to create. Indeed, another reason for the weakness of contemporary Christian radicalism is the sense that many radicals see ecumenism as raising the truth-question, not as solving it.

For John Paul II, on the other hand, as distinct from Hans Küng, 'infallibility' symbolizes the renewed claim that Christianity 'knows' what we should otherwise be doubtful about, the supernatural terms of human existence. Critical theologians have never been able to free themselves entirely from the charge that, if they want to call themselves 'Christian', they *ought* to hold a similar view of the absoluteness of the Christian revelation. This attack has been made not only from the 'orthodox' side. When *Honest to God* was first published Alasdair MacIntyre wrote a review in *Encounter* which began: 'What is striking about Dr Robinson's book is first and foremost that he is an atheist',[4] and at the time this trenchant attack was regarded in many quarters as something of a put-down, richly deserved, of radical religious writers in general, who were held to be *less* than honest because they refused to admit the validity of MacIntyre's charge. It was typical of the time that a *Daily Telegraph* journalist, T. E. Utley, should begin an article on *Honest to God* with the challenge: 'What should happen to an Anglican bishop who does not believe in God?'[5]

Later reflection suggests that MacIntyre, who wanted Christianity to be either 'orthodox' or untrue, and who certainly thought that it was untrue if it were 'orthodox', had failed to grasp the difference between the radical and orthodox positions. Radical theology sprang and springs from deep anxiety about what can be honestly *said*, whether in specifically Christian terms, or in a more general religious sense. Nothing has happened to lessen that anxiety since 1963, least of all in the sphere of Christian dogma, where the pressure has been increased by a growing recognition that other world-religions have systems of theology which cannot just be dismissed in cheerful Victorian style as false, that plurality entails more than peaceful co-existence: this kind of anxiety was ably expressed in John Hick's *God and the Universe of Faiths* (1973). What has changed is the temper of British society, in which radicals of all kinds are now only entitled to their doubts as long as they keep them private, and in which both nationalism and racism flourish, setting another limit to the influence of religious radicals who choose to sympathize with concepts like 'black theology'.

In any case, to hesitate about what can be said in the late twentieth century in the theological terms authorized by the orthodox tradition does not imply atheism, as MacIntyre asserted: it implied no more than an awareness that after two thousand years of Western Christian history the theologian now had to lay his dogmatism aside and ask what he could still say, in however qualified a form, about the significance of Jesus for religiously-minded people in the West. It did not follow that because one was anxious about what could be honestly said, one was unable to say anything at all. Orthodox writers, on the other hand, while often recognizing and giving full value to the difficulties which radicals confronted, deny that these problems called in question the simple truth of the Christian system. They cling to the belief that, if one only waits long enough, a post-modern, 'mediaeval' world-view will grow like grass through the ruins of contemporary culture, until the new order set in motion by the Enlightenment and the French Revolution ('we all know what that led to'), not to mention the Protestant Reformation and the Communist Manifesto of 1848, has been submerged and forgotten. In that new mediaevalism, doubt will no longer be a serious matter, or, just perhaps, a matter for punishment. In the nineteenth century this romantic baroque approach was already familiar; it was the Ultramontane 'politique du miracle'. The strength of such opinions in the Church of Rome helps to explain the decline of radical theology in a religious sub-culture in which Catholicism now predominates.

From another point of view, it is the expansion of radical theological interest which has worked against its popularity in the churches. Feminist theology is inherently radical, and emerges as such in the writings of Elisabeth Schüssler Fiorenza and Sharon D. Welch, for example. Sharon Welch summed up her general position in the statement that 'instead of finding what it is in Christian texts that condemns sexism in advance, radical feminists question the texts from the stand-point of sexism, asking what it is about Christian concepts of God, of history, of human nature that made it possible for sexism to operate in the life of the christian community';[6] one could multiply quotations of this kind, which assert that there is no real possibility of reconciliation between the patriarchal past of Christianity – texts, institutions, metaphorical and eth-ical systems combined – and a feminist theological system. Such a conflict cannot make radical theology popular in the mainstream churches. It is interesting that when SCM Press published *Honest to God* as a paperback in 1963, the illustration on the cover was of a bronze sculpture, *Seated Youth 1918*, by Wilhelm Lehmbruck: the seated, naked, thoughtful figure, resting its elbows on its knees, was that of a solitary man, and the God about whom the book was being honest was, in its way, masculine too. I doubt if one would use that symbol now, if one were seriously thinking about honesty and the divine. We have changed, and radical theology made its contribution to that change, and today's radicalism has transcended the dialogue between MacIntyre and John Robin-son. One is reminded of George Steiner's words: 'The flower-child in the western city, the neo-primitive chanting his five words of Thibetan on the highway, are performing an infantile charade – founded on the superfluous wealth of that same city or highway. We cannot turn back. We cannot choose the dreams of unknowing. We shall, I expect, open the last door in the castle even if it leads, perhaps *because* it leads, on to realities which are beyond the reach of human comprehension and control. We shall do so with that desolate clairvoyance, so marvellously rendered in Bartok's music, because opening doors is the tragic merit of our identity'.[7] Steiner is no theologian, but he is expressing the impulse behind radical theology, an impulse which MacIntyre missed altogether.

Even in its less extreme forms, feminist resistance to the mainstream Christian tradition is bound to stir up counter-resistance to the radical point of view. Marina Warner, for example, in her study of Mary, *Alone of All her Sex* (Weidenfeld & Nicholson 1976), said that from the standpoint of the

twentieth century the concept of Mary was a human construct, a power in reserve to which the Catholic Church
always seemed to return when the times were dangerous.
Whatever the value of the metaphorical statements involved
in the Marian dogma, Our Lady does not bring us a substantial
body of 'revealed' knowledge, which she has further guaranteed in such famous incidents as when she appeared to
Bernadette at Lourdes and said that she (Mary) was the
Immaculate Conception. Our Lady brings only human images
of woman, images which have often distorted human behaviour, male as well as female, and which are now increasingly seen to have done so by feminist writers. In his
recent brilliant analysis, *The Cult of the Virgin Mary. Psychological Origins* (Princeton 1986), Michael Carroll suggested that
the hold of Mary on the Catholic imagination had been
weakened by the more christocentric approach of the Second
Vatican Council, but John Paul II has reaffirmed, both by
preaching and by pilgrimage, the central vitality of all the most
important Marian sites in Europe, from the Rue du Bac in Paris
(the Miraculous Medal) to Fatima. The full weight of Catholic
popular religion, emotional and institutional, is bound to be
thrown against radical criticism of the Virgin's theological
significance. The human investment in the cult of Mary is so
great that the consequence of her dismissal to the margin of
the religious sub-culture, to the edge of the mythical, and even
beyond, is incalculable.

Radical theology, then, has run against the grain for
something like twenty years: against the essentially conservative mood both of the churches and of society. British society
has turned sour in the long-term aftermath of political defeat;
the churches, though willing to accept the welfare state as the
social consequence of that political upheaval, are still roman-
tically opposing themselves to man's coming of age. This
atmosphere was pervasive enough to affect John Robinson
himself: his radical impetus slowed as he grew older. And
liberation theology, which at first sight might look as though it
were a reinforcement of the critical approach, was not a *radical*
alternative to 'orthodoxy' but one way of politicizing

orthodoxy. The manifold problems about Christianity as a religion were submerged in genuinely serious problems about society; the 'option for the poor' was a reasonable political choice, though hardly as novel a choice as some liberation theologians seemed to think it to be, but it gained little from being related to a naive use of biblical texts. The flaw in an interpretation of the Bible from a left-wing point of view is that it is equally possible to interpret the Bible from a right-wing point of view; moreover, nothing in the modern history of the church inclines one to trust the judgment of the priest in politics (see my study of modern church history, *The Unacceptable Face*, SCM Press 1987, for further discussion of the tangled relationship between the churches and politics). Politics is a familiar place in which to search for ecstatic common action, revolution and counter-revolution, for utopias and police-states. But politics does not solve religious questions; at some stage or other, what emerges from the political dialectic is a demand for the end of discussion, for conformity, for individual submission to those who know better where the true interests of society lie. The 'politicization of orthodoxy' was an attempt to make 'orthodoxy' more palatable by gently secularizing it; it was also a retreat from radical theology as such.

What the history of the past twenty years suggests, then, is that the critical theologian should be content to go against the grain. Radicalism was briefly popular in the 1960s because it was seen as another method of trying to halt the loss of members and priestly vocations which was increasing at the time and which has never entirely stopped since. If radicalism had proved effective in rescuing institutions in decline it would have continued to receive ecclesiastical support, but when the decline continued, writers like Edward Norman soon discovered that radicalism was one of the major causes of the problems of the churches. There were obvious advantages in the discovery that it was not the 'orthodox' but the radical minority which bore the responsibility for the churches' weakness. The institutions regrouped, persuaded that the fall in numbers and influence could only be checked by reasserting the absolute truth of their interpretation of Christianity.

The ambiguous and financially profitable growth of American television evangelism was seen, incredibly, as further evidence of the power of a return to 'orthodoxy'. Similar views lay behind the Papacy's switch from a 'Roman' to a global, television-based context. Theology has ended in politics, and that always leads to tears.

The radical theologian must recognize that, in all but rather specious circumstances, he will always be going against the grain, against the 'orthodox' impulse towards certainty, institutional authority and political engagement. The radical must keep his head and stay loyal to his fundamental *aperçu*: that there is no easy escape-lane out of the problems of being religious in the twentieth century either by appealing to theology-as-tradition, or by reliance on supernaturally inspired texts, or by turning to religious experience, however allegedly christocentric. *Honest to God* summarized modest objections to all those routes out of trouble, and many who had tried them and become dissatisfied were greatly relieved to find their problems part of a common stock. For that very reason, however, the problems remain.

Thérèse of Lisieux may seem an unlikely example of radicalism. Yet, in the last year of her life, when she was dying of tuberculosis, the conflict between her past passionate Catholic religious experience and her growing sense of a divine absence pointed to the heart of the radical theological experience itself. She dismissed as irrelevant her poetry, with its suggestion that at times for her the veil of faith was torn aside: as far as I am concerned, she said, it is no longer a veil but a wall which reaches up to heaven and blots out the stars. She told her sister Pauline, pointing to a well of shadow under the chestnut trees at the bottom of the convent garden, that she herself lay in similar blackness, body and soul. Her prayers to the saints fell, as it seemed to her, on deaf ears. Thérèse was canonized very quickly after her death, partly because of the cures which were rapidly associated with her cult, partly because in the First World War she seemed to replace Joan of Arc as the chosen 'saint' of the French fighting forces, and partly because she seemed at the same time to be exactly the kind of ecstatically loving, obedient, self-obliterating yet maternal figure (she was no child nor was she childlike in her dying months) around which the ideal of modern feminine holiness had been constructed. Nevertheless, her role in the history of modern Christian spirituality probably rests more securely on an unconsciously 'radical' understanding of her as one who endured the darkness of the grove of chestnut trees and watched the bright night-sky turn utterly black.

Less than a hundred years have passed since the death of Thérèse of Lisieux, but they have darkened the sky as much as they have bloodied the ground. 'There is a storm blowing out of paradise . . .'

John Lee

◆

Honest to What?

'But why this prejudice against books in some Christian quarters? For me a book is simply another human being talking to me as clearly as he can: and if I had never received such communications I would never even have started on this journey.'

Philip Toynbee[1]

The church hall was packed to the doors, something like two hundred people, huddled together in mutual suspicion of a bishop who had dared to question their faith. The vicar rose, then member after member of this well-attended evangelical suburban church, and all had one aim in common: to denounce a man and his book and to affirm their own faith in the face of such flagrant atheism.

I remember, as a fifteen-year-old, observing this angry gathering, having two thoughts which struck me as highly amusing. One was that nobody in the hall seemed to have read this awful book; and, secondly, the beginnings of a wonderful feeling that this Christianity had holes. It was vulnerable; and if a bishop could have a go at it then so could I! I laid more plans, but they didn't involve reading anything religious, certainly not with a title which included the name 'God'. I wanted to get away: to flee from this 'peeping Tom' called Jesus. I lived for the day when I could be free, little knowing that in my later attempts at rebellion I would be confirming the shape and the power of the spectre who could reach into my soul and strangle me. This God was spiteful and malevolent. It hounded me and it would kill me. I also remember, several years later at university, being prayed for by a Christian gathering, who, through a concerned messenger, informed me that my behaviour was indicative of a 'backslider', and that I was in danger of eternal punishment. The following term my name was removed from the prayer list and, I presume, from the Book of Life. What is it that makes us so sure of our own rightness and of others' wrongness? Or, deeper still, why can a name that means freedom to one mean prison or death to another?

Towards the end of 1971, when I was twenty-four, I found myself walking along Margaret Street in Sydney, Australia, and I felt the chains tighten again as I could not pass a particular church bookshop without looking in. There was a book on one of the shelves called *But That I Can't Believe*! I bought it and consumed it with a joy which was verging on hysteria. I went back to the same bookshop the following day and purchased *Honest to God*, *In the End, God* and *Letters and Papers from Prison*. I could not pretend to understand all that was written on these pages, but they echoed a voice that had been crying inside me for as long as I could remember.

The shameful irony of my situation was that I had already discussed with several people the idea of training for the priesthood; so deep was my guilt at hating this God I was even prepared to devote my life to the Almighty as a sort of eternal sacrificial hell. My 'vocation' was based on a form of intense hatred. John Robinson began to question this arrangement and Dietrich Bonhoeffer worked quietly on my self-made prison.

Psychiatry, and particularly psycho-analysis, has always been regarded with intense suspicion in Christian circles, and one

quotation from *Honest to God* seems to sum up the core of this
suspicion. John Robinson used John Wren-Lewis' contribution to *They Became Anglicans* (p. 42):

> Christian writers . . . still feel constrained to produce
> 'refutations' of the Freudian case against religion, although
> in fact a very large proportion of what passes for religion in
> our society is exactly the sort of neurotic illness that Freud
> describes. . . . It is not merely that the Old Man in the sky is
> only a mythological symbol for the Infinite Mind behind the
> scenes, nor yet that this Being is benevolent rather than
> fearful: the truth is that this whole way of thinking is wrong,
> and if such a Being did exist, he would be the very devil.

Christian faith is something which seems to be an excluding
concern, continually whittling away all external and threatening influences, until the man or woman of God is seen as
heaven-centred and earth-repelled. If we take the concentric
circles of vocation in the church as the orders of deacon, priest
and bishop, the 1662 Book of Common Prayer (which was
used at my ordination) asks in the Litany at their ordination or
consecration for them to be delivered from 'the deceits of the
world, the flesh, and the devil . . . from all false doctrine,
heresy and schism'. The priest must endeavour to lay aside
'the study of the world and the flesh', and the bishop and
priest must be persuaded that 'the Holy Scriptures contain
sufficiently all Doctrine required of necessity for eternal
salvation', and be determined 'to teach nothing, as required of
necessity to eternal salvation, but that which you shall be
persuaded may be concluded and proved by the Scripture'.
Although we may argue that this is open to interpretation, the
major thrust of religious organization and expression within
the Christian church is towards the rejection of the world and
its replacement with spiritual concerns, thus ushering in a
very primitive but powerful impulse to deal with individual
and communal psychic conflict in a projective system which
can only lead to the shutting down of healthy human
intercourse. This has some very serious implications for
Christian practice and life-styles.

The process of analysis or analytic psychotherapy is in major part to allow the inner and outer world of the individual or the small group to come closer together. As unconscious or preconscious material is made available through the therapeutic alliance, so the discontinuity between what is 'inside' and what is 'outside' becomes recognizable and can be used to effect change, particularly the reduction of anxiety (often expressed somatically) or action which may be dangerous to oneself or others. Now this is quite an inadequate summary of what psychotherapeutic work is all about, but even with the vast range of competing theories which this century has produced, and the disagreements which exist between 'organic' psychiatry and the 'talking therapies', it is impossible to ignore the fact that Freud and his successors have opened up a new and invaluable way of looking at human motivation and action.

However, the claim which analysis has made to being 'scientific' is now open to the most telling criticism, and the basic mechanisms, which include terms such as transference, counter-transference, projection and introjection, seduce the unaware (who include some excellent practitioners) into pronouncing on the total objectivity of the 'science'. H. J. Home, in his seminal paper 'The Concept of Mind', is quite clear on which side he would place this discipline. Freud's discovery was a restatement of an ancient insight in a new language: 'the symptom could have meaning . . . Freud took the psycho-analytic study of neurosis out of the world of science into the world of the humanities, because a meaning is not the product of causes but the creation of a subject'.[2] Home continues his argument: 'The subject of meaning is known to us through an act of identification and not through an act of sense perception or scientific observation,' and anyway 'we can never observe the "I" that observes' (p. 47).

Christians have always been wary of scientists. As John Robinson said in *Honest to God*, God is seen to be 'constantly pushed further and further back as the tide of secular studies advances . . . he is not required in order to guarantee anything, to solve anything, or in any way to come to the rescue'.

So why isn't psycho-analysis more of an ally than an enemy? Anthony Clare drives the point home: 'One does not ask whether prayer or religious faith "works" in the sense that we ask whether penicillin or an antidepressant or aversion therapy works. It could be argued that our remarkable ignorance concerning the actual effectiveness of psycho-analysis and psychotherapy persisting well into the last decades of this century owes something to the fact that such activities belong more properly to religion than medicine.'[3] But religion does not regard psycho-analysis as an ally, and theological study is not conducted alongside the various theories and practices of individual and group process. Religious practice and much popular theological elaboration, whether from the conservative or liberal standpoint, specific-ally and deliberately exclude the questions 'Why?' and 'What do the images, symbols, rituals, and, most importantly, the words mean in terms of our inner motivations and desires?'

William Fried has written a fascinating paper about resis-tance among some patients in group therapy. He says that he works with groups 'composed predominantly of narcissistic neuroses, relatively severe character disorders, and border-line personalities', and yet the ubiquitous resistance he high-lights is certainly amongst my repertoire and is owned by everyone I have talked to who has read the paper. Briefly, Fried concentrates on the inability of these patients to symbol-ize and therefore have an 'as if' understanding of the transferences within the group. The transferences become what he calls a 'compelling reality' and therefore there can be no spontaneous play; which brings in some of the ideas of Donald Winnicott who did, and wrote about, such marvellous work with children. The concept of Winnicott that Fried highlights is the transitional phenomena associated with play in the infant, where symbolization and language have an essential role. If the 'good enough' mother has provided an environment which will allow a tolerable anxiety to be worked with between what is external and what is internal to the infant, then the transitional space becomes an area of creativity, 'in which inner and external reality can be played with, juxtaposed, matched, mismatched, dismantled, reorganized, created, destroyed and recreated'.[4] If not, and survival anxiety predominates, then there can be no enjoyment of space and time, and the inner world of the infant becomes full of persecutory feelings which need to be pacified if there is to be any psychic rest. The transitional area is of no real use to the infant, and the search is continually for an external reality to provide the security which is desired so deeply. The ultimate experience is the one which gives a sense of elation that accompanies fusion with the thing which is totally gratifying. In order to conduct the search, 'the infant must first accomplish a kind of fission by which his personality is divided into a precociously operative False or "caretaker" Self and the more passive, yearning True Self which requires care' (p. 101).

We all cover our true and yearning selves with a façade which is desirous of relationships and meaning but is actually a caretaker for something which is much more vulnerable and frightened. This self is soul-deep.

The child who has had a good enough mothering experience is able to carry out experiments on the nature of reality, whereas the child who has not, and operates in the False Self mode, uses language as a means of denying separation and, in fact, confuses it with the experience. The purpose of language is then 'to conserve and preserve rather than to explore. It contracts all meaning (that is to say – all experiences of external objects) into its needs rather than expanding its needs into meaning . . . [the] confusion of words with the object itself is the result of languages being founded on the principle of hallucinatory gratification and not, as under more facilitative conditions, on an accepted need for communication' (pp. 101f.).

We are now squarely in the area of religious communication and experience and, quite simply, of how two opposing parties can look at the same passage of scripture and start a war over its interpretation. It would be easy to dismiss this link by either denying the model presented above as in any way representing what goes on in us all to a greater or lesser extent, or by appealing to the ultimate Authority and stating that He or She has been left out altogether. My point is that the model does not just deal with a mother/infant relationship; its validators are operative in our experience at this very moment. Moreover, no matter what the Almighty may wish to communicate through us, it actually has to be put into words, and words are part and parcel of our total life experience. It therefore follows that if what we want to communicate to others is a wish to avoid intolerable anxiety through 'religious experience' (for want of a better phrase), then this will find a ready home amongst those who share the psychopathology. The theological message becomes enmeshed with an emotional message, and slowly, as we have seen on the American stage, the figure of Jesus becomes unrecognizable in a sea of projections which have him blessing the dollar and protecting the American Way, very much like Superman does – to the obvious pleasure of my six-year-old son!

Religious language is very often a way of denying separation, and, as many of us know to our cost, separation from God is the definition of hell. It brings up our most primitive, non-verbal feelings, which search desperately for containment. The cruel and slow death of crucifixion, when all meaning seems to have been washed away like one's friends and followers, beckons us with the word 'forsaken' ringing loudly in our ears. Abandonment comes up very often in the consulting room but hardly ever in the church.

The language becomes confused with the experience, and its purpose is to conserve and preserve rather than to explore, to requote Fried; and so the life of Jesus becomes a dead and lifeless experience, because we dare not accompany him along the road, look into his eyes, feel the warmth of his body; we dare not accept that he is the Word made flesh. The church looks upon the study of the mind, whether through medical, psychological or psycho-analytic language, with the greatest suspicion, simply because the insights gained threaten to expose the false self-representations of dogma and much doctrine as being language divorced of intimacy. And here the science and the art come together, because both the organic psychiatrist and the psycho-analyst could agree when the patient has lost touch with reality and some sort of psychotic mechanism is being employed to fulfil the demands of a bizarre inner world. The treatment of such a condition is always open to debate, but its existence is unlikely to be denied by either practitioner.

The world of scientific endeavour, as well as the world of Mind, has had to undergo some very strange contortions in the present century. Our Newtonian eyes find it difficult to assimilate the new and threatening dimensions of quantum mechanics. Niels Bohr has said: 'Anyone who is not shocked by quantum theory has not understood it.'[5] At the heart of the matter is the question: is an atom a thing? If it is, then it should have a location and a definite motion. But quantum theory denies this; it says you can have one or the other but not both. The celebrated Heisenberg's principle of indeterminacy says that position and momentum form two mutually incompatible aspects of reality for the microscopic particle, and the observer determines which will be observed. Fritjof Capra, with whom John Robinson was well acquainted, has written two very interesting books on the elaboration and meaning of such discoveries, using systems theory and the spiritual insights of Eastern philosophies, and this must also have an effect upon the way we view Christian theology.[6] In *Truth is Two-Eyed* John Robinson regarded Capra's work *The Tao of Physics* as 'sometimes facile' (p. 22), but went on to paint a beautiful picture in words of why absolutes will no longer do for physics or for Christian theology. 'The behaviour of things and objects is to be viewed as the behaviour of "fields" in which everything ultimately interconnects with everything else. Reality is multi-polar, and its unicity comes not from a single fixed point but from its co-inherence at every level . . . its seeming permanence reflects a dynamic balance, not a static equilibrium' (p. 23).

Such new ways of thinking are also present in recent developments in psycho-analytic theory, with particular reference to narcissistic transferences present in dyadic and group contexts. Kohut refers to the self as a 'psycho-analytic abstraction . . . a content of the mental apparatus. . . . To be more specific, various – and frequently inconsistent – self-representations are present not only in the id, the ego, and the super-ego, but also within a single agency of the mind. For example, contradictory conscious and pre-conscious self-representations – e.g. of grandiosity and inferiority – may exist side by side.'[7] As the physicist Ernest Hutton has written: 'The important link between human beings is communication, not mere energy; meaning, and not cause, is what predominates. The changing pattern of relationships rather than linear movement in space-time describes human behaviour.'[8]

All this seemingly diverse material (and I do not claim any absolutes myself) may lead us to a radical restructuring of our ways of believing, and points us towards self-knowledge, with all its ambivalence and false trails, as a vital component to any exploration of what and who God is, and how he reveals himself to us. Feelings, words and rituals are amongst the time-honoured ways of incorporating the numinous into our lives, and intimacy is often the state to which we aspire, intimacy with God and intimacy with our neighbour; and yet this intimacy, by its very nature, must be of essence the most honest and true part of ourselves meeting the most honest and true part of another. Intimacy contains ambivalent and often contradictory feelings, and if we are really to be 'seen', then we will be both angry and sad, powerful and weak, joyful and depressed, together and alone. It is the greeting of our contradictions which makes for a truly intimate relationship, and it is within a system of belief and unbelief that the person of Jesus draws near.

I believe this to be amply illustrated by the story of the raising of Lazarus in John 11. It is neither to elaborate on the record nor to project on to Jesus something which is not there to say that Jesus was intimately involved with Mary, Martha and Lazarus. The record (RSV) also states that 'the dead man came out' (v. 44). As Jesus had predicted, 'This illness is not unto death' (v. 4). And yet we have three explicit references to the grief of Jesus:

v. 33 he was deeply moved in spirit and troubled.

v. 35 Jesus wept.

v. 38 Then Jesus, deeply moved again, came to the tomb.

One of the theological messages of this passage is the journey from death to life, and one of the intimate messages is that Jesus was moved to tears. One cannot be viewed without the other. In *The Priority of John*, John Robinson has written: 'The materials clearly fail for reconstructing Jesus' self-consciousness in psychological terms, for analysing his psyche, its history or its type. The Gospels are no more in the business of supplying answers to psychological questions than they are to sociological or economic questions – though this does not mean that it is illegitimate *for us* to ask them' (p. 354). But psychological study is only a way of moving us on to a deeper and more enriched encounter with ourselves and another; and if we then filter and process this incident with Lazarus into the realm of 'miracle divorced from feeling', then we have what is to some a faith and what is to others a farce. In moving from God to Jesus to ourselves we fulfil the super-naturalistic 'parody' which John Robinson put so clearly in *Honest to God*, 'that Jesus was really God almighty walking about on earth, dressed up as a man. . . . The traditional view leaves the impression that God took a space-trip and arrived on this planet in the form of a man' (p. 66).

It is most interesting that in the development of the Lazarus incident the chief priests and the Pharisees took counsel to kill both Jesus and Lazarus, thus trying to make dead (again) him who had been made alive. It was not the miracle that threatened them; that was not even questioned. In fact, it seems rather bizarre to try and kill somebody and his friend if it has been amply illustrated that this somebody can raise people from death. No, the threatening part was the life of Jesus and Lazarus set against the dead considerations of politics and religion.

Taken nineteen centuries on, we seem almost to do the same thing with Jesus. H. J. Home tackled the area of scientific objectivity in the world of the psycho-analytic study of the mind and said that 'a divine science is heir to all the logical difficulties of religion'. Home called this process one of 'reification' and it is 'a process of killing. . . . It has its own peculiar necrophilic flavour'.[9] By the very act of refusing to feel Jesus crying, we deny him life, and so all else becomes a projective fantasy, placed beyond reach in the realm of dead and powerless miracles, which we can cling on to in the vain hope that by touching them we can cheat death ourselves. This is what is ushered in by our rejection of 'the world' and our anxiety-ridden attempts to replace all individual and communal psychic conflict with a projective system which can no longer allow us to be intimate creatures.

What then of the product? It is a Christian church which cannot begin to address the emotional and physical proximity of women, of homosexuals, of people with AIDS, of people who are alive, because it has relinquished the language of intimacy. The church has always settled, and probably will continue to settle, for the false self-representations which have many answers but few questions. It cannot stand the pain. I am always saddened, but now not so surprised, at the sparseness of the congregation on Good Friday and a church bulging to the doors on Easter Sunday. Easter communicants are even accepted as an indication of a particular church's health. Where did that one come from?! Sadly, the compromise of settling for many false self-representations is only maintained at great cost, and this is at the margins and at the centre. The cost at the margins is paid for by women, gay people, divorced people and those who bear obvious wounds. The cost at the centre is sometimes the living of a double life or paid for through the classic exchanges of denial, repression or displacement. And then we have to risk the words of Jesus 'Truly, I say to you, I do not *know* you' (Matt. 25.12).

That is one view of the product; but there is another. The Church of England is the established church of the realm, and therefore its parish priests are often privileged to conduct many rites of passage. Birth, marriage and death are times at which the priest is present. But how is he present? Those of us who are priests have the unique opportunity to accompany people through some very traumatic events in their lives; but what is the quality of our presence at such occasions? Is it the presence of false self-representations which are covered by endless references to scripture and the appropriate vestments? When we take the child in our arms and look into the face of the mother are we moved? (She may not be, in which case we should be moved even more for the infant's future!) Do we look into the eyes of the couple before us and wonder at what is in the future for them both? Or do we talk past them to the third brick down on the west wall? And, even more importantly, do we accompany the dying in their rage, or their acceptance, and can we stay with the ones who are left behind to curse God or thank him? These are times at which those on the margins do not have to pay the price for visible wounds, and the centre can be true to itself and its calling through the example of Jesus.

There is, however, one activity where intimacy is offered in a most explicit way, and that is through the sacrament of bread and wine. Whether these elements are considered simply as reminders of the body and blood of Jesus or as transubstantial in essence, the words of Jesus as reported by Paul in I Corinthians 11.23–26 are the most intimate expression of his desire for union with us. It is in no way blasphemous to suggest that such sharing is of the same order as a sexual union, where body fluids are mixed and exchanged. Sadly, copulation can be a meaningless activity, where one person acts sexually upon or within another and there is no exchange of intimacy – this can occur throughout a long and seemingly secure marriage – or it can be the outward sign of a blend of desire which enriches and enhances the two selves who come together. So with the sacrament of Holy Communion. Jesus can be received as a sterile and separated entity, enclosed within the amber of dead religious language and ritual, or he can be the lover who offers his body fluids to be incorporated within our own, thereby sharing the most intimate parts of himself with us in a supreme act of solidarity.

As a priest, this is forcibly brought home to me at communion each time I have to consume the remaining elements. It is not uncommon to have the pieces of half-eaten bread which have accidentally fallen back into the chalice floating on the surface, and it is also possible to make out the different refractive indices of saliva within the wine. If I am truly in solidarity and love with my brothers and sisters in Christ, then my consumption of the remains is a parable of exactly the relationship that Jesus meant. The debate within the church about the shared chalice and AIDS is very interesting when viewed from this not unimportant angle.

I started this essay with an outline of some of my own internal conflicts about God and what he was within my limited self-knowledge at the time of reading *Honest to God*. The direction in which I have tried to take the reader is towards the thesis that self-understanding and personal revelations are just as important as any statements about the nature and action of God and Jesus in the world. I believe that theological language of any variety can often have little or no value because, for the user or reader, it has no clusters of associative intimacies with which to surround it, and both the religious image or the religious idea loses all its power because of this false separation. I also believe that it is often the expressed wish of the church to communicate only in such a language and specifically to exclude the challenge of self-examination in its sons and daughters who train for the ministry. The effect of this deliberate act is to produce the false self-representatives, who actually are in desperate need but who cannot share their real and intimate selves for fear of being abandoned by the church, which demands faith and not doubt, and by a God who punishes more often than he forgives. Inappropriate guilt may be a fertile ground for many who choose to minister in the church, but narcissistic injury and associated envy are the deeper and more primitive channels by which we may discover true salvation.

John Robinson wrote that 'theological statements are not a description of "the highest Being" but an analysis of the depths of personal relationships – or, rather, an analysis of the depths of *all* experience "interpreted by love". Theology, as Tillich insists, is about "that which concerns us ultimately".'[10]

I understand from several people who knew John Robinson personally that he sometimes found the intimate face-to-face encounter quite difficult, but what is patently obvious from his writing is that he found that an intimate medium.

John Robinson was released by the written word in a way that he could not achieve sometimes in the personal meeting. My thanks to God for his work may have a large element of projection, and it is up to the reader to assess the health of this statement, but I am sure that I would not have found my way back towards a wholesome relationship with God so quickly had it not been for this remarkable and emotional theologian and bishop.

Dennis Nineham

What Happened to the New Reformation?[1]

The theologians by whom John Robinson was influenced in the 1950s and 1960s, and whose thinking he sought to deepen and popularize, were all in their various ways preoccupied with a single question. That question concerned the nature and scope of the problem posed for religion by the unprecedented movement of cultural change which has swept over Western Europe since about the middle of the eighteenth century – and which, incidentally, shows no signs of slowing down; quite the reverse.

The point still needs to be made strongly that John and those who thought like him were quite right to take this movement with the utmost seriousness and to recognize it as an irreversible and far-reaching process which is highly problematic for religion. A good deal of nonsense has been talked by those who have mounted rearguard actions of various kinds, seeking to exploit the heterogeneity and rapidly changing character of modern culture. They have repeatedly quoted Dean Inge to the effect that 'he who marries the spirit of the age will soon find himself a widower', without giving any indication of an appropriate response to the situation, apart from the implied suggestion that, since modern outlooks change so rapidly, we should stick with an outlook which is incompatible with them all!

One aspect of the current situation John and his colleagues pin-pointed very accurately. Traditional Christianity was formulated on the basis of an outlook which could accept the biblical record more or less exactly as it stood, and which understood the universe along lines not so very different from those followed by the New Testament writers themselves. Since this outlook persisted for many centuries without really serious modification, orthodoxy, and whatever else was taken to be involved in being a Christian, came to be defined in terms of it. As a consequence, the church was ill-prepared for a quite new cultural situation in which a very different approach to the Bible, the historico-critical approach,[2] was available and had to be adopted as the price of integrity, and which had an understanding of reality almost *toto coelo* different from any in the Bible or the classical Christian period.

By the mid-twentieth century all this had long been recognized, especially by German theologians; but English theology had tended to fight shy of it and to concentrate on attempts to contain individual symptoms by the condition rather than on diagnosing and facing it in itself. So when John Robinson exposed the matter in its full dimensions, not only from within the English theological establishment but as a bishop of the Anglican church, there were bound to be considerable surprise and some consternation.

In some areas John showed himself fully alive to the implications of what had happened – to the implications for morality, for instance, in his writings on 'situational ethics'. If he was not perhaps quite so clear in other areas, that is something he shared with many of the other theologians he admired. Bultmann and his school, for example, believed it possible to retain for the Bible, or at any rate for the New Testament, a status as the exclusive source of revelation not so very different from the status accorded to it in traditional Christianity; and they defended strongly the uniqueness of the Christ of faith (though not of the historical Jesus). John was not particularly attracted by many of the categories with which they worked in this connection. He attempted to vindicate uniqueness for the historical Jesus, an attempt which was not easy to square with a thoroughgoing accept-ance of the historico-critical method;[3] and in general he perhaps underestimated the depth of the cultural gulf sep-arating us from the biblical writers, especially where their attitudes to the past and the reporting of it are concerned. Some (though by no means all) of his work on the Bible has a distinctly old-fashioned air, and he was inclined to feel that if a particular biblical writing could be shown to date from a period not long after the events with which it dealt, its assessment of those events could be quite confidently accep-ted. Even now the implications of modern cultural develop-ments for the Bible itself have been less fully grasped than its implications for the way the Bible has been handled down the Christian centuries. This is no doubt an inheritance from the sixteenth-century Reformers, who felt free to criticize what the church had made of the Bible in a way they would never have dreamed of criticizing the Bible itself.

Nevertheless John's overall assessment of the situation was extremely perceptive, and a great deal of interest was also aroused by one of the key moves he (and others) advocated for dealing with it. This was the proposal to move from the model of height and 'out there' to the model of depth, in our attempts to envisage the supernatural.

Such a proposal implied an awareness that the religious problem today is most intense at the level of the *imagination*. What people need is some approach to envisaging realities such as God, creation and providence imaginatively in a way which does no violence to the rest of what they know to be true. At that level it is easy to see the suitability of the depth model for a culture deeply influenced by Freud and depth psychology and by the other depth metaphors analysed by Lionel Trilling and others.

If the suggested change of model has not quite fulfilled all the hopes once entertained for it, that is perhaps because the proponents of it somewhat mislocated the real centre of the modern religious problem. Probably most people were more alive than John supposed to the purely symbolic and non-literal character of spatial metaphors in this connexion. On the other hand the work of both historians and scientists seemed to suggest that all events are parts of an interrelated web of natural causality, so that any event can be sufficiently accounted for on the basis of some combination of physical causality and human intentional behaviour. In the light of that, a great many people felt considerable difficulty over the claim that God intervenes in history and changes the course of events. Although such feelings had been very clearly exposed by Bonhoeffer, among others, John and most of the other advocates of the depth model did not succeed in showing that it was any great improvement on the height model in this respect. Defining God in terms of 'a dearest freshness deep down things' and talking of reality – the only reality we experience – as being at its deepest level personal, concerned and gracious has the undoubted advantage of eliminating the need to envisage God as a separate individual being alongside all other beings; but for it to be fully convincing, it must be supplemented by a plausible account of how the personal and gracious character of innermost reality manifests itself in practice and makes a difference to the quality and outcome of life at the historical level. Otherwise we are back with the nightmare vision described by T. W. Manson, in which God 'appears for all practical purposes to be a *roi fainéant*' with a thick plate-glass window between him and the world. 'The eye of faith can see through the window and observe that there is a God and that he appears to be benevolently disposed towards men; but nothing more substantial than signals of paternal affection and filial trust and obedience can get through.'[4]

What is the 'cash value' of the various 'levels' in the depth analogy; and in particular what is the relation between reality 'at its deepest level' and reality at the more superficial levels, where it often seems anything but caring and gracious?

With his usual intuitive insight, Austin Farrer recognized this as the key problem and manfully confronted it head-on in his book *Faith and Speculation* and elsewhere, though he can hardly be said to have reached a satisfactory solution, any more than F. R. Tennant had done before him. In his recent Bampton Lectures *God's Action in the World* (SCM Press 1986) Maurice Wiles advocates cutting the Gordian knot and acknowledging that there have been no divine interventions in history of the sort proclaimed in the tradition. However, he does not share the vision of things T. W. Manson attributed to the 'liberals'; he clearly believes in 'a divinity that shapes our ends, rough-hew them how we will' and is clear that what he claims as the unique phenomenon of Christ was not just a contingent event, but was directly due to the divine will. He gives no indication how he envisages this divine impingement, and the problem of the relation between supernatural and natural causality still remains to be resolved; yet for many this, rather than the issue of spatial metaphors, is the nub of the matter. Which in part accounts for the fact that the New Reformation never quite took off.

John Robinson's appreciation of the imaginative side of religion is also evidenced by the amount of attention he gave to liturgy. Though his writings on the subject and his practical liturgical experiments in Clare College Chapel and elsewhere have not been without their influence, they were within a fairly traditional framework, and nothing he did or said has prevented the churches from saddling themselves in the past twenty years with liturgies which, for all the modernity (and often poverty) of their language, are scarcely less foreign to our culture than the liturgies they displaced. Essentially what seems to have happened, at any rate in the Church of England, is the substitution by experts in liturgiology of patristic for late mediaeval models – not an obvious improvement so far as the ordinary worshipper is concerned. What linguistic discrimination and philosophical sophistication are required, for example, in order to be able to repeat with integrity:

Christ has died
Christ is risen
Christ will come again.

Perhaps, as Father Harry Williams suggests, better at this point in the service to keep silence even from good words! The result of all this is that liturgy has been of no help in forwarding a religious reformation. Quite the reverse, in fact.

As already suggested, John was in some areas rather a reluctant changer, and it is paradoxical that Leonard Hodgson, to outward seeming a very traditional and establishment, even pedestrian, figure, was towards the end of his life the most radical of them all. 'For too long', he wrote in his last book, 'study of the biblical writers (and, for the matter of that, of patristics, scholastics, reformers and the rest) has been based on the assumption that someone, somewhere, at some time in the past, really knew the truth, what we have to do is to find out what he thought and get back to it.'[5] At any rate on one interpretation of it, such a statement is simply packed with dynamite, but similar statements are to be found in the later writings of Geoffrey Lampe, and the considered views of such men deserve to be pondered with full seriousness. The issue they raise is surely a crucial one: in determining the Christianity of the future what part should be played by the tradition, including the biblical tradition, on the one hand, and what part by contemporary experience and insight, secular as well as religious, on the other? The suggestion clearly is that contemporary insight should play an altogether greater part than it has ever been allowed to do in the past. It may be doubted whether John Robinson's position was quite as open-ended as that, though the fact that he was moved to write about the relationship between Christianity and other religions, for example in *Truth is Two-Eyed*, suggests that he recognized the significance of one area for which the question raised by Hodgson and Lampe had important implications.

What moral can be drawn from all this? Three reflections may be offered.

It could be argued that one of the reasons why the theological reformers of the mid-century have not carried their point more decisively is because they proposed reforms for a situation they had not subjected to sufficiently careful and detailed analysis, analysis which might have shown conclusively the need for reform and have suggested what sort of reform was called for. That sort of criticism has frequently been made, for example, in connection with Bultmann's programme for demythologization.

It is, relatively speaking, a new thing for the church in the West to be in a cultural context not largely under its control, and indeed largely of its devising. What strategy should it adopt?

Should it not devote sizeable resources to the organization of a thorough and detailed investigation of the current situation, instead of encouraging individuals to come up with instant remedies? Such an investigation would need to be a corporate exercise involving a considerable amount of inter-disciplinary co-operation. Many investigators would be needed and the primary qualification they would require would not in most cases be a grounding in theology – though they would need that – but sufficiently deep immersion in some element of modern culture for them to be able to appreciate what was really going on in it, to distinguish the solidly based from the ephemeral and still experimental, and above all to uncover the unspoken assumptions and presup-positions that lie behind current theories and discoveries and are essential to their validity.[6]

As an excellent example of the sort of investigator needed, we might cite the American sociologist (and first-rate 'amateur' theologian) Peter Berger (cf. his book *Facing up to Modernity*, Penguin Books 1979). Significant is his account in his book *The Heretical Imperative* (Collins 1984) of how fuller exposure to various aspects of the modern world led him to change his theological stance from that of a disciple of Barth to that of a disciple of Schleiermacher; though it is also significant that he still looks to the past for illumination and does not propose a new and fully contemporary stance. In relation to the natural sciences, John Bowker's Wilde Lectures might be cited as another example,[7] but the most remarkable achievement in this field to date is surely that of Don Cupitt, who in a long series of books has tried to lay bare the real situation in a number of areas of our culture and to show how it came to be as it is. Needless to say, he may be wrong in some of the conclusions he draws from his studies, but those who think he is should surely undertake further comparable studies to show where he has misread the situation, rather than complain because his account of religion differs from that given in earlier and quite different cultural situations.

A further way of approaching the problem may also be suggested. Would it not be well if a number of scholars each took a cross-section through Christian history and examined in detail what beliefs and practices were involved in being a Christian at that particular time and place; and in what ways these were conditioned by the circumstances of the day, the science, technology and means of production, the social, economic and intellectual climate and so on? (The present writer is engaged in an attempt to analyse what it meant to be a Christian in northern France in about AD 1000 from that point of view.) Such studies might be expected to do at least three things:

1. To show beyond a peradventure that every expression of Christianity has been culturally conditioned.

2. To suggest the *sorts of ways* in which culturally conditioning factors influence religious belief and practice.

3. By showing in detail the points at which traditional Christianity was moulded by cultural circumstances which no longer obtain, to suggest areas in which change might now be expected to be necessary.

A third reflection is this. Unless the omens are entirely misleading, the Christianity of the future is going to be more open-ended than the Christianity of the past. On a whole range of issues where there can be no question of knock-down answers, increasingly educated Christians will quite properly claim the right to judge for themselves, and unanimity in their conclusions is not to be expected.[8] What sort of unity and institutional coherence will be possible for the church in such a situation? How far are they really necessary and how are they to be secured? To answer those questions will require a prolonged period of sustained and corporate consideration. What is worrying is that there seems little sign at the moment of its even being contemplated. There is still far too great a tendency to suppose 'that someone, somewhere, at some time *in the past*, really knew the truth' and that all we have to do 'is to find out what he thought and get back to it'. Hodgson's demurrer cannot be too strongly sustained.

J. C. O'Neill

Simplicity, Intricacy and Complexity

Dennis Nineham used to say that you could not understand John Robinson until you had seen him in cope and mitre. The winning verbal simplicity, the ability to go to the root of a question, which used to hold us spellbound in Clare Chapel from 1956 to 1959, was the simplicity of a man who had roots deep in the richness of the English church. He might be simple; but what he was being simple about was nothing less than the seemingly remote and intricate doctrine of the last things!

Here is a parable. The Australian thriller writer André Jute wrote a successful book called *Reverse Negative* (rewritten forty-three times, turned down by forty-four publishers and now available from Methuen) which included not only the diary of the hero but also a separate computer-generated probability study in which the hero wore the black hat. He aimed the book at 'the well-educated and highly intelligent middle-class professional who doesn't mind having his mind stretched a little of an evening'. Some friends, mainly academics, said it was too hard, and 'for the upper intelligentsia only'; so they ran a test. Over five hundred people who

said they read fiction were found by enquiry in libraries and at
paperback book stands. Seventy-five were selected from these
as being demographically representative: twenty-five belonging to Jute's own target group of middle-class professionals
(lawyers, doctors, upper civil servants etc.); twenty-five
intelligentsia (mainly university teachers with post-graduate
degrees); twenty-five others as a control group (housewives,
primary school teachers, nurses, office workers, eighty per
cent without university degrees). These seventy-five were
given the novel up to the point where all the clues were
presented and asked, Whodunnit? The middle-class professionals for whom the book was written scored twenty per
cent; the intelligentsia twelve per cent; and the control group
of 'other readers' sixty-four per cent.[1]

When we think about it, this result is not really surprising.
The intelligentsia is trained to make quick plausible
hypotheses about a great number of different subjects, and
the thriller was just one more field in which to exercise their
undoubted gifts. The 'other readers' loved the one genre, and
devoted all their time to reading in it; and they were able to
master easily the intricacy of Jute's new book.

I begin to ask myself whether we members of the intelligentsia who are theologians, in our laudable desire to be
simple, are missing the actual intricacy of the universe and its
Creator; and I begin to ask myself if our 'other readers' are not
capable of comprehending the intricacy of things better than
us, who have lost the art.

We members of the intelligentsia simplify because only by
framing simpler hypotheses do we discover new laws and so
advance our mastery of the world; we need to find the
fundamental unity below the apparent diversity. We also
want to communicate, to teach; and simplicity discovered
seems to be simplicity waiting to be conveyed.

Perhaps we are like André Jute's intelligentsia who could
not spot who dunnit; that is my growing worry since *Honest to
God* was published, since I began my own new theological
voyage in 1964, which has somehow taken me away from the
normal shipping lanes.

Here are some incidents that made me wonder. A friend once said to me, 'We are all utilitarians now,' and I thought to myself, 'I'm not.' Why not? Because no decision I have ever taken has turned out as I expected. If no decision ever turns out as expected, how can we rely on our expectations as a measure of the utility of the decision we are considering whether or not to take?

A second example. Renford Bambrough entirely convinced me that all moral decisions are objective in his classic book, *Moral Scepticism and Moral Knowledge*, published by Routledge and Kegan Paul in 1979. He showed me that subjectivists come to their false position by noticing that moral decisions are relative to circumstances and thinking that that implies subjectivity; by noticing that moral decisions involve complex situations, and thinking that objectivity would require an impossible 'absoluteness'; and by noticing that enquiry is inexhaustible and thinking that that makes moral judgments inconclusive. Bertrand Russell, for example, 'supposes, as many subjectivists do, . . . that the objectivity of moral enquiry is bound up with the "absoluteness" of moral rules or principles, with a kind of "universality" that will involve us in imposing on the actual complexities of life and conduct, motive and circumstances, a rigid, cramping, stultifying simplicity' (p. 47).

That is well said, and obviously fits my thesis. I am reminded of theologians who always quote the saying 'Nor do they put new wine into old bottles', and forget to quote 'No one puts a patch of undressed cloth on an old garment' (Matt. 9.17 not Matt. 9.16).

I keep wondering, however, whether Bambrough himself had not simplified one of the intricacies of moral argument. Most of our arguments about moral questions are conducted by proposing to each other a different sort of example, said Bambrough, and I agree. ('A main cause of philosophical disease – a one-sided diet: one nourishes one's thinking with only one kind of example', Wittgenstein, *Philosophical Investigations*, Remark 593). The foundations of our knowledge are to be looked for usually in the soil, I agree; but not also in the sky?

I proposed this question. Isn't it true that you must *always* in a serious philosophical argument tell your opponent you have changed your mind? Is not this an absolute, that admits no exceptions, whatever the circumstances? Is not this law written in heaven?

A third example. I was fascinated by the necessary incompleteness of our knowledge which accompanies the necessary absoluteness of our judgment. If the Cretan who says 'All Cretans are liars' is speaking the truth, he is lying; and if he is lying, he is speaking the truth. Yet he and I and all of us continue to make absolute judgments that include all possible cases. Again, no possible series of experiments could prove that a perfectly unbiased penny, when tossed, will land heads in exactly fifty per cent of the cases, without a hair's breadth deviation. Yet the whole of our calculations of probability, upon which our lives are based, depends on the unchallengeable certainty that a perfectly unbiased penny, when tossed, will land heads in exactly fifty per cent of the cases, without a hair's breadth deviation.

These are three incidents in my intellectual voyage since *Honest to God*: my coming to see that while we must try to calculate the result of our actions, we are inevitably surprised by their outcome; my recognition that all moral judgments were objective but that while most were relative not all were relative; and my discovery that the very process of thinking was based on certainties impossible to prove.

In short, the universe seems to me to be both intricate and simple. The tendency of the intelligentsia is to simplify and to think that simplicity excludes intricacy. We also tend to think, as part of our simple view of the world, that the 'other readers' cannot understand intricacy.

Vices tend to produce their appropriate disease. I think our simplicity's disease produces a judgment of poetic justice, the disease of complexity. I remember the BBC producer addressing a distinguished assembly of theologians in the School of Pythagoras, St John's College, Cambridge. 'When I ask you theologians, Do you believe in God?, you say to me, It depends what you mean by God.' Of course the answer may have to be intricate, but I wonder if it need be so complicated? Of course we should be prepared to reflect on what it is to reflect on what it would be to answer such a question, if the situation requires it. That is perhaps part of what I am doing in this article. But does that entitle us to baffle people who ask straight questions with impenetrable complexity? They, after all, are usually well-versed in the intricacy of holding that there is an order of angels as well as men and God; that God is three-in-one and one-in-three; that the world is regular, one cannot trust every miracle story, and miracles happen sometimes, if rarely; and that most decisions are a matter of moral indifference, some a matter of moral prudence where one must calculate on a sliding scale of moral rightness, but that there are a few cases where there is no choice but to take one line, even if it means death.

John Robinson, I suspect, used to be rather looked down on in his third Cambridge life as a popularizer who over-simplified. He was more highly regarded the further from Cambridge he travelled. I suppose there was something in the charge made against him. But of course we usually detect in others the fault to which we ourselves are the most prone. I wonder whether the world is both a simpler and a more intricate place than what we intelligentsia are by training and habit fit to detect.

Ronald H. Preston

Honest to God, The New Morality and the Situation Ethics Debate

At first sight, the sixth chapter of *Honest to God*, 'The New Morality', seems an intrusion into the main theme of the book. Indeed it is. But John Robinson was always alert to the changing emphases in current theological moods and writings, and he had a bold and synoptic mind which sought to relate them to one another as part of a larger spectrum. In this case, he explained the connection by saying that the new understanding of the transcendent which he was exploring meant that the understanding of morality was also in the melting pot, and that in this respect the winds of change had already become a gale. In his view, the old morality was the counterpart of the 'supranaturalist' way of thinking which he was challenging.

The chapter is short. John was to elaborate it, later in the year, in three lectures given in Liverpool Cathedral on 'Christian Morals Today'. They were published at the time, and included later in his book *Christian Freedom in a Permissive Society*. There are shades of difference between them, but it suffices to concentrate almost entirely on the argument in *Honest to God*.

Robinson describes the old morality as one of absolute standards, according to which some actions are always right or wrong. In Roman Catholic thinking this is because the network of empirical human relationships is a void concealing a world of occult realities which lie behind the outward order of life. The indissoluble marriage bond is an example. This is simply the metaphysics of a pre-scientific age. In Protestant thought, the absolute rules are seen as the command or law of God as found in the Old Testament or the teaching of Jesus in the New. On the contrary, the Sermon on the Mount is not a new law (even if Matthew may have so interpreted it), but an illustration of what love *may* require but not what it always demands. The parables of the Kingdom are not the source of rules to be generally applied, but a call to a specific group or individuals. The ethical teaching of Jesus, furthermore, makes no attempt to deal with the needs of third persons or to adjudicate between conflicting claims. There is a need to move from the 'heteronomy' of obedience to commands to the 'autonomy' of personal decisions in different contexts. This does not mean a slide into relativism but a move to 'theonomy', that is to a personal response to the uncondi- tional, the sacred, the holy in the particularity of concrete relationships. In less abstract terms, it is to share the 'mind of Christ', as Paul expresses it in I Corinthians 2.16, or to follow the injunction of Jesus to 'love as I have loved you', as the Johannine writer puts it in his gospel at 13.34. St Augustine's phrase is quoted: *dilige et quod vis fac*, best translated as 'love, and *then* what you will, do'. Love has a built-in moral compass enabling it to 'home' intuitively upon the deepest needs of the other, and so it can allow itself to be utterly open to the situation. Nothing is prescribed except love; nothing in itself can always be labelled as wrong. Nevertheless, laws and conventions are dykes of love, providing guiding rules arising from accumulated experience; but they are constantly in need of re-examination.

The main writings referred to in this chapter are C. H. Dodd's *Gospel and Law*, Paul Tillich's *The Protestant Era*, Emil Brunner's *The Divine Imperative*, and especially an article of Joseph Fletcher in 1959, 'The New Look in Christian Ethics'.

Christian Ethics was not a major focus of John Robinson's

intellectual concerns. In his younger days he distinguished himself in the area of philosophical issues involved in Christian theology and later became primarily a New Testament scholar. But his wide-ranging mind and concern for the witness of the church, which underlay his efforts to understand our empirical situation in Britain in the 1960s, made him take an informed interest in most aspects of contemporary life and culture. Ethical issues loomed large among his subsidiary interests, and he wrote quite a lot in this area in his various books and articles. This brief sixteen-page chapter does cover most of the issues of the situation ethics debate, even though it is flawed as it stands. Paul Ramsey, in discussing John in *Deeds and Rules in Christian Ethics* (first published in Britain in 1965), says: 'What Bishop Robinson has written on theology, liturgy and prayer seems to me far more significant and worthy of attention than what he has written in Christian Ethics.' He goes on to make rather heavy play with the mixture of the voice of Jacob preaching pure act-agapeism and the hands of a rule-agapeistic Esau which co-exist uneasily in Robinson's text, and asks: 'What is the relation between his voice and the skins of goats upon his hands and the smooth of his neck; and where in fact does he get these skins and the goodly garments of Rebekah's elder son?'[1]

Further, there is not any necessary connection between the new morality and Robinson's plea for a new understanding of divine transcendence. R. A. McCormick, the American Jesuit whose surveys of current writing on moral theology were such a distinguished feature of the American Jesuit quarterly *Theological Studies*, made this point when he wrote in an American survey *The Situation Ethic Debate*, edited by Harvey Cox in 1968, 'Except for a few absolute negative prohibitions I believe that Catholic Moral Theology is quite as situationist as Fletcher at his best.'[2]

We shall need to put John Robinson's chapter in the context of the situation ethics debate immediately before and after 1963, and to ask where the debate got to. But we can say at this point that, leaving aside flaws of exposition, John's essential case is a strong one. A powerful witness to this is Bishop Ian

Ramsey. In 1966 he edited a weighty symposium on *Christian Ethics and Contemporary Philosophy*. In his introduction he says that 'Christian morality is no morality of rules, no morality of mere obedience to commands'.[3] In his concluding chapter 'Towards a Rehabilitation of Natural Law' he elaborates the point. He says that we need principles, and we need to be cautiously conservative about the principles we hold at any given time. It is true that rapid social change may cause them to need revision, but there are some which are virtually sacrosanct. He adds: 'We need moral principles, and there are moral principles. But they are not copy-book principles, any more than morality is a slavish following of rules. They each point back to an obligation revealed through and around the empirical facts of countless situations, an obligation matched only by a decision in which we realize ourselves characteristically as persons. This is the core of truth, I would suggest, in the claims of those who sponsor "situational ethics" and talk of an "existentialist" approach' (p. 394). We may note in passing that it would have been better if Ramsey had written 'or talk' instead of 'and talk', for, as we shall see, the 'situationists' we are concerned with were not existentialists.

In the chapter 'The New Morality' Robinson was 'homing in' (to use his phrase) on a debate which was already raging in Protestantism in the United States, or in a different form in the Roman Catholic church in the course of the drastic reforms of traditional moral theology which were furthered by the Second Vatican Council 1962–5. It hit Britain only in 1966, with the publication by SCM Press of Joseph Fletcher's *Situation Ethics* in that year followed by his *Moral Responsibility* of 1967 (though this mostly contained material which was earlier than the 1966 book). The terminology associated with the debate was, in many respects, unfortunate. The 'new morality' itself was not a new term. It had been used more than a generation earlier to refer to the views on sex and marriage of Bertrand Russell. This associated it overwhelmingly with sexual morality. So in practice did the term 'permissive'. Both became journalistic phrases suggesting lax sexual conduct, and set off defensive reactions, especially among the many who had genuine fears of what damage human beings might do to one another in their sexual relations, or among those who themselves had various sexual 'hang ups'. 'Permissiveness' is not in any case the right term. 'Plural' would be a better one. Modern society has not become in all respects more permissive. For example, its sensitivity to racist attitudes and practices has greatly increased. The antisemitic side of a G. K. Chesterton or a John Buchan is now disapproved when formerly it passed without comment.

In sexual ethics, however, attitudes have changed, because the 'official' position in this country was a legacy of the Christendom situation in which the Christian sex ethic seemed to be summed up in a series of negatives: no masturbation, no sexual intercourse outside marriage, no contraception, no sterilization, no abortion, no divorce (as distinct from separation), to which we could now add no artificial insemination. Moreover, the understanding of human sexuality had been overwhelmingly expressed by males. Practice was indeed far from corresponding to theory and, in so far as it was observed, it was largely through fear of the physical and social consequences which were thought likely to follow from infringements. In this respect the situation has clearly changed. Respect for traditional Christian authority has declined to such an extent that it is hard to get a hearing for new and creative thinking on human sexual fulfilment which has been coming from Christian sources in recent decades and which has tried to face the current situation creatively, and re-think the Christian understanding of human sexuality from its roots. When he wrote or spoke on sexual ethics John was one of those who contributed to this rethinking. He stressed continually the fact that he regarded himself as a radical, in the sense of one who was concerned with the roots of Christian faith and life, the contingent expressions of which would vary.

Furthermore, our society is less characterized by a general permissiveness than by plural sources of authority in morals. Many church-goers hanker after the old Christendom situation. The outward system of the Church of England still reflects it, and conceals from many of its adherents the fact that the inward reality is almost eroded. This is a dangerous source of self-deception. A social ethic for Britain today must arise out of what common understanding of the human person can be achieved among the various communities in our country whose moral understanding is in a framework of different faiths. It will be found that there is fortunately a considerable overlap between them in their understanding of the nature and status of the human person. This applies also to many humanists. Humanism is also a faith, in the sense of interpreting the mystery of life on the basis of an ultimate presupposition behind which one cannot go, for it cannot be 'proved' because the evidence is ambiguous. Humanist faiths vary, but many are close to the Christian. We can see signs of this in the continual debate on abortion. It is largely one between different Christian and different humanist positions as to which policies are *in*human and which more truly human.

The situation ethics debate centred on whether there are absolute rules of Christian conduct which are timeless and context-free. Their source could be the Bible or Natural Law as interpreted by the church, or a combination of the two. The limits of the expression of a homosexual orientation in sexual activity has become a test case for many. Can the moral status of such actions be settled by a biblical text or texts? Or can it be settled by calling them unnatural? Again, the prohibition of the consumption of alcohol, or of gambling, has been widely taught in evangelical circles on biblical grounds. Quakers have usually advocated pacifism on the same grounds. For centuries usury was forbidden by traditional moral theology, on the grounds that money cannot breed so that a charge for the use of it is unnatural. Again, one of the three arguments used against contraception in the Papal Encyclical *Humanae Vitae* depends upon the view that it is unnatural. Such positions have been increasingly criticized. The detailed ethical injunctions of the Bible are being seen as related to the context out of which they came. Those of Paul in I Corinthians, on women, marriage and slavery, are good examples. And nature is seen less as a fixed reality and more as subject to human control, in aid of a fuller realization of the divine intention in creation, according to criteria which arise from an increased understanding of the potential creativity of human beings under God. Moral theology has been coming to realize that *if* there are moral absolutes expressed in detailed rules of conduct, they are very few, and that the moral life is overwhelmingly made up of decisions where they do not apply. Extreme boundary situations are also quoted when even such few rules as have been suggested might be called in question.

The problem then is, on what basis to decide what to do? The proponents of situation ethics have not been against moral principles. One of Robinson's confusions, as we have seen, was to suggest by making an antithesis between love and law that the advocates of situation ethics were against moral principles. They have not been existentialists, who write as though the moral life is like living as an extemporary speaker, forging ahead into the unknown without any precedents as a guide. To think that they are is a common mistake. It was a mistake made by Pius XII when, in 1952, in an address to the World Federation of Catholic Young Women, he condemned situation ethics on this ground. Karl Rahner tended to take the same line. The question has rather been about the status and limitations of moral principles, what to do when principles appear to conflict and, in general, on what basis to decide a particular ethical question when grounds for uncertainty appear. In particular, new situations crop up where no principle has yet been formulated. Bioethics has thrown up a number of these recently.

The discussion of these questions has been paralleled by debates in moral philosophy which face the same problems. Is one to follow a rule in these difficult cases, or try to estimate the likely consequences of feasible ways of acting and choose the one which seems likely to maximize the good, the values, involved and minimize the disvalues? Sometimes following principles leads to behaviour which seems hard and unloving; sometimes following likely consequences does. Kant's teaching against telling lies for benevolent motives is a classic instance of the former. We can see what he is concerned about (as St Augustine was in his day), but few are convinced by his rule. Similarly, classic cases are brought against consequential-ist policies followed by all forms of utilitarian ethics, such as punishing an innocent person, if an example is needed to strengthen law and order in a particular situation, and so promote the common good.

Moreover, the common features of moral situations are more prominent than their unique features. That is why stability and continuity in the moral life are so important. Words like virtue, character, fidelity, loyalty, trustworthiness reflect this, to say nothing of the term covenant with its strong biblical notes. Rules may have to be broken, but we must not make the exceptional the norm. The recent discussions in moral philo-sophy were conveniently covered in two books of readings, both from the USA, *Moral Rules and Particular Circumstances* edited by Barnet A. Brady (Prentice Hall 1987), and *Situationism and the New Morality* edited by R. L. Cunningham (Appleton-Century-Crofts 1987).

Christian ethics could not be exempted from wrestling with these problems. A lively debate continued throughout the 1960s and into the 1970s. If one stresses deciding by likely consequences in a particular situation, how is a situation to be circumscribed? One feature can lead to another until the future of the globe itself is involved. At some point a line must be drawn beyond which no estimate of likely consequences is made. Again, it is possible to re-describe the elements in a particular situation in such a way as to reformulate a moral rule, so that what was an exception is incorporated in a refined rule. A symposium which dealt with most of the approaches to Situation Ethics was *Norm and Context in Christian Ethics*, edited by Gene Outka and Paul Ramsey and published by SCM Press in 1968. In fact, a percipient article by J. M. Gustafson summed up the issues almost before the debate got going in Britain.[4]

By the middle of the 1970s, the debate had petered out. Proponents of traditional morality still abound. Protestant biblicists still want to move directly from a biblical text to some detailed ethical rule, though their use of scripture is selective. I have seen many examples of attempts to move directly from the Priestly code in Leviticus to the modern world, but I have never seen anyone make such a jump from the so-called 'communism' of the early church in Jerusalem, referred to in chapters 2 and 4 of the Acts of the Apostles. The Sacred Congregation for the Defence of the Faith continues to issue Instructions on detailed issues of sexual ethics, on the basis of a view of natural law with which a great many Roman Catholic moral theologians disagree. Among those who disagree, a lively debate is going on as to whether there are basic values in our understanding of what is distinctively human, none of which must be directly infringed in any moral decision, which leads to the assertion of some incorrigible principles, or whether one should act to maximize the realization of values. But to pursue this would take us too far.

The situation ethics debate was mistaken in so far as it concentrated on a meagre harvest of moral absolutes. It got this issue out of perspective and distorted the debate. All normative ethics have to ask themselves to what sort of rules their basic affirmation leads. In the case of Christian ethics it is what sort of rules *agape* requires. In practice, we tend to follow whatever moral rules we were brought up with or have come to accept, until we reach a difficult situation which brings us up sharply. Then we have to decide whether to carry on following the rule, or, on this occasion abandon it, and decide according to our estimate of the consequences of feasible courses of action. There is no rule for deciding when to break a rule. This was a root issue between Jesus and the Pharisees. They were quite ready to agree that the Sabbath was made for man and not man for the Sabbath, but they wanted a rule for breaking the rules, and this Jesus would not give them. Discernment is needed. Moral judgment is an art. Of course, knowledge of a situation is required, and that is why as much relevant information as possible is needed, whether the issue involves only one or two people or whether it is one of public policy in the social, economic, industrial or political realms, involving inter-disciplinary study. But more than knowledge is needed. Wisdom, discernment is also required. Moral issues are rarely simple. That is why there has been a tendency in Christian ethics in the last decade to turn away from preoccupation with what should be done in particular circumstances to what kind of person should we be, so that faced with ethical decisions we shall be persons of discernment. We should hope to contribute a depth of understanding which is the fruit of living within, and drawing upon the graces mediated by, Christian fellowship and worship. Questions of character, virtue, the education of conscience and all that in Roman Catholic circles is termed personal formation are involved. This is admirable, in that the Christian life involves acting from the right motive as well as working out what is the right action in the circumstances. Both need attending to. We should not pay attention to one and neglect the other. The danger of a stress on character is that of falling back into the old pietistic error of assuming that if someone is a 'converted', 'consecrated', or 'changed' person there is no more ethically to be bothered about. He or she intuitively 'home' on to a situation (to use Robinson's dangerous term), and know what *agape* requires to be done. But merely to mean well is the road to sentimentality, or to disastrous mistakes born of factual ignorance.

To return, in conclusion, to the place of moral principles in morality. They have a fourfold role. 1. They are a distillation of moral experience drawn from personal reflection and choice and the collective wisdom of the church; without them we should never learn from experience. Existentialism is no basis for ethics. 2. They support us and save us from disaster when our weakness tempts us to wrong-doing. For instance, the temptation to tell lies usually comes upon us suddenly: a steady rule of truthfulness helps us not to fall when in nine cases out of ten truthfulness is required. Children, too, need moral rules, but as they grow up they need to acquire a mature attitude to them. 3. Rules prevent us thinking of ourselves too easily as exceptional people or as in an exceptional situation: the temptation to weigh the balance in favour of our wishes is very great. 4. Rules give guidance when the consequences of an action are so long-ranging and wide that they are impossible to estimate. The classical Marxist has been particularly prone to advocate or condone the most hideous acts if they could be said to further the ultimate utopia of a classless society. The era of Stalinism provided many examples in Russia and the Communist parties outside it.

Nevertheless, moral rules, though good servants, are bad masters. They need to be kept under review. Whether there are any incorrigible ones is an important but subsidiary question. Examples of ones which have been quoted are 'Do not punish an innocent person', 'Do not force sexual intercourse on someone unwilling'. Whether they are incorrigible is debatable, but in any event they cover only a tiny part of the vast area of moral life.

Furthermore, *agape* is seen at its deepest in the shadow of the cross of Christ and in the light of his exaltation. Christians will be alert to the difference this may make to the weight they attach to facts, and to their estimates of the likely consequences of ethical decisions. It is part of their task in bringing a vision of goodness alongside the details of a situation, and in making decisions in the boldness of those who are justified, or accepted, by faith in matters of ethics as well as doctrine. They are ready to live with the inevitable uncertainties in obtaining and assessing details, in estimating consequences, and in living with Christians who may come to different conclusions even if they agree on the same method and are not adherents of the old morality. These latter must be opposed with charity. The moral task of Christians is not to fulfil moral norms but to take a given reality and form it into something worthy of human beings and therefore of God in whose image they are made. The old morality at its best aimed at this, with its teaching that 'circumstances alter cases', but it was hampered by its beliefs in universal negative prohibitions. The new morality is the recovery of a more authentic Christian ethic.

Alan Race

◆

Truth is Many-Eyed

One sign of vitality within a religious community is its ability
to adapt, critically, to changing circumstances and new
experiences. When this does not happen a community is likely
either to atrophy and become irrelevant to the lives of its
people, or to assume an arrogant triumphalism and dominate
them.

John Robinson's *Honest to God* was supremely an experiment in presenting Christian faith in the context of a culture
which was unable to live with ready-made answers from the
past. The crisis related chiefly to how Christians could
reappraise their tradition so that it cohered at the deepest level
with a range of human experience in the present. The new
accounts of reality describing that experience, especially
prominent in the fields of existentialist philosophy, historical
science, sociology and psychology, all seemed to require the
revision of faith if it was to continue to command respect.

There is every reason for pressing ahead with this critical
method in theology which *Honest to God* embraced. If the issue
of the nature of God is the central question of theology, then
the context in which it arises is no less important. Today this
must include the realization that the world is ineradicably

plural. That is to say, in the context of world religious pluralism, being 'honest to God' from now on must include the recognition that for many people their 'salvation' takes place within other equally powerful and vibrant religious settings. When the *dharma* travels West, and when the Christian missions in the traditional cultures of the East have met with only minor success, Christian faith can no longer assume a monopoly of religious truth or think of itself as rightfully supreme.

We have been made aware of the new context for theology by various means. Through travel, we are confronted by whole civilizations where religions have fostered the transformation of human beings by spiritual practice without any reference to Christianity. Through the historical and phenomenological study of the world religions, we are inspired by literature and reflections of deep wisdom, comparable to much that the Christian tradition has produced. Through personal friendships, we are impressed by the strong faith of human beings who espouse a religious pathway which for them is noble and life-giving, and which remains sufficient for their aspirations. As a result of new experiences, we are forced to recognize the degree to which religious truth is also a function of birth-place. A satisfactory account of Christian faith cannot now be given without simultaneously showing how it relates to the vast range of religious experience outside the Christian framework. The Christian *darśan*[1] is in need of expansion.

John Robinson began to face this frontier in his book, *Truth is Two-Eyed*, given first as the Teape lectures in India in 1977. The title itself contains an explicit repudiation of the attitude which has characterized much of Christian thinking in the past, namely, the exclusivist view which holds that the knowledge of God has been confined to one stream of cultural religious history alone. In retrospect, one could be forgiven for thinking that the problems surrounding *Honest to God* were fairly parochial, compared with those that arise when pluralism is placed on the Christian agenda.

Given the new awareness of religious pluralism, the one-eyed view of religious truth seems more and more moribund. Sheer experience tells against it. Moreover, the foundations on which the most recent forms of exclusivism were built, in the middle years of the present century, now seem untenable. The shape of both the biblical and dogmatic arguments have changed. Developments in biblical studies, for example, have shown us the problematic nature of deriving answers to modern questions, such as the Christian response to a religiously plural world, from literature which was not designed to answer them, at least in the form in which they now present themselves. So a recent study of the theology of mission, facing the question of the missionary relationship with the other world religions, concludes that 'No comprehensive solution to this issue can be found in the Bible, but it does offer some leads.'[2] Interestingly, however, the leads the authors of this book suggest we follow speak positively of discovering the love of God beyond the boundaries of Israel and the church. Second, developments in systematic-dogmatic theology point out the role of the human religious imagination in describing religious experience. The distinction between 'religion' and 'revelation', a device which enabled exclusivists to promote Christianity as *sui generis* among the world's religions, now appears as an attempt to circumnavigate the human element in interpreting Christian faith. It seems dangerously anachronistic, and might even be a form of religious imperialism.

Rejecting exclusivism closes off one avenue of approach; it does not in itself solve the problem of the Christian response to religious pluralism. It is worth setting out the position of *Truth is Two-Eyed* in a little more detail, both as a window on to the issues involved, and in order to demonstrate alternative avenues of exploration.

Experience, combined with the thrust of the universalist strand within Christian belief, compelled Robinson to recognize the unity of the divine life lying behind the world's religions:

The God who discloses himself in Jesus and the God who discloses himself in Krishna must be the same God, or he is no God – and there is no revelation at all. *Ultimately* for both

sides there are not 'gods many and lords many' but one
God, under whatever name . . . (p. 98).

But within this all-encompassing affirmation there was room
for distinctions. The model Robinson used to clarify this was
that of an ellipse. Here two centres (eyes) of religious truth,
each representing a dominant, though not uniform, religious
cluster, characterized roughly as prophetic (West/Semitic/
Christian) and mystical (East/Indian/Hindu), could co-exist in
a creative tension. The worth of the model lay in the fact that it
overcomes the isolation between religions yet also respects
their differences. Moreover, it could claim some validity in
actual reality. The dividing line between the two religious
types ran not only between, but also within East and West. In
a twofold observation, Robinson showed first how each
religious 'eye' in practice had developed elements of its
opposite mode in the ellipse – e.g. prophetic religion
harboured mystics and mystical religion made space for
prophetic voices; and second, how when each 'eye' on truth
was treated in isolation it led to a distortion – e.g. the West has
often expressed itself myopically in a 'historical positivism or
fundamentalism of an all-or-nothing kind', and the East at its
worst has been tempted by a 'dangerous historical absen-
teeism, making for a quietist indifference and fatalistic irres-
ponsibility', (pp. 54, 56). Overall, the model countenanced
religions as complementary witnesses to the one divine reality
which animated the heart of all religions, and yet it was also
alert to the remaining unease in the tension that exists
between the different philosophical and theological affir-
mations stemming from those witnesses. It would not appeal
to everyone as a viable way forward in an age of comparative
religious studies, but it was an extremely imaginative proposal, and could take its place as a serious contender among a
number of experiments emerging at the time.[3]

Robinson stopped short of affirming a full pluralist theory,
which is the view that the different world religions represent
different religious paths of normative value for those who
follow them, none reducible to another, each bringing

salvation/liberation/enlightenment, according to its historical and cultural setting. It accepts the person of Jesus as one norm among other norms, one uniqueness among other uniquenesses, in a world context where the fullness of religious truth is pursued in a spirit of mutual respect and shared criticism. The clue to why Robinson shied away from this conclusion lay in his christology. He was fond of using the description 'decisive' (borrowing from the process theologians) to explain the impact and importance of Jesus, both for Christians and for the world. In other words, Jesus was not the exception to the human race, but its true representative. In him the intended goal of creation in the relationship between God and human beings came to fruition. This way of expressing belief in the incarnation was in line with a certain fruit of New Testament studies, which reports Jesus as the eschatological agent of God's kingdom, and not as the God-Man of subsequent doctrinal development. In philosophical terms, this means that in Jesus the self-expressive activity of God in creation reached a climax. Now this may be an improvement on the older apologetic which talked of two natures in one person, but in the context of a positive approach to inter-faith relations it created an ambiguity. For the implication of this shift (and Robinson was not alone in this move), in the direction of what can be called the historicizing of the incarnation, is that the way is opened up for there to be other saviours and revealers, other incarnations in other times and places, other normative representations of the meaning of human life under God. Yet Robinson did not quite follow through these implications. He admitted that his christology did not confine God to Jesus, and that whatever was glimpsed of God in Jesus was always open to 'completion, clarification and correction' in dialogue with others, thus maintaining the complementarity between religions in line with the belief that 'truth is two-eyed'. But he also maintained, as a matter of confession, that in Jesus the love of God was present to the highest degree, the 'profoundest clue to all the rest' (p. 129). Thus he maintained a hold on the uniqueness of Jesus, albeit in an untraditional form.

Robinson's discussion highlights the ambiguity of the term 'decisiveness' as this is applied to Jesus in the light of the positive impact of living in a religiously plural world. On the one hand, as a function of dogmatic theology, 'decisiveness' means that Jesus remains *a priori* the ultimate norm for all humanity and all other potential revealers. This gives the impression of pursuing the Christian judgmental attitude in a milder form. If the concept of incarnation includes other religious representations than that in Jesus, who by definition is the 'completion' of God-with-humanity, then this merely repeats the pattern of Christian superiority. At this point exclusivism and inclusivism look like two versions of the same approach. On the other hand, as a function of experience, 'decisiveness' points to Jesus as the 'profoundest clue', on the basis of at least implicit historical comparisons. This gives the impression of being sensitive to historical enquiry as a means of demonstrating the value of the term, in relation to different religions, but it is likely to claim too much. In this respect, Robinson contended that Christianity has the potential to incorporate, more satisfactorily than other religions, those factors which are inimical to religion, which he names as evil, the impersonal, and the feminine. This was a bold act of faith, but requires much more prolonged and careful enquiry than Robinson ever gave it, before it could command widespread support. Many would contend that it could never prove anything worthwhile in any case. If this is correct, then Robinson was open to embracing a full pluralist position without too much adjustment in his overall model, though he remained reluctant to do so. It may be that the ambiguity of the term 'decisive' is less helpful than at first it looks.[4]

At this juncture, before we spell out the pluralist case, it is worth enquiring further into the meaning and consequences of living in an age of historical consciousness. For much of the argument for a shift in the Christian response to a multi-religious world depends upon accepting certain premises in relation to it. Two implications of the rise of the modern historical consciousness strike me as pertinent to our discussion.

First, historical reality as, in Ernst Troeltsch's phrase, 'a continuous connection of becoming', contravenes the older view of religious truth which was grounded in an interventionist supernatural account of its origins. We have come to see that religious truths are more humanly constructed truths than we once thought. It is from within historical time and space that women and men have constructed the means for interpreting and acting upon their experience. Patterns of meaning and understanding have developed, directly related to the needs, institutions, perceptions and religious ideas of a society at any one particular period in history. Religions have provided frameworks within which human life and struggle can have meaning and orientation. If we accept that this process describes the history of all religious communities, including the Christian – and we have no reason to think otherwise – then we must find a way of incorporating this knowledge into our own Christian self-understanding. The implications of this historicist picture for the sense of absoluteness which has traditionally been attached to Christian faith have been summed up by Gordon Kaufman:

> We now see the great theologians of Christian history, for example, not simply as setting out the truth that is ultimately salvific for all humanity (as they have often been understood in the past), but rather as essentially engaged in discerning and articulating one particular perspective on life among others.[5]

A historicist perspective which values religious truths as radically human constructs begs the question of the role of divine revelation in religious life. Yet it need not necessarily undermine the concept of revelation altogether, as point up the need for its reinterpretation in the light of new knowledge. What is seriously called into question, however, is the sense of exclusive absoluteness that religions have traditionally accrued to themselves.

The second effect of historical consciousness relates to its bearing on change in the identity of Christian faith, and concerns the distinction between faith and its interpretation in

limited, partial, and culturally conditioned forms, each circumscribed by its own reference points and assumptions about
reality. In Christian discussion at present the search for a
coherent understanding of the person of Jesus, one not bound
by the philosophical categories of the ancient world, is one
example of how this impact has been felt. But historical
consciousness presses further than the need to find some
comparable restatement of the two-natures doctrine. It looks
behind that doctrine at the concept of 'finality', a concept which
the doctrine of incarnation was designed to embody from
within the different philosophical assumptions of the subsequent early centuries. This oldest view of the 'finality' of Jesus
derives from both the impact of the figure of Jesus himself and
the background Jewish apocalyptic view of history, with its
attendant expectations of the 'final' messianic figure, which
was the matrix for Christian belief at this earliest time. Deep as
the hold of that view of history has been on Christian
consciousness, so that the modern clamour for 'decisiveness' is
a latter-day instance of it, it nevertheless sits odd with modern
perceptions of history as the 'continuous connection of
becoming'. Given a different setting for Christian faith in the
present, there is no reason why attachment to the way of Jesus
should express itself in a framework involving that same sense
of finality. In an age when religious pluralism is accorded
positive value for so many reasons, Christians can feel freed
from that ancient 'finality' to work out their commitment to
Jesus alongside and in dialogue with other religious commitments, and not against them. Nor is this a matter of adjusting
Christian faith simply in order to accommodate other religious
ways, as it is sometimes said. It is a recognition that changes in
Christian self-understanding, as a result of the developing
historical consciousness, make possible a positive global
recognition of the place of many religions in the purposes of
God. Coupled with the first effect of historical consciousness,
outlined above, it could be even said to demand it.

My contention then is that, under the pressure of historical
consciousness, with both internal changes in Christianity's
perception of its own identity and the positive valuation of a

vital pluriform religious world, Christian theologians (and the same will be true for theologians from other traditions) are required to construct a new theology to fit the new experiences. What shape might such a theology take?

A number of theological models in this vein have been advanced now, and there is no need to repeat them here in detail.[6] My own view has the features of what has been called 'unitive pluralism'.[7] This recognizes that the world religions reflect genuine experiences of the divine life at their roots, and that these experiences have generated differing philosophical patterns of belief and community life. It accepts Wilfred Cantwell Smith's observation that 'faith is a global human quality', and that 'God has participated more richly in human affairs, man (sic) has participated more diversely in God, than we once knew'.[8] It holds that 'salvation', or its various cognate terms such as 'liberation' and 'enlightenment', is taking place within the various world religious patterns of thought and practice, to varying degrees which are virtually impossible to grade. It retains the uniqueness of each tradition, but not their unrelatedness, and the elliptical model of John Robinson's proposal is most helpful in picturing this aspect for us. It is more at home with metaphor, symbol and parable as the chief vehicles of religious truth, each bearing the linguistic quality of both representation and instrumentality, than with purely metaphysical descriptions. It believes that the person of Jesus is both a parable of God's love and care for the world and a door of human response to the divine mystery. He is of universal importance, thus providing Christianity with a foundation for mission, which in relation to the other world religions, assumes a dialogical character. Equally, it holds the Buddha's enlightenment, for example, as indispensable for human well-being, and as universally binding, to be learned from and celebrated. Such a shift is now possible if Christian faith is to take full cognizance of the dominant historical consciousness of our time. It is also necessary if we are to do justice to the new data made available as a result of growing contacts and dialogue between people of faith.

The pluralist model is constructed inductively, and is not

without difficulties of its own. Some have said that it represents a move to a supposed Olympian point, a kind of meta-
position beyond the positions of any of the world religious
traditions themselves – in effect, a new religion! The argument continues that the pluralist case is incoherent because
religious traditions speak out of particular and unique centres, which, theologically, are simply part of what is 'given'
in those traditions. So, Christianity relates to the world by
virtue of its concept of 'the Christ', Islam through 'the
Qur'an', and so on. I think this objection overstates its case,
and it is dependent on too static a view of religious tradition.
What the pluralist model asks of us is that we engage in the
new world of religious dialogue with, as it were, one foot in
the Christian circle and the other in a circle which encompas-
ses an unknown quantity. It is an engagement which exper-
ientially we know to be valid (true) even though it remains,
for the time being, still something of an analytical puzzle.
Some have attempted to provide epistemological backing for
the enterprise. Perhaps the most well-known of these
schemes is that of John Hick, who makes use of a Kantian
distinction between the noumenal and the phenomenal
world. The former applies to Reality ('God') in his (her, its)
inner being and therefore strictly speaking unknowable, and
the latter applies to 'God' as imaged from within particular
historical and cultural settings and therefore known diversely in human response.'[9] Paul Knitter speaks more loosely
when he says that 'in the new model of religious truth . . .
absoluteness is defined and established not by the ability of a
religion to exclude or include others, but by its ability to
relate to others, to speak to and listen to others in genuine
dialogue'.[10] Cantwell Smith prefers not to speculate about
epistemology, believing most Western epistemology to be
orientated on things rather than persons.[11] It must be said
that these suggestions have not found common acceptance.
That does not invalidate them *tout court*, so much as sound a
note of warning. As an alternative route, others are exploring
a liberation perspective for an ethical foundation for affirming a pluralist position.[12]

Those who are sympathetic to viewing religious pluralism, and therefore inter-religious dialogue, in a positive light but who refuse to espouse a full pluralist theory, because of the fear of a meta-position, are exercising a rightful caution.[13] But caution need not become an unnecessary obstacle. For pursuing some kind of dialogical relationship between religions does seem to harbour an expectancy which implies some provisional relationship between the different traditions, some relationship between transcendence and varied global religious life. Being open to receive truth from whatever quarter it comes has its own virtues, but being open to another religious perspective surely carries a different expectation about what can be learned from dialogue and openness. Otherwise, why should there be anything special in inter-*religious* encounter as such? The pluralist model, therefore, does not propose that Christians participate in a meta-position, but perhaps suggests something like a meta-tradition. We have a foot in two camps. We celebrate and share what we know of God through the impact of Jesus in our world. We also wait to hear, learn and be judged by others who tell of a different experience, without defining their experience by virtue of our criteria of the Christ. We participate according to the Christian norm, yet with other norms which are also universally binding. It is the difference between what Cantwell Smith has called 'a "Christian" theology of comparative religion' and 'a theology of comparative religion for those among us who are Christians'.[14]

A related criticism of the pluralist model could be aimed like this. The problem is that it solves the question of conflicting truth-claims between religions too easily. It seems to ignore the very real diversity of the language and symbol systems of the different traditions. It looks as though what is being proposed is a view which holds that all religions are the same thing underneath, all equal, so that what a person believes is of no real significance. Despite the caricature in the latter part of that argument, it does hold some force. But pushing this criticism all the way would mean living with an unsatisfactory relativism, such that religions must remain for ever locked in their own language boxes. This is untrue to history, where religions have often borrowed from one another and absorbed different insights from other traditions. It is also untrue to experience, where the practice of 'passing over' to another tradition has enabled a richer faith to emerge, an enlargement and exchange that implies a deeper grasp on religious life and truth. More theologically, the criticism ignores the radical relativity of religious symbols, themselves pointers to divine reality rather than replicas of it in contingent form.

The stress on religious belief and practice as relative to the divine Absolute enables the uniqueness of the different religions to be affirmed, while also allowing the possibility of their complementarity. As William Thompson says: 'It is the commonality of the one God which finally undergirds the complementarity of the religions.'[15] He also adds a further function in the model, which is an insistence on mutual *criticism* between the traditions, as a means of keeping the bad aspects of relativism at the door. So, for example, he adds that Judaism's stress on covenant ought to criticize and correct Christianity's lapses into individualism, while in turn Judaism can ponder Christianity's insistence on a Messiah who suffers and empties himself. Similarly, we could add that Christianity could learn from Buddhism's insistence on the human heart as the locus of the solution to the human predicament, correcting Christianity's tendency to opt out and leave everything to divine intervention. Simultaneously, Buddhism could be made to ask itself about the reality of the world as a place of real process, where things go wrong, where evil does pervade. A critical dialogue would quicken the unique centres of the world's religious traditions, while teaching them to shed the vestiges of exclusiveness and intolerance. In short, the dialogue would show how each needs the other to be itself. To that extent the question of whether there is salvation in the church is not answerable independently of the question of whether there is salvation outside the world! To be fully Christian in the future will, paradoxically, involve living out of more than Christian resources alone.

I admit that the proposal for a pluralist approach in the Christian response to a multi-religious world is a new venture for Christian faith, and Christians have generally been trained to see newness as a threat. But an alternative reading of Christian history is possible, one which sees it as marked by radical newness and change more than we have cared to recognize. Christian terms and expressions, including even central doctrines such as the belief in God as Trinity, which have been thought to body forth the essence of Christian truth in a claim to continue the line of authentic tradition, can easily be read as innovations in their time. That of course does not necessarily discredit them. But it does leave a sense of relativism, where hitherto theologians have thought of themselves as handling stable tradition.

Such a reading of history can induce vertigo. It can also release us from the restrictions of the past, and enable faith to find its appropriate expression with reference to the dominant realities which inform our world in our own time. These are irrevocably multi-religious. Being 'honest to God' now implies being 'honest to Gods'. Affirming religious pluralism as 'God's' manner of dealing with our world, in all its exuberant variety, can be a valid Christian option and, for the reasons given above, becomes a necessary one. Radical novelty, given a certain perspective on history, is not sufficient reason for being wholly mistrustful. The vulnerability of the pluralist theory, and the intellectual pit-falls surrounding it, are only too obvious, not to say overwhelming.[16] For Christians, the life of vulnerability Jesus himself lived and the universalism he achieved can be our guide on the way.

The pluralistic 'theology of comparative religion for those among us who are Christians' is, I repeat, constructed inductively. If it is problematic for some, it is also provisional and open to revision. Part of the test of its adequacy is whether it will turn out to be valid in practice, whether it will hinder, pre-empt, or enable the dialogue to proceed. Whatever the intellectual reasons for being cautious, they should not be sufficient to stand in the way of embracing the positive good of partnership between religions as the next phase of Christian involvement in history, now begun. The two great threats to a sustainable life on the planet earth, death by poverty and nuclear catastrophe, are reasons enough for religions to co-operate, learn mutually and act.

Ruth Robinson

───────◆───────

A Question of Trust

'What became of *Honest to God*?' has sometimes been asked in the past twenty-five years. This attempt at further exploration is undertaken out of loyalty to its author and its readers, especially perhaps those who have written to me in the last few years, some of whom were still children or not yet born when the book was published.

John Robinson suggested in the Preface to *Honest to God* that 'there is a growing gulf between the traditional orthodox supernaturalism in which our Faith has been framed and the categories which the "lay" world (for want of a better term) finds meaningful today' (p. 8). We are now a whole generation further on and, as he suspected, the gulf is now very much wider. Just how wide it can be I am uncomfortably aware in the secluded dale where I now live. To find some means of bridging the gulf from the farther bank on which I stand sometimes seems impossible. Words tend to fray and break. Trust, hope, compassion, especially the last, are the ones that give the surest grip. So let us begin there.

Trust is a very personal matter, but being personal does not necessarily make it private. Christian trust has always been a corporate one, having its human focus in a man, Jesus of

Nazareth, who lived 2,000 years ago. The basic character of this trust remains the same through succeeding ages: that the universe into which we are born is at its heart trust*worthy* in a personal sense. But in order for this trust to be a living reality, each generation needs to interpret and express it in terms that have present meaning and intelligibility; each individual must be able to know it personally. Human language developed to a large extent as metaphor derived from the impact of the external world on the physical senses ('I see what you mean', 'I understand', 'I feel happy', 'I am touched by your kindness'); that is, we describe our inner world in terms that are intelligible in the external world. How we define our trust depends on our experience of the world we are born into, which includes its inherited culture and religious background. Had I been born in the East or Middle East or into a Jewish family, my intuitive spirituality would probably have been expressed in terms of Hindu or Buddhist, Jewish or Islamic mysticism. I cannot imagine myself as a fundamentalist adherent of any religion. But I was born in a Christian culture, though it was never pressed upon me; I chose it for myself as a young adult because then as now it most aptly focussed and enlightened my understanding.

In the early centuries of Christianity, the trust experienced by Christians and centred in Christ was defined in terms of a cosmology then universally intelligible; above the earth was heaven, the abode of God or the gods; beneath was the underworld of departed spirits. In terms of this cosmology the Christian 'good news' or gospel was that God, the loving Father who created us, sent his only Son who had been with him from the beginning to be born on earth as a human being. This man, Jesus, lived a life of total loving response to his Father and faced death rather than betray that love. In dying he offered his life as a ransom so that all might be reconciled to the Father from whom they had cut themselves off. Three days after his death Jesus was raised from the dead and received by God at his right hand in heaven. Thereby the sacrifice that had been made on behalf of all was vindicated and accepted; all who placed their trust in Christ would be eternally saved from damnation and united with him in heaven, themselves made sons of God by adoption.

This 'model' or interpretation of inner experience is still used by Christians today but in many different ways, mostly figurative or imaginative, but often literal. Too often the model is insisted on as itself the focus of the trust, and to question the model appears to threaten the very heart of the trust. This leads to much confusion and misunderstanding. In our day we need to ask ourselves again what is the nature of our trust in Christ and how our experience of it can be defined in a way which is intelligible in a world of quantum physics.

In 1859 our understanding of the book of Genesis was transformed by the publication of Darwin's *Origin of Species*. This has proved a liberation and an enrichment. Our idea of God has been released from the constriction of a cosmology which placed the beginning of the world at some 4,000 years BC and from a literal interpretation of the Bible account of creation. A hundred years and more on, it is perhaps time to look at the New Testament with new eyes and to free it from restrictions comparable to those from which the nineteenth-century scientists freed the Old Testament. It is not simply a question of re-defining old doctrines but of transposing the Christian experience within its first-century context together with the interpretation then given to it and having sufficient trust to allow it to confront us *as a whole*. We do not keep the mind of Christ within us or live according to his spirit by adopting a first-century world view. We need to ask: how did Jesus understand himself in terms of the world he lived in and the cosmology with which he was familiar, and how did he respond to it? And what is our comparable response to our world in terms of the cosmology we understand? We should take the New Testament seriously as history by seeing it whole and seeing it in depth. For at the heart of the history is a story, a real-life story about a real human being, and we are implicated in it. It is our own story and without it we are likely to find ourselves as homeless and disorientated as the remaining bushmen of the Kalahari often are now from theirs. But how to keep it, and us, 'alive'?

It must be stressed to begin with that I shall not be writing about facts to be believed in. My concern, on the contrary, is that the language we use to transmit and share our corporate and individual Christian experience should alert and nurture our spiritual perceptiveness and not simply petrify it. I have been greatly encouraged since completing the work on this essay by the publication of a book by Edward Robinson, *The Language of Mystery* (SCM Press 1987), in which the author explores a similar theme in his own sphere of spirituality and the arts. He affirms with delicacy and precision the necessity both for communication, which reassures me (it is tempting to feel that silence is the only safe option), and for the exercise of our creative imagination. I rely on that of the reader to 'lift' my otherwise pedestrian text.

Two further things encourage me. The first is that the Doctrine Commission of the Church of England recently published its report *We Believe in God*. I find this a heartening document because it allows me to assume a greater measure of understanding than there was twenty-five years ago. Base camp is established further along the route, so I do not have to start so far back and can explore further without fear of losing touch. The second is that we are learning from our physicists new ways of looking at the physical world. The language they use is often tentative and undogmatic; the results of their experiments are intriguingly ambivalent and sometimes mysteriously contradict each other; they are gaining fresh insights about the way the observer seems to affect what happens. All this gives me hope both that Christians may have the confidence to be less dogmatic and that intuitive language may be understood more sympathetically by Christians and non-Christians alike.

Paul Davies says that 'science distinguishes itself sharply from religion. Religion is founded on dogma and received wisdom, which purports to represent immutable truth.'[1] This needs to be questioned. Religions may *develop* from dogma but the root of dogma is a deeply significant corporate experience; for 'the Christian doctrine of God is not a speculative theory. It is an attempt at understanding a profound religious experience, centred in the life and teaching of Jesus'.[2]

David Bohm, the theoretical physicist, speaking of scientific research, explains the word 'theory' as having the same root as 'theatre', in a word meaning 'to view' or 'to make a spectacle'. 'Thus it might be said that a theory is primarily a form of *insight*, i.e. a way of looking at the world, and not a form of *knowledge* of how the world is.'[3] We should consider *dogma* in a similar light. The word is derived from the Greek *dokein*, 'to seem', 'seem good' or 'to think', 'suppose', which better expresses the tentative and provisional character of theological statements, and 'doctrine', which we usually take to mean something unconditionally laid down, simply means 'the teaching', 'that which is taught'. The purpose of religious doctrine is not to promote intellectual assent but to record and nurture a spiritual response to the world. But the terms by which we express this inner activity depend very much on how we understand the physical world and the sort of metaphors consequently available to us. We should heed David Bohm's warning at the end of his illuminating chapter on the way we use language, for it applies, I think, to all aspects of our world as we experience it, to religious doctrine as well as scientific theory: 'It is thus essential to be aware of the world view implied in each form of language, and to be watchful and alert, to be ready to see when this world view ceases to fit actual observation and experience, as these are extended beyond certain limits' (p. 47).

We should therefore expect the form of our doctrines to change. This does not mean that earlier teaching is proved wrong or discarded, any more than Einstein has proved Newton 'wrong', or that quantum theory has displaced relativity, but rather that 'one may expect the unending development of new forms of insight' (p. 5), each gathering up and carrying forward what has gone before. To deny a growth in the spiritual as in the scientific understanding of the world we live in is, for Christians, to deny that the Spirit is active. The world is all of a piece, spiritual and physical; metaphors must be living ones if they are to fit both observation and inner experience and be true to what we believe in. But what is believing?

Here again I would want to go back to the root of the word 'believe', of which there are traces in the still remembered 'lief' and 'liever' ('I had as lief' or 'I would liever' meaning 'I would like' or 'I would rather'). The root meaning was 'to hold dear', 'cherish', 'trust in'. This is the sense in which I believe; it is initially an activity of the heart and will rather than the head. When we say we believe in someone it means we trust them. We are not making a statement about their existence. To believe in God is to trust that the universe *is* trust*worthy* in a personal as well as a mechanical way. For Christians, the focus and definition of this trust is the man Jesus whose compassionate power in the manner of his living and dying and teaching was recognized by his disciples after his death as active in their own lives. Succeeding generations have known this same spiritual presence and by sharing in its activity, in loving, caring, forgiving, suffering, have begun to learn what it may mean to be human. Believing in God is to trust that the universe – all that is – is 'made', 'meant', 'has it in it' to be like this.

Trust cannot be separated from hope in its fulfilment, and the expression of this hope depends on the differing expectations of each generation. The first disciples expected the end of the world in their lifetime. In the Middle Ages, when the earth was thought to be flat, with heaven above and hell beneath, hope was popularly deferred to a life after death with God in heaven 'above the bright blue sky', a cosmology adopted by many of our Victorian hymns. This is a pale reflection of the underlying Christian hope: that our trust in the prevailing power of compassionate love is, and will be, vindicated in a cosmic sense. What models can our world today provide to express this hope? We should not be denied the right to explore this question by too slavish a dependence on models from a previous age. Some who would dearly wish to call themselves Christians, who are already in the trusting sense 'believers', cannot conscientiously commit themselves to statements which seem to assume a cosmology that has been superseded. Clauses like 'maker of heaven and earth', 'came down from heaven', 'ascended into heaven', 'is seated at the right hand of the Father', 'will come again with glory', especially when set among statements of simple historical fact ('suffered under Pontius Pilate', 'was crucified', 'was buried') are misleading to those, whether Christians or not, who do not discriminate between factual and intuitive language. We do not believe the universe is physically managed like that, but it sounds as if we do, and the Christian experience is consequently misunderstood and discredited. It is necessary now to ask how the spiritual content of such phrases might be expressed in language that can convey it today.

The church has always affirmed that Jesus was truly human, though only apparently on his mother's side. This was all very well in an age that believed that women embodied the material aspect and men infused the spiritual essence of human nature. It won't do in an age that knows about genes and has, with regrettable exceptions, a more enlightened view of the equality of men and women. We can believe neither that Jesus inherited human genes from his mother alone, nor that the other set was implanted ready-made, as fossils in the rocks were supposed to be by those who could not accept the evidence of evolution a hundred years ago.

All human beings inherit features and personality traits from their forebears and are conditioned by the assumptions, expectations and accumulated knowledge of the age they live in. They make mistakes, change their mind, do things they are sorry for; how else can they know how to forgive and be forgiven? There is no other way to be human than to learn, often the hard way, how to *become* human in the fullest sense: in other words, how to be a whole person. No human being is born perfect, without any flaws or failings, but it is possible so to fulfil our humanity as to be directed towards wholeness, to becoming a complete person, acknowledging that the authority for our life lies within the intimate centre of our own being and not on rules imposed from without. That Jesus was such a man is what 'comes through' the New Testament and is of 'crucial' significance in the history of our spiritual evolution.

Being human means sharing an evolutionary past, not only in a biological sense but also mentally and spiritually. If only we could free ourselves of the constraint to define what Jesus has done for us in terms of a metaphysical transaction (making atonement to God for our sins), we might better appreciate what he accomplished in making us conscious of ourselves as spiritual beings 'at one' within ourselves. Teilhard de Chardin sees evolution as an ascent towards consciousness. 'Man discovers that *he is nothing else than evolution become conscious of itself*, to borrow Julian Huxley's concise expression.'[4] One scientist who sees Jesus as marking the shift to conscious spiritual awareness is the American research psychologist Julian Jaynes, whose book with the rather daunting title *The Origin of Consciousness in the Breakdown of the Bicameral Mind* (Penguin Books 1982) is an illuminating study of the growth of human consciousness. It is important for us to understand our inner past, for we are as prone to regress to an archaic spirituality as we are to infantile behaviour and we need to be conscious of our motivations.

Jaynes suggests that Man (in the generic sense of *anthropos*, human being) has not always been conscious, aware that is, of himself and other people. Archaic Man had no sense of space and time to enable him to relate, no memory or capacity to learn from experience, to imagine or expect the future. Even today, consciousness is a much smaller part of our life than we think it is. I can drive my car without being aware of all the stimuli I am automatically obeying; I can ride my bicycle without being conscious of how I'm staying on. In fact it is when I think about it that I tend to fall off. Man operated very well without thinking about it until as late as the second millenium BC, the time varying in different cultures and individuals and generally coinciding with the widening of social contacts and the development of writing. Before this time the human brain operated in two hemispheres or chambers (hence '*bi*cameral'), an executive part functioning like a god who gave instructions and the obedient servant who carried them out. The instructions were heard as voices, much the same as Joan of Arc's voices and the voices experienced by schizophrenics. The system operated very well while people lived in small wandering groups, but as they settled in cities and social life became more complicated; the voices from different cultures became confused (the Tower of Babel). The link that men and women felt with their own inner god were loosened as those with their fellow-men were strengthened by trade and writing; the voices grew weaker as they grew in awareness first of others and their surroundings, then of themselves. The gods withdrew more and more, to woods and streams, mountains and awesome places and eventually to another world. Man was left with a sense of a lost paradise where his god had walked with him 'in the cool of the day' and felt abandoned and rejected (compare Ps. 22.1, quoted by Jesus: 'My God, my God, why hast thou forsaken me?').

Physiologically, according to Jaynes, the gradual loss of these inner voices and the growth of consciousness meant the breakdown of the communication links between the two hemispheres of the brain. Throughout the Old Testament we see evidence of the birth-pangs of this consciousness. Amos still shows the true bicameral voice: 'Thus saith the Lord'; his thinking is done for him and he obeys directly. Ecclesiastes, on the other hand, expresses feeling and understanding in an entirely subjective way and shows a vivid awareness of space and time, as for example in the famous passage: 'To every-thing there is a season, and a time to every purpose under heaven.' Jaynes sees Jesus as offering a religion for conscious rather than bicameral humanity. 'The divine kingdom to be regained is psychological not physical. It is metaphorical not literal. It is "within" not in extenso' (p. 318). But he goes on to say that Christianity does not remain true to its founder but 'returns again and again to this same longing for bicameral absolutes, away from the difficult inner kingdoms of agape . . . to an archaic authorization in an extended heaven' (pp. 318f.). However, I would say that Jesus does more than offer a religion for conscious humanity. In Jung's words: 'He preserves mankind from loss of communion with God and from getting lost in mere consciousness and rationality. That would have brought something like a dissociation between consciousness and the unconscious, an unnatural and even pathological condition, a "loss of soul" such as has threatened man from the beginning of time.'[5] In other words, he makes us whole. He restores our 'inner voice' but transformed, integrated with our true self; no longer an unconscious authority to be unconsciously obeyed, but a living gracious presence to which we are consciously responsive.

In such ways Jesus reveals and 'inspires' us to share his full humanity, by living as a wholly compassionate person and rising above the restricted religious attitudes of his time to a new awareness of our inner nature. He 'saves' us by enabling us to become what we are: true human beings.

A further question remains: How can we speak of *God* intelligibly today? John Polkinghorne, who is both physicist and priest, says: 'There is this remarkable congruence between our inward thought and the outward way things are.'[6]

So, to speak of God we should first consider how things are. Physicists offer different theories or scenarios to account for the 'big bang'. Particles can appear at random with no apparent cause, so perhaps the total universe doesn't have a cause. In any case, cause and effect are temporal concepts and time/space originated with the big bang, so asking what 'caused' it seems to be a meaningless question. There is no longer any way we can think about God 'existing' 'before' 'creation'; all these words are time/space concepts. Questions about accident and design, chaos and order, in the universe are real ones for scientists, but however far back there may seem to be a gap for God, the probability is that it will one day be closed by a physical explanation. Nicholas of Cusa in the fifteenth century already understood this: 'While I imagine a Creator creating, I am still on this side of the wall of Paradise! . . . Wherefore albeit without Thee naught is made or can be made, Thou art not a Creator, but infinitely more than a Creator.'[7]

One could almost say that it is among physicists, as well as among poets and artists, that we find our present day mystics. To try and follow their explanations of how things are is to

enter a world of wonder, mystery, contradiction and ambivalence. Mind and matter are understood as aspects of a cosmic
whole; physical reality as we imperfectly apprehend it appears to be partial or illusory; the world can more appropriately be described in terms of flux and movement, that is, of
'being' in the verbal sense, than of what 'is' in the static sense.
Sharing their language is perhaps to find a common tongue in
which a spiritual response to the world can be expressed in an
intelligible way for our age. Adapting models which make
sense to physicists may be a good way for us to put believing
into words which will be provisionally authentic.

Hitherto we have generally understood the world as fixed; it
has simply been a question of discovering how it permanently
is. Consequently our language is correspondingly fixed and
static. We say for example 'God is Love'. But, as David Bohm
suggests (pp. 27–47), in a world which is understood to be in
constant flux, nouns seem too rigid and miss the flow. It is like
hearing in isolation each separate note of a piece of music
without being aware of the concerto that is being played.
Verbs are perhaps more fitted to describe how we relate to the
world as we perceive it. (Indeed, this would be to recover an
awareness we seem to have lost. We are told the Hopi Indians
referred not to 'a tree' but to 'treeing', as if to say 'there treeing
is happening', just one aspect of the total cosmic activity.)
Perhaps we can better understand God, not as *a* being, but as
be-ing (in the continuing present tense) and to say God is
Loving (as an active verb). Praying can then be more easily
understood not as addressing a person ('But who are you
praying to?') but sharing in a personal activity.

In Bohm's study of the enfolding-unfolding universe and
consciousness he describes all that is, including inanimate
matter, life and consciousness as an unbroken whole in which
everything enfolds and is implicated in everything else (pp.
172–213). Life is 'implied' in the universe from the beginning;
there is a continuous flow among organic and inorganic
particles; creatures are enfolded into their surroundings as,
for example, we breathe in and out the air about us; inanimate
matter is simply a grouping of particles in which life is not

manifest. Consciousness also is involved in this process as our senses 'feel' our environment, and memory enfolds our past with our present. Consciousness can be described in terms of a serious of 'moments' which may vary in extent and duration: '(even a particular century may be a "moment" in the history of mankind). As with consciousness, each moment has a certain explicate order, and in addition it enfolds all the others, though in its own way. So the relationship of each moment in the whole to all the others is implied by its total content; the way in which it "holds" all the others enfolded within it' (p. 207).

This model of Bohm's is perhaps one we may adapt for describing God as Loving activity, God-being-God, enfolded into the total structure of all that is, both intimately and infinitely; caring, reconciling, healing. According to this model, nothing is outside this enfolding compassion and we, implicated in its activity, enfold all that is within our care, giving to everything its proper reverence, whether it be other creatures, the environment or simply the objects we use in our daily life. This same compassion enfolds, too, the terrible aspect of all that is, the evil men do to each other and the randomness and chance of accident and natural disaster; it is implicated not by causing suffering but by actively suffering with and within the sufferer.

We can also perhaps understand 'the Christ moment' as 'holding' all moments of history and human lives within itself. As Jung put it, 'That is to say what happens in the life of Christ happens always and everywhere'.[8] It is not only the response of Jesus' disciples to their experience of his life and death that is held within this moment. So also is the subsequent teaching together with the later explicit doctrines of Incarnation, Atonement, Resurrection, Ascension. More and more is enfolded into the original 'moment' as time goes on.

For Christians today, the total content of this historic 'moment' is enfolded within our present one as we make our response to it. We may find a searing and costly love tearing through our defences and know it within our own life as incarnation; we may be able to accept forgiveness for a terrible hurt we have done and know it as atonement, come through suffering with a joyful acceptance we had thought beyond us, or find new life through a desolate loss, and know this as resurrection. And because of all that is enfolded in these moments they will be focussed for us in Christ's 'moment' and we will find ourselves saying: 'That is what is happening.'

The church has always affirmed that Christianity is rooted in history, that Christ died for all men once for all and that therein lies our salvation. But do we not restrict the loving activity of God to a too narrow view of history? Using Bohm's model we may rather think of 'God' acting within history, in and through us, in an interflow of enfolded moments involving past and present. One of the disturbing results facing physicists in their quantum experiments is that the observer appears to affect what has already happened. That is, the observer is implicated in the results of his experiment. Perhaps we can understand from this how Christ's loving activity can be a saving event for us as we are implicated in it by our response to it and it is enfolded in our present living.

You may ask, then, what difference there is in practice between a caring, compassionate person who is a Christian and one who is not. Explicitly, there is no difference at all. There is no Christian monopoly in caring. Indeed if, as we trust, compassion enfolds all that is, we must hope that everyone will exercise it, for to do so is to follow our true human nature; to act caringly is to find ourselves in our natural environment. The only genuine reason for being compassionate is because someone needs our compassion; the only honest caring is for the other's sake, regardless of religious belief or motivation. The difference is *implicit* in the particular Christian consciousness of what is happening when compassion is asked for or offered and in the trust and hope that the response matters infinitely. It may be explicit in distinctive practices such as prayer, liturgy and contemplation.

To pray is to recognize that caring involves some basic words such as 'thank you', 'I'm sorry', 'please', 'I love you', 'how wonderful' spoken from the heart, not only to each other but as an affirmation of the whole being without limit. It is to trust that speaking these words changes how things are both intimately and ultimately. Praying for other people involves action on their behalf. It lies in doing what we can for them, including holding them consciously and lovingly in our hearts. This often turns out to be a very practical form of help. How it works is often a mystery, but many know their lives to have been changed by it and because of it have been upheld when they have been at their weakest and most vulnerable. A child once said to me: 'I think prayer works because it increases the amount of caring in the world'.

The eucharist (thanksgiving) or communion is the liturgy, literally 'the work', which enfolds the Christian past within the Christian present. It is not simply a notional remembering of Jesus but a re-membering of the risen Christ in the lives of those gathered in his name, who offer themselves to be broken and used for the reconciling and making whole of the world. Christ is made present when he lives, dies and rises in those who are at-one with him. Christian liturgy is atonement actually working: bread being shared, shattered lives made whole, relationships mended.

Contemplation is that alert and attentive waiting upon stillness that has been known as the practice of the Presence of God. Here we make our direct response to the inner 'Thou' that meets us; there is no more talking about 'It'. In retrospect there is only the personal language of relationship to describe the intimacy of the encounter, only the language of cosmic unity and wholeness to describe the ultimacy of it. The language used by Christians in recalling these moments is sometimes remarkably similar to that used by physicists to describe the mysteries of the physical world confronting them:

> God is nearer to us than our own Soul: for He is the Ground in whom our Soul standeth, and He is the Mean that keepeth the Substance and the Sense-nature together so that they shall never dispart (Julian of Norwich).

> Thy natural senses cannot possess God or unite thee to

Him; nay, thy inward faculties of understanding, will, and memory can only reach after God, but cannot be the place of His habitation in thee. But there is a root or depth in thee from whence all these faculties come forth, as lines from a centre or as branches from the body of the tree. This depth is called the centre, the *fund* or bottom of the soul (William Law).

There is an existence, a something higher than soul – higher, better, and more perfect than deity
(Richard Jefferies).

Our overall approach has thus brought together questions of the nature of the cosmos, of matter in general, of life, and of consciousness. All these have been considered to be projections of a common ground. This we may call the ground of all that is, at least in so far as this may be sensed and known by us, in our present phase of unfoldment of consciousness. Although we have no detailed perception or knowledge of this ground it is still in a certain sense enfolded in our consciousness in the ways in which we have outlined, as well as perhaps in other ways that are yet to be discovered.

Is this ground the absolute end of everything? In our proposed views concerning the general nature of 'the totality of all that is' we regard even this ground as a mere stage, in the sense that there could in principle be an infinity of further development beyond it (David Bohm, pp. 212f.).

Both mystic and physicist recognize the limits of human language and thought in attempting to plumb the depths of existence. For both there is always a beyond to what can be intuitively sensed or proposed.

How then is the Christian hope to be defined? St Paul gives its most powerful affirmation in his Epistle to the Romans: 'For I am convinced that there is nothing in death or life, in the realm of spirits or superhuman powers, in the world as it is or the world as it shall be, in the forces of the universe, in heights or depths – nothing in all creation that can separate us from the love of God in Christ Jesus our Lord' (8.38–39).

The interpretation of this hope varies widely among Christians. For many it has come to mean the assurance of a life after death in which they will be reunited with their loved ones. For the New Testament, the resurrection body has nothing to do with the individual's moment of death. It is both corporate and cosmic. As John Robinson commented in *The Body*, it signifies rather 'the *solidarity* of the recreated universe in Christ' (p. 79). 'And as the Christian hope of resurrection is fundamentally social, so it is inescapably historical. . . . The building up of the Church is not the gathering of an elect group *out of* the body of history which is itself simply for destruction. It is the resurrection body of history itself, the world as its redemption has so far been made effective' (p. 83).

Pierre Teilhard de Chardin, in his magnificently poetic study of human evolution *The Phenomenon of Man*, describes the Kingdom of God as 'a prodigious biological operation – that of the Redeeming Incarnation' (p. 293). His vision is of 'an advance of *all together*, in a direction in which *all together* can join and find completion in a spiritual renovation of the earth' (pp. 244–5). The focal point of this advance, 'that mysterious centre of our centres which I have called Omega', he sees as a convergence of all consciousness, involving not a loss but a fulfilment of personal identity. Omega is not simply a point at the end of time; if it were, we could have no perception of it. It is also a present reality drawing every-thing to itself by the energy of love. 'Love alone is capable of uniting living beings in such a way as to complete and fulfil them, for it alone takes them and joins them by what is deepest in themselves' (p. 265).

One of the implications of 'incarnation' is that humankind is responsible for sharing in this activity of unifying love. Possessing reflective consciousness we have the manipula-tive power to direct our future; evolution is in our hands. Fear, hatred, cruelty and selfish ambition, individually and collectively, tend towards fragmentation and disintegration, threatening to turn this unifying, holistic process into reverse. The Christian hope, trust and will lies in that unifying activity of love which is enfolded into our very existence. For here lies our only means of spiritual survival in what Teilhard calls 'a personalized universe'; not personalized in the sense of becoming a person but 'by charging itself at the very heart of its development with the dominating and unifying influence of a focus of personal energies and attractions' (p. 267n.).

The function of the Christian church is to be the instrument of this unifying activity; to promote healing and wholeness in all communities, intimate, local and world-wide, and to be not so much the moral conscience of the world but its unified consciousness, nourishing both creative imagination and spiritual perceptiveness. The churches as institutions, alas, often betray or decline this role, and its members opt for what is least demanding. Edward Robinson in *The Language of Mystery* presents a telling indictment of the way we have allowed kitsch to corrupt both art and ritual (pp. 60–9), and in *We Believe in God* the Doctrine Commission finds that many people prefer to evade the fundamental issues, settling for the 'unreflective maintenance of generally good habits'. But, the Report continues, 'the present age is one in which such habits are increasingly hard to sustain in the absence of deliberate decision. Explicit challenges increasingly demand explicit choices' (p. 50). The body of Christ is to be discerned where explicit challenges are being met, not with 'a sort of gentle philanthropism',[10] but with an active, purposeful and costly love. It is to be discerned where the intuitive life of the Spirit is shared and explored, in silence, prayer or liturgy, and earthed in an acknowledged corporate concern for the growing together of humankind in love and trust.

Trust for me lies in the inescapable possibility that life coheres in the way of Christ. There is no intellectual certainty here; to believe so would be wishful thinking. There is only trust, however frail, or cynicism. In the language of the spirit, we can choose to live or die. But to trust is to be answered by a 'yes', a recognition within the heart that can be known only as a mystery. The metaphors I have borrowed and used may be appropriate for a time but they are expendable. Trust is not fixed there. To trust is to welcome the mystery at your hearth.

Peter Selby

Truth and Resistance

Evensong. St John's College, Oxford. Sunday after the Ascension, 1963. 'It seems,' the preacher said, 'that St Luke has pulled Dr Robinson's leg, and it has come off in his hand.' We laughed, of course, as we were meant to, not being particularly aware how the academic debate was going and of the code according to which it was being conducted. Everybody knew, we were being told, the significance of the spatial imagery in the Gospels, that it was not offered literally, and that its significance was theological, not geographical.

Ten years or so later. The conference room of the Southwark Diocesan Training Centre, where many of John Robinson's initiatives were pursued. The Management Committee is discussing the use of the place. One member asks passionately, 'What *has* happened to all the people who bought and read *Honest to God*?' The silence suggested that that was, as they say, a good question. Presumably in 1963 they had not been part of the 'everybody' who already knew that St Luke (and a lot of other people) had not meant to be taken literally. And presumably in the intervening ten years it had come home to them that not everybody did know and not everybody wanted to know.

Fifteen years further on, with *The Myth of God Incarnate* and the 'Durham affair' behind us, it is not easy to believe that much has been learned. The comments of professional theologians about these debates sound no less Olympian than that 1963 sermon; the Church of England (at least) can be guaranteed to get completely stuck every time some issue, doctrinal or pastoral or ethical, arises because of the problem posed by its tradition, and those who read *Honest to God* may now be reading Don Cupitt, but who knows? Certainly if they are, there is less sign than ever that the Church of England can really relate to them and to their search. Maybe we get some kind of theological incident every four years or so, and we just have to accept the cycle, just slightly rewriting the script each time, prepared to hear the same responses, churchpeople arguing, theologians disdaining, while out there the uncertain melt quietly away, wondering whether their neighbours are after all right in thinking that ultimate questions are not worth bothering about.

There are other reasons too for a loss of nerve and commitment in pursuing the agenda which 1963 opened up: there is a lot of superficial evidence that it is certainties that sell, and old certainties that sell best of all. The 1960s are seen by Government as a low point of loss of vigour and greatness, and its certainties are clearly very marketable indeed. Consultation and thinking, considering the complexities of situations, are processes despised as simply 'avoiding the issue'; first comes the green paper, and then, in no time, the bulldozer. There is no sense that political exploration is anything other than a sign of the disarray of the Opposition. For those in power, the certainties are there, waiting to be imposed. And in the churches it is the certain ones who can tell you they are growing.

So what did happen to those who read *Honest to God* and found it striking a chord in relation to their own religious search and their vision of what church might be like? As one of them, I remember being struck at the time, even as a student, by the gentle optimism that pervaded it. The belief that comes across is that things will change if enough people think they should. And a belief, too, in the power of the liberal idea in itself. Put like that, it sounds vastly more naive than John Robinson could possibly have been, and yet that is how it reads. The proposals for the revision of doctrine, for the updating of ethics, and for the modernizing of the life of the church, all seem to have a lot going for them, and they still strike a responsive chord. They seem only to have one thing going against them, and that is their underestimation of the struggle that would be needed to make any move forward on any of those fronts. The flaw is fatal. It takes no account of the reaction likely to take place to any such proposals, and could obviously take no account of the radical changes in consciousness that have taken place in the last decade. Maybe that just means that the ideas of the *Honest to God* era were good ideas but ones which happened to come before their time.

Sadly, that estimate will not do. Perhaps for some of the intervening twenty-five years it would have done; it was possible to hope that at some point the truth would dawn on society, on believers, on the church, and that change would happen. But not now. Change in the direction of a faith that took modern critical approaches seriously, of a society that took seriously the needs of the most vulnerable, and of a church that would structure itself for the evident missionary needs of our time rather than hold on to patterns that ministered to those of a previous time – such changes are not by any means merely delayed but substantially reversed. What has taken place is not just a series of individual developments but a change of consciousness, so that within the heart of people in our small part of the Western world has been born a new attitude to living, and a new set of assumptions about what can and should happen. That must raise questions about the truth of the faith and hopes of the *Honest to God* era, even for those of us who found and still find them stimulating and truth-bearing. If John Robinson's beliefs and values are being so virulently rejected, is there not some reason to ask whether they were not in some sense and as he put them inadequate expressions of a Christian faith for our time? If they had been true, would there not by now be some greater evidence that they would be winning people's hearts?

The most original contention of *Honest to God*, as its author often said, was the holding together of Paul Tillich's theology and Dietrich Bonhoeffer's estimate of humanity as 'come of age'. So abandoning the 'God out there' had two particular motives. First, it was so that Christianity could be expressed in terms of responses to the ultimate questions of human beings, and secondly, so that it could be presented as true in a world which no longer held religious presuppositions. Both those motives struck deep chords in me and in many others who responded warmly, without previously having had much acquaintance with the work of either of those theologians, to what John Robinson was saying. It made sense that ultimate questions could be answered without recourse to spatial metaphors, and it also seemed extremely hopeful that the 'adulthood' of humanity and the secularity of our age were being recognized. Further reflection at the time began to cast doubt on that crucial synthesis, and the pressures and attitude-changes of the intervening years have rendered it quite untenable. It looks now simply part of the gentle optimism of that time.

Some of those who read the book must still be asking ultimate questions, but they can be under no illusion that such questions are being widely asked or that the answers of the 1960s carry weight. More recent theological storms have not elicited the public interest, let alone the *Observer* headlines, of 1963, but have tended rather to turn into domestic squabbles within the church, allowing an opportunity for the traditionalists to have another go at the 'liberals'. Those debates have not produced a new theological language which would bridge the gap between Christianity and those outside it for whom ultimate questions are still matters of deep concern, and if they have not found their way to accepting the language and symbol that the church has on offer by now they must surely be very sceptical whether there will ever be anything new under the sun.

Meanwhile 'adulthood' has been deeply corrupted. The language of self-reliance and non-dependence has become too much part of the propaganda of our time to serve as a serious invitation to mature faith. It stands as part of a go-getting culture, for the ideal of self-advancement, removed a long way from faith in the person-for-others, servant of a God edged out of the world on to a cross. If any ultimate questions are left in people's minds they are supposed to be settled by recourse to a traditional religious frame of reference, which in turn is not expected to find its expression in any kind of common life. Ethical questions of the sort which occupied my student mind seem to have been resolved either by people going off in their own directions or by a strident summons to return to the old ways as though there never had been any real reason for doubting their continuing validity. Sexual morality is seemingly decided by a combination of public moralizing by some while others 'do their own thing'; the middle ground of serious debate seems largely, like most other middle grounds, to have been vacated.

If therefore in 1963 it was possible to hope that a humanity come of age would pursue the possibility of a common destiny with a serious commitment to the search for common answers, the dawn of 1988 hardly seems a time when that hope is being realized. Such signs of religious growth as there are occur under the aegis of a conservative theology and spirituality, one that seeks to leave on one side, or take a short cut through, the intellectual questions raised by Christian belief. Meanwhile, in the pursuit of a sustainable common life for humanity, the possibility of there being a hopeful consensus that would allow a gradual increase of wealth to be used for the gradual relief of the sufferings of the poor seems to have evaporated for the foreseeable future; there is no question where the high ground of the political argument lies, and it is not with social consensus.

In which ways, then, does the theological agenda proposed by John Robinson, and his perception of the human situation, need revision, if it is to serve us twenty-five years on? It was in the later part of the *Honest to God* decade, as I pursued my own theological study, that I first began to put into words (I think in the question period after an Old Testament lecture) my sense that what was lacking in his theological synthesis was anything that could be felt as *authoritative*. It was possible to speak such truth to power while the power would listen. But what was its cutting edge if the times grew urgent and the powers that be less amenable to persuasion? Was there not in the biblical recital of God's action and God's Word (however philosophically problematic they might be) at least some sense that there was something (Someone) with which human beings *had* to do, whether they chose to or not and whether it accorded with the point they had arrived at in their spiritual pilgrimage or not. The status of what was being recited might indeed be open to questions of many kinds, but the language and the symbols certainly 'spoke'. Indeed my experience was that a critical approach to the Bible and to the tradition, so far from preventing it from 'speaking', gave it a new and more powerful voice. Certainly there were questions about what, within the total narrative, was true and in which sense true; but the problems seemed to be there no less in a theology purged of myths (or replaced with new ones) and the price paid in loss of authority seemed far too great. The human spiritual search, and the human experience of shared compassion, seemed to be available only the other side of a sense of transcendence which the biblical tradition, speaking for itself, seemed to contain. My contact with the Civil Rights movement, and through it with black spirituality, seemed to reinforce that sense. And so there seemed to be a choice between what Bonhoeffer perceived as the need to find an articulation of the Christian gospel that would confront human beings not naturally religious and Tillich's response to what he saw as the ultimate questions inherent in human existence. I do not now think that there are ultimate questions *inherent* in human existence until and unless human beings are specifically and authoritatively addressed. In the terms in which John Robinson tried to effect a synthesis, I have found myself having to choose, and have opted for Bonhoeffer.

Part of that choice lies in some of the perceptions already mentioned, which make our time look far more like the one which led Bonhoeffer to the prison cell in which his seminal ideas were written than the atmosphere of secure post-war consensus. For all the manifest differences, the liberal ideal and the hope of justice seem in our society to face many of the overpowering challenges of fifty, rather than twenty-five, years ago. Our search is for a language that will speak not just to those who in the privacy of their own reflection are still engaged in a spiritual search, but to those also who dismiss such a search as a diversion from the cynical exercise of power and to those whose need is for a word of hope in their situation as members of a permanently poor and powerless class. More is needed to preserve the ideals of a free-thinking and open society than free-thinking and openness themselves can muster.

'What *has* happened to all the people who bought and read *Honest to God*?' The setting in which that question was first expressed to me, the Southwark Diocesan Training Centre, Wychcroft, has itself undergone a transformation. When the question was expressed, its chapel had a central altar, surmounted by a mural of Christ the Worker, expressive of the Christ in our midst and the people of God gathered around. It has been odd to find the building refurnished, and reorientated through ninety degrees. The mural is the same, but now on ahead of Christ's people, far more their Saviour and their Judge than their companion. And the people are no longer naturally gathered around but addressing and being addressed, needing to be made into what they no longer appear naturally to be. On the wall is a notice to the effect that this reorientation has been partly done in memory of the same John Robinson whose inspiration and theological agenda had lain behind the original conception of the Training Centre and its chapel. The other side of an awareness of transcendence? I have never checked what was in the mind of those responsible for the refurnishing; but for me there is a symbol here of what has happened to the theological agenda of twenty-five years ago.

None of this is to question either the humane instincts or the spiritual perception of that time, far less to suggest that John Robinson himself was unwilling to be faithful to them in the intervening period. It is to say that the language and symbol offered in *Honest to God* have been found lacking for the spiritual crisis which actually faces us. It is to say that the qualities of authority and directness to be found in the biblical narrative and proclamation may be more needed at this hour than a scrupulous quest for the boundary between faith and history, and it is to face the fact that the creation of a humane society, one in which people can engage in their spiritual quest, lies the other side of the contemplation of God as judge and the confrontation with some very intransigent and intractable realities of power.

Nor does this realization settle the hard philosophical questions about the meaning of God's judgment or God's activity; it highlights the fact that the issues of religious truth which troubled the author and readers of *Honest to God* are not to be solved in isolation from the struggle to prevent the poor having their resources and possibilities for housing or education or whatever snatched from their grasp for the profit of the few with the connivance of the many. The task as it now appears is to enable the language of faith to speak with immediacy and power in a context where the danger to liberty and peace is not yet seen but is more and more menacing. If we do not notice the change in the agenda it will impose itself upon us. It has yet to be seen whether *Faith in the City* raises the issues of justice with sufficient clarity or whether, as I am inclined to suspect, it too contains too much optimism about the reasonableness of those enjoying the fruits of power and those whom they represent.

It is clear that John Robinson arrived to serve as a suffragan bishop in the diocese of Southwark with a great deal of optimism about the church's situation, as his biography shows. Even if *Honest to God* now appears to carry on too much of that optimism, it no doubt represented for him a radical reappraisal of his initial view after somewhat more than two years in office. It is about the same time since I came to serve as a suffragan bishop in the same diocese; as I reflect on my initial sense that it was important to speak to people of the Durham affair, and so of some of the questions of meaning and truth that lay behind *Honest to God*, that too requires reappraisal. Is it responsible to suggest to people that it is very important for them to be clear about the impact of critical thinking on our understanding of the meaning of doctrine when a vastly more serious crisis looms for the future of Christian belief?

The fact is that the era through which we are living is so spiritually corrosive that by comparison with our duty to find ways of resisting that corrosion other theological tasks have to take a much lower priority. Certainly the boundary between faith and history, between myth and chronicle, needs investigating; but where we now stand, that issue stands out in sharp relief as having to do with the very possibility or impossibility of still entertaining, in our historical circumstances, belief in the sovereignty of a God such as Jesus Christ revealed God to be. For those who would hold to that belief, the absolutely overriding priority must be given to the search for a language powerful enough and a discipleship committed enough to counter the seemingly overwhelming viewpoint – it is indeed a form of religious conviction – that banquets for some and crumbs for others is not merely the only possible common life we can have in view for the human species, but is as such actively to be sought after. There is not much point in any version of the Christian proclamation, whether demythologized, conservative or whatever, that does not bring that issue out into the open.

It is only necessary to keep your eyes open to see what is the cost of discipleship for those who, whichever corner they inhabit, resist the religious blandishments of our all pervading individualism. Whether their resistance is on behalf of the homeless or refugees or the poor or women or black people, if they are resisting on behalf of the belief that human beings are, contrary to all we are being told day after day, made for a wholesome and peaceable common life, they will need all the resources and support they can find if they are not to go under. They will in particular need the constant refreshment of their religious conviction, if that is where they are starting from, that the shape of Christianity is a corporate one, or else they will by degrees find their belief subverted till it wears the dress of Christianity but is at heart (even if it is not recognized as such) merely an English version of the German Christian Movement, salt without any taste.

There is no doubt that *Honest to God* was written by a person much exercised by the responsibility belonging to a bishop. Certainly John Robinson believed he had a very clear vocation to teach the truth. There is much that he did that involved taking sides about issues; but I am not completely clear that he displays a recognition that the issue of truth is also, and always, related to somebody's interests, and is never therefore completely abstract or objective. It is certainly not possible to avoid that awkward fact now, because the struggle about the nature of Christian truth is becoming so closely related to questions of power in our society. In that setting, anybody with a concern for truth, and certainly anyone with a role like that of a bishop charged with maintaining it, will have to give priority to those truths which will defend the growing number of the victims of politically and religiously supported individualism, and at the moment they may not in the main be those who bought and read *Honest to God*. They are likely to be people who never saw themselves as having much investment in the religious quest under whatever guise, and they only will if it can be clear that there is in Christianity a language and a life-style which stands with them in their trial.

I have the good fortune to know that among those who bought and read John Robinson's book are many who have noticed very clearly how the theological agenda has shifted and in their living pay the price that is required of them. I do not yet see the emergence in our country of a theological language that might do for us in our situation what the language of liberation theology has done for Latin American Christians or, for that matter, what Catholicism has done for Polish ones. Insofar as John Robinson had a basic concern for the discovery of a language equal to the religious quest of his readers, I believe the discovery of such a language is not only vital in our time but is the proper continuation of the enterprise to which he was committed. I fancy it may have to be the kind of language the Confessing Church spoke, and that was in many ways lacking in refinement, though it was never lacking in passion. And above all it met the need; and telling the truth in a way that meets the need of the hour is, when all is said and done, what the church is for.

Select Bibliography

To avoid unnecessary duplication in the Notes, this Select Bibliography contains publication details of the main works of John Robinson and other books which are regularly cited.

Books by John A. T. Robinson

In the End, God . . . A Study of the Christian Doctrine of the Last Things, James Clarke 1950, revised ed. Fontana Books 1968
The Body: A Study in Pauline Theology, SCM Press 1952
On Being the Church in the World, SCM Press 1960, reissued Penguin Books 1969
Liturgy Coming to Life, Mowbrays 1960
Honest to God, SCM Press and Westminster Press 1963
The Honest to God Debate, edited by John A. T. Robinson and David L. Edwards, SCM Press 1963
Exploration into God, Stanford University Press and SCM Press 1967
But That I Can't Believe!, Fontana Books 1967
Christian Freedom in a Permissive Society, SCM Press and Westminster Press 1970
The Human Face of God, SCM Press and Westminster Press 1973
The Roots of a Radical, SCM Press 1980
The Priority of John, SCM Press 1985
Where Three Ways Meet, edited by Eric James 1987

Books about John A. T. Robinson

Eric James, *A Life of Bishop John A. T. Robinson: Scholar, Pastor, Prophet*, Collins 1987

A. Alistair Kee, *The Roots of Christian Freedom: The Theology of John A. T. Robinson*, SPCK 1988

Richard H. McBrien, *The Church in the Thought of Bishop John Robinson*, SCM Press 1966

Notes

———————◆———————

T. G. A. Baker *Is Liturgy in Good Shape?*

1. H. Nouwen, *Reaching Out*, Fount 1980, p. 44, quoted in Robin Green, *Only Connect: Worship and Liturgy from the Perspective of Pastoral Care*, Darton, Longman and Todd 1987.

2. *Liturgy Coming to Life*, p. 35.

3. A good example is provided by the post-communion prayer in Rite A which begins 'Father of all, we give you thanks' and ends with the highly evocative words 'so we and all your children shall be free, and the whole earth live to praise your name, through Christ our Lord'.

4. This is happily the present policy of the Royal School of Church Music.

Tim Beaumont *John Robinson and the Radical in Politics*

1. Christian Schumacher, *To Live and Work*, Marc Europe 1986.

F. W. Dillistone *Recasting the Mould*

1. Susanne Langer, *Philosophical Studies*, Oxford University Press 1962.

2. Francis Thompson, 'The Kingdom of God. In No Strange Land', *Selected Poems*, Methuen and Burns & Oates 1909.

3. *Truth is Two-Eyed*, p. 143. The quotation comes from P. Chenchiah, *Rethinking Christianity in India*, p. 162.

Alan Ecclestone *Religious Truth Must be Lived*

1. Michael Roberts, *The Modern Mind*, Faber and Faber 1937, p. 251.

2. John Wren-Lewis, 'On Not Going to Church', *Prism*, February 1962, p. 28, quoted in *Honest to God*, pp. 9of.
3. Sebastian Moore, *God is a New Language*, Darton, Longman and Todd 1967.
4. *Liturgy Coming to Life*, p. 106.

J. L. Houlden   *Frontiers of Honesty*

1. Alec Vidler, *A Variety of Catholic Modernists*, Cambridge University Press 1970. For Turmel's career see pp. 56–62; he lived from 1859–1943.
2. See F. A. Iremonger, *William Temple*, Oxford University Press 1948, Chapter VII; Owen Chadwick, *Hensley Henson*, Clarendon Press 1983, Chapter 6.
3. The cases of Hans Küng at Tübingen, of the contributors to *The Myth of God Incarnate*, SCM Press 1977, of Don Cupitt, and perhaps of John Robinson himself.
4. The cases of Michael Goulder and Antony Kenny spring to mind.
5. These considerations have been close to the surface in numerous modern theological storms: over *Honest to God*, 1963; Maurice Wiles's *The Remaking of Christian Doctrine*, SCM Press 1974; *The Myth of God Incarnate*, edited by John Hick, SCM Press 1977; and David Jenkins's utterances, leading to *The Nature of Christian Belief*, Church House Publishing 1986, a statement by the bishops of the Church of England.
6. Adrian Hastings, *A History of English Christianity 1920–1985*, Collins 1986, pp. 152f.
7. Raymond E. Brown, *The Birth of the Messiah*, Geoffrey Chapman 1977, see especially Appendix IV.
8. See my editorial in *Theology*, Vol. XCI, January 1988.
9. See especially E. P. Sanders, *Paul and Palestinian Judaism*, SCM Press and Fortress Press 1977; id., *Paul, the Law and the Jewish People*, Fortress Press and SCM Press 1983; Heikki Räisänen, *Paul and the Law*, J. C. B. Mohr (Paul Siebeck), Tübingen 1983; Francis Watson, *Paul, Judaism and the Gentiles*, Cambridge University Press 1986.
10. See Gerd Theissen, *The Social Setting of Pauline Christianity*, T. & T. Clark 1982, especially Chapter 3.

Alistair Kee   *Mystery and Politics. The Explorations Continue*

1. *On Being the Church in the World*, p. 9.
2. Rudolf Otto, Introduction to *Friedrich Schleiermacher: On Religion*, Harper and Brothers 1958, p. viii.
3. Jon Sobrino, *The True Church and the Poor*, SCM Press and Orbis Books 1985, p. 135.
4. Alfredo Fierro, *The Militant Gospel*, SCM Press and Orbis Books 1977, p. 344.

5. Johannes Metz, *Theology of the World*, Herder and Herder 1969, p. 109.

6. Eric James, *The Roots of the Liturgy*, Prism Pamphlet no. 1, 1962, p. 5.

John Kent   *The Shadow of a Grove of Chestnut Trees*

1. Alec Vidler et al., *Objections to Christian Belief*, Fontana Books 1963, p. 99.

2. Paul van Buren, *The Secular Meaning of the Gospel*, SCM Press 1963, pp. 90f.

3. Friedrich Nietzsche, *Daybreak*, translated by E. J. Hollingdale, Penguin Books 1985, p. 191.

4. Alasdair MacIntyre, in *The Honest to God Debate*, p. 215.

5. Ibid., p. 95.

6. Sharon Welch, *Communities of Resistance and Solidarity: A Feminist Theology of Liberation*, Orbis Books 1985, p. 68.

7. George Steiner, *In Bluebeard's Castle*, Faber 1971, p. 106.

John Lee   *Honest to What?*

1. Philip Toynbee, *Part of a Journey. An Autobiographical Journal 1977–1979*, Collins 1981, p. 343.

2. H. J. Home, 'The Concept of Mind', *International Journal of Psychoanalysis* 47.1, 1966, p. 42.

3. A. W. Clare, 'Psychology', in *Encyclopedia of Medical Ignorance*, ed. R. Duncan and M. Weston-Smith, Pergamon Press 1984, p. 6.

4. K. William Fried, 'Within and Without. The Examination of a Ubiquitous Resistance in Group Therapy', in *Group Therapy*, ed. Wolberg and Aronson, Stratton Intercontinental, New York 1979, p. 99.

5. P. Davies, *God and the New Physics*, Dent 1983, p. 100.

6. Fritjof Capra, *The Tao of Physics*, Collins 1976; id., *The Turning Point: Science, Society and the Rising Culture*, Wildwood House 1982.

7. H. Kohut, *The Analysis of the Self*, The Psycho-analytic Study of the Child, Monograph no. 4, Universities Press Inc, New York 1971, xv.

8. Ernest Hutton, 'The Self in the Group', *Group Analysis* XVII.2, 1984, p. 132.

9. H. J. Home, 'The Concept of Mind' (n. 2 above), 47.

10. Paul Tillich, *Systematic Theology* Vol. 1, Nisbet 1951, p. 15, quoted in *Honest to God*, p. 49.

Dennis Nineham   *What Happened to the New Reformation?*

1. To a considerable extent, the success or failure of John Robinson's projected 'new reformation' will have depended on the tenability of the ideas and theories he put forward. Though a thoroughgoing critique of his thought would be very worthwhile (e.g. was he in the last resort a pantheist?), nothing of the sort was possible in the course of this short article.

2. In the widest sense, as including literary, sociological and many other sorts of criticism.

3. For more on this see my contribution to *The Myth of God Incarnate*, ed. John Hick, SCM Press 1977, esp. pp. 186ff.

4. T. W. Manson, in *The Interpretation of the Bible*, ed. C. W. Dugmore, SPCK 1944, pp. 97, 93f.

5. Leonard Hodgson, *Sex and Christian Freedom*, SCM Press 1967, pp. 42f.

6. For a much fuller working out of this suggestion, see my essay in *Imagination and the Future*, ed. J. R. Henley, 1980, pp. 189–203.

7. J. W. Bowker, *The Sense of God*, and *The Religious Imagination and the Sense of God*, Clarendon Press 1973 and 1978.

8. The refusal of large numbers of Roman Catholics in the West to accept the papal line where sexual mores are concerned and to feel no guilt for their refusal, surely foreshadows the shape of things to come.

J. C. O'Neill   *Simplicity, Intricacy and Complexity*

1. André Jute, *Writing a Thriller*, A. & C. Black 1986, p. 79. *Reverse Negative* was first published by Hyland House, Melbourne in 1979: then by Secker and Warburg 1980: Methuen 1987.

Ronald H. Preston   Honest to God, *the New Morality and the Situation Ethics Debate*

1. Paul Ramsey, *Deeds and Rules in Christian Ethics*, Scribner 1967, p. 22.

2. R. A. McCormick, in *The Situation Ethic Debate*, ed. Harvey Cox, Westminster Press 1967, p. 279 n. 11.

3. Ian T. Ramsey, *Christian Ethics and Contemporary Philosophy*, SCM Press 1966, p. 13.

4. J. M. Gustafson, 'Context v. Principle: A Mistaken Debate', *Harvard Theological Review* 58, 1965.

Alan Race   *Truth is Many-Eyed*

1. *Darśan* is a Sanskrit word which means 'seeing', especially seeing the divine reflected in an image, a set of ideas or a person. Cf. Diana L. Eck, *Darśan: Seeing the Divine Image in India*, Anima Books, Pennsylvania 1981.

2. D. Senior and C. Stuhlmueller, *The Biblical Foundations for Mission*, SCM Press and Orbis Books 1983, p. 345.

3. During the 1980s a number of books have surveyed the field and staked out their own positions. Cf. Harold Coward, *Pluralism: Challenge to World Religions*, Orbis Books 1985; Kenneth Cracknell, *Towards a New Relationship*, Epworth Press 1986; Gavin D'Costa, *Theology and Religious Pluralism*, Blackwell 1986; Paul Knitter, *No Other Name?*, Orbis Books and SCM Press 1985; Alan Race, *Christians and Religious Pluralism*, SCM Press

1983. From his experience in the WCC sub-unit on dialogue S. J. Samartha sets out many of the issues very clearly in *Courage for Dialogue*, WCC, Geneva 1981.

4. Robinson's position here is not dissimilar from that of Hans Küng. Cf. Hans Küng, *On Being a Christian*, Fount Books 1978, Ch. A. III; id., *Christianity and the World Religions*, Collins 1987. See also my discussion of Küng in 'Christianity and Other Religions: Is Inclusivism Enough?', *Theology* LXXXIX, May 1986, no. 729.

5. Gordon Kaufman, 'Religious Diversity, Historical Consciousness, and Christian Theology', in *The Myth of Christian Uniqueness*, edited by Paul Knitter and John Hick, Orbis Books and SCM Press 1988, p. 9.

6. John Hick, *God Has Many Names*, Macmillan 1980 and Westminster Press 1982; Paul Knitter, *No Other Name?*, SCM Press and Orbis Books 1985; Wilfred Cantwell Smith, *Towards a World Theology*, Macmillan 1981. The most recent exploration of the pluralist model from the American scene has involved many leading theologians and shows the diverse approaches to it: cf. Paul Knitter and John Hick (eds.), *The Myth of Christian Uniqueness*.

7. Alan Race, *Christians and Religious Pluralism*, SCM Press and Orbis Books 1983; also Paul Knitter, 'Catholic Theology of Religions at a Crossroads', in *Concilium* 183, 1986, pp. 99–107; William M. Thompson, *The Jesus Debate*, Paulist Press 1985, Chapter 13.

8. Wilfred Cantwell Smith, *Towards a World Theology*, Macmillan 1981, pp. 171f.

9. John Hick, 'Religious Pluralism', in F. Whaling (ed.), *The World's Religious Traditions*, T. & T. Clark 1984, pp. 147–64; id., 'The Philosophy of Religious Pluralism', *Scottish Journal of Theology* 37, 1984, pp. 229–36.

10. Paul Knitter, *No Other Name?*, p. 220.

11. Wilfred Cantwell Smith, *Towards a World Theology*, Chapter 5 and p. 189.

12. See the essays in *The Myth of Christian Uniqueness* by Rosemary R. Ruether, Marjorie H. Suchocki, Aloysius Pieris SJ and Paul Knitter.

13. See John B. Cobb Jr, *Beyond Dialogue: Toward a Mutual Transformation of Christianity and Buddhism*, Fortress Press 1982.

14. Wilfred Cantwell Smith, *Towards a World Theology*, Chapter 8.

15. William M. Thompson, *The Jesus Debate*, Paulist Press 1985, p. 388.

16. See the reflective summary by T. Driver in *The Myth of Christian Uniqueness*, pp. 203–18.

Ruth Robinson   *A Question of Trust*

1. Paul Davies, *God and the New Physics*, Dent 1983, p. 220.
2. *We Believe in God*, Church House Publishing 1987, p. 102.
3. David Bohm, *Wholeness and the Implicate Order*, Routledge and Kegan Paul 1980, p. 3.

4. Pierre Teilhard de Chardin, *The Phenomenon of Man*, Collins 1959, p. 220.

5. C. G. Jung, *Answer to Job*, Collected Works II, Allen and Unwin 1978, p. 429.

6. John Polkinghorne, *One World*, SPCK 1986; see also his *The Way the World Is*, Triangle Books 1983.

7. Quoted by F. C. Happold, *Mysticism*, Penguin Books, revised edition 1970, p. 339.

8. C. G. Jung, *Collected Works* II, p. 89.

9. I have taken these three quotations from F. C. Happold, *Mysticism*, pp. 327, 379, 392 respectively.

10. Pierre Teilhard de Chardin, *The Phenomenon of Man*, p. 293.